Studying Law

www.skills4study.com – the leading study skills website

Palgrave Study Skills

Authoring a PhD
Business Degree Success
Career Skills
Critical Thinking Skills (2nd edn)
Cite them Right (8th edn)
e-Learning Skills (2nd edn)
Effective Communication for Arts and
   Humanities Students
Effective Communication for Science and
   Technology
The Exam Skills Handbook
The Foundations of Research (2nd edn)
The Good Supervisor
Great Ways to Learn Anatomy and Physiology
How to Manage your Arts, Humanities and
   Social Science Degree
How to Manage your Distance and Open
   Learning Course
How to Manage your Postgraduate Course
How to Manage your Science and Technology
   Degree
How to Study Foreign Languages
How to Study Linguistics (2nd edn)
How to Use your Reading in your Essays
How to Write Better Essays (2nd edn)
How to Write your Undergraduate Dissertation
Information Skills
IT Skills for Successful Study
Making Sense of Statistics
The International Student Handbook
The Mature Student's Guide to Writing (2nd
   edn)
The Mature Student's Handbook
The Palgrave Student Planner
The Personal Tutor's Handbook
The Postgraduate Research Handbook (2nd
   edn)

Presentation Skills for Students (2nd edn)
The Principles of Writing in Psychology
Professional Writing (2nd edn)
Researching Online
Research Using IT
Skills for Success (2nd edn)
The Study Abroad Handbook
The Student's Guide to Writing (2nd edn)
The Student Life Handbook
The Study Skills Handbook (3rd edn)
Study Skills for International Postgraduates
Study Skills for Speakers of English as a
   Second Language
Studying Arts and Humanities
Studying the Built Environment
Studying Business at MBA and Masters
   Level
Studying Economics
Studying History (3rd edn)
Studying Law (3rd edn)
Studying Mathematics and its Applications
Studying Modern Drama (2nd edn)
Studying Physics
Studying Programming
Studying Psychology (2nd edn)
Teaching Study Skills and Supporting
   Learning
The Undergraduate Research Handbook
The Work-Based Learning Student
   Handbook
Work Placements – A Survival Guide for
   Students
Writing for Law
Writing for Nursing and Midwifery
   Students (2nd edn)
Write it Right
Writing for Engineers (3rd edn)

Pocket Study Skills
Series Editor: Kate Williams

14 Days to Exam Success
Blogs, Wikis, Podcasts and More
Brilliant Writing Tips for Students
Completing Your PhD
Doing Research
Getting Critical
Planning Your Essay

Planning Your PhD
Reading and Making Notes
Referencing and Understanding Plagiarism
Science Study Skills
Success in Groupwork
Time Management
Writing for University

Studying Law

Third edition

Simon Askey
Deputy Director of the Undergraduate Laws Programme
University of London International Programmes

and

Ian McLeod
Visiting Professor of Law
School of Social Sciences and Law
Teesside University

Senior Associate Research Fellow
Institute of Advanced Legal Studies
University of London

palgrave
macmillan

First published 2011 by
PALGRAVE MACMILLAN

Palgrave Macmillan in the UK is an imprint of Macmillan Publishers Limited, registered in England, company number 785998, of Houndmills, Basingstoke, Hampshire RG21 6XS.

Palgrave Macmillan in the US is a division of St Martin's Press LLC, 175 Fifth Avenue, New York, NY 10010.

Palgrave Macmillan is the global academic imprint of the above companies and has companies and representatives throughout the world.
Palgrave® and Macmillan® are registered trademarks in the United States, the United Kingdom, Europe and other countries

ISBN-13: 978-0-230-30279-2

This book is printed on paper suitable for recycling and made from fully managed and sustained forest sources. Logging, pulping and manufacturing processes are expected to conform to the environmental regulations of the country of origin.

A catalogue record for this book is available from the British Library.

A catalog record for this book is available from the Library of Congress.

10   9   8   7   6   5   4   3   2

20 19 18 17 16 15 14 13 12 11

Printed in the UK by CPI William Clowes, Beccles, NR34 7TL

Contents

Preface

Law teachers and examiners often complain that many students fail to do themselves justice. More particularly, they complain that although many students have learned a great deal of law, they have simply not mastered the skills of using the law to deal with the kind of tasks that they have to perform. While these skills may be practised and developed in the context of tutorials and seminars, they must ultimately be demonstrated in assessed work of one kind and another. Additionally, for those students who go on to pursue careers with a law element (whether in the legal profession or elsewhere) these skills will continue to be invaluable in the much longer term.

This edition continues the structure of the previous one by beginning with an introduction to some basic ideas which underpin both law itself and the English legal system, before explaining how lawyers find and cite the sources of law. There is then a discussion of the basic principles of legal method, followed by a chapter on how to read law reports and statutes. The case we have chosen to illustrate the way in which law reports should be read is *Henthorn v Fraser* [1892] 2 Ch 27 and we are grateful to the Incorporated Council of Law Reporting for England and Wales, Megarry House, 119 Chancery Lane, London, WC2A 1PP, publishers of *The Law Reports* and *The Weekly Law Reports*, for permission to reproduce the text. The statute we have chosen is the Dealing in Cultural Objects (Offences) Act 2003, the original text of which was printed under the superintendence and authority of the Controller of Her Majesty's Stationery Office, being the Queen's Printer of Acts of Parliament. The Act is Crown copyright and is reproduced by permission. After a chapter on how to write formal English, the final three chapters explain how to answer essay questions and problem questions, and how to make oral presentations. The chapter on oral presentations includes guidance on mooting.

The major updating for this edition centres on the Treaty of Lisbon and the coming into operation of the Supreme Court. Additionally, of course, we have tried to reduce the infelicities which inevitably seem to slip through any process of writing, rewriting and proof-reading.

Although we have each been responsible for originating individual chapters, we have jointly revised the whole book. Accordingly, convention requires that, publicly at any rate, we must each accept full responsibility for any remaining defects. Of course, this will not stop us privately blaming each other if any such matters are subsequently brought to our attention.

We are grateful to Jacqui McLeod for continuing to act as our editorial assistant, to Suzie Burywood for her cheerful support at all times and to Ian Kingston for taking care of the copy-editing and type-setting.

If this book helps students to find their feet in the early stages of their studies, and to develop their skills in such a way as to improve their performance in assessed work, we will have achieved our aim.

Simon Askey
Ian McLeod
March 2011

1 Studying Law: What's It All About?

What law does, how it does it and how it should do it, are all basic questions that have engaged the minds of philosophers and lawyers for more than two thousand years. For students with the right aptitude, who are prepared to work hard at developing their analytical and linguistic skills, the academic study of law offers the possibility to engage with challenging questions such as these and to develop the kind of transferable skills which many employers value highly.

● Introduction

What is law *about*?
The best way to approach the academic study of anything is to ask: *what is this subject about*? This question may be important for two reasons.

First, those who start to study a subject like law without giving at least some thought to its nature are likely to find themselves adrift upon a vast ocean of apparently random – and therefore confusing – detail. Some knowledge of the nature of law, even if only in outline, will help to provide a framework within which you can organise and understand as much of that detail as possible. More particularly, this understanding will enable you to see how the detail contributes (or, in some cases, fails to contribute) to the coherence of the body of law as a whole.

Secondly, it will give you an important insight into how you will be required to think and the intellectual skills you will need if you are to study the subject successfully.

So, returning to the initial question, what is law *about*? We will approach this question by asking two further questions:

- What does law do? and
- How does it do it?

We will consider these questions in turn.

What does law do?

Although there is a great deal of academic debate about the nature of law, for the moment we can assume that law consists of a body of *rules*. In practice, of course, those rules will need to be *made*. Additionally, having been made, the rules will need to be *interpreted*, *applied* and *enforced* in a wide variety of factual contexts; and they may need to be *changed* from time to time. It follows, therefore, that there must also be a set of *institutions* whose function it is to make, interpret, apply, enforce and change the law. There are many such institutions, with Parliament, the courts, central government and local authorities being among the most obvious examples.

The fact that law involves both rules and institutions still leaves open the question of what it is that law actually *does*. An outline answer to this question is that *law regulates social conduct with a view to enabling (or at least helping) people to live peaceably in a well-ordered society*. In practice, this means that the law must *identify* the *duties* and *powers* of both *government* and *individuals*, as well as *enforcing* the *duties* and *regulating* the *exercise* of the *powers* in both cases.

More specifically, constitutional law deals with the allocation of power between different institutions (such as central government departments like the Home Office) and local authorities (such as county councils and London borough councils) as well as a range of other public bodies (such as the Environment Agency). Once constitutional law has allocated public powers to various institutions, administrative law seeks to control the way in which those institutions exercise their powers.

Moving to the level of relationships between individuals, the range of law is truly vast. Taking only a few examples at random, the law regulates matters as varied as:

- the ownership and transfer of property and rights in property;
- the creation, functioning and winding-up of companies and business partnerships;
- the right to privacy;
- the rights of people who are not British citizens to enter the United Kingdom and their status when they have done so; and
- the relationships which arise from marriage and cohabitation.

Of course, these categories are by no means watertight. (For example, marriage may well affect existing property rights, or bring new ones into being, or both.) However, the vastness of the law's range is seldom reflected in the way students are introduced to it, which generally relies very heavily on a few traditional categories.

Of all the categories of law which regulate relationships between individuals, the two which you are most likely to encounter at an early stage are *contract* and *tort*, which may sometimes be put together to form the bulk of a single subject called *obligations*. (The idea of *contract* is probably obvious even to non-lawyers, but it may be worth saying that the word *tort* describes particular kinds of unlawful conduct, such as trespass, negligence, libel and so on, where the legal relationship between the parties arises simply as a matter of law, rather than arising from an agreement between them.) The placing of these subjects at an early stage within your studies is far from arbitrary. The fact of the matter is that they underpin many of the specialised subjects which you will encounter later on. They are, therefore, literally *foundational* in nature.

So far, we have approached the question *'What is law about?'* in terms of *'What does law do?'* but this is only a partial answer because it still leaves the more practical question of *'How does law do it?'*.

How does law do it?

Introduction
One useful way of approaching the way in which law functions is through the distinction between *criminal* law and *civil* law.

The distinction between criminal law and civil law
Criminal law prohibits certain types of anti-social conduct such as murder, rape, theft and dangerous driving. By way of contrast, civil law deals with conduct which, while still anti-social, is rather less so, such as breaching contracts and trespassing on other people's land.

The policy decision as to whether a specific type of conduct should be classified as criminal or civil will depend on how harmful to society and its members the conduct in question is thought to be. In order to understand how this policy decision is made, it will help if you first understand the practical consequences which flow from something being classified as either *criminal* or *civil*.

The first practical consequence is that, in the case of *criminal law*, the state itself (acting mainly through the police and the Crown Prosecution

Service, but sometimes through other institutions such as local authorities) will investigate allegations of illegality and also bring legal proceedings. On the other hand, where conduct is classified as a *civil wrong*, it is left entirely up to the victims to assemble the evidence and formulate the legal arguments which will be necessary in order to support their claims, and to decide whether to bring proceedings in the courts.

The second practical consequence is that where guilt is either admitted or proved in criminal proceedings, the court will impose sanctions which will be enforced automatically. Moreover, these sanctions will usually be intended, in principle, to be either punitive (such as fines), or reforming (such as probation) or perhaps even an uneasy combination of the two (such as imprisonment). The fact that the courts exercising criminal jurisdiction may also be able to award compensation for financial loss represents only a small exception to the general nature of criminal sanctions. In practice, they make such awards only in very straightforward cases, leaving the victims of crime to pursue more complicated claims by way of civil actions.

On the other hand, where judgment has been obtained in civil proceedings, it is left entirely to the victims to decide whether to enforce whatever orders the courts may make. Moreover, these orders will very seldom be intended to be either punitive or reforming, but will focus instead on compensating claimants or protecting them against further wrongdoing; or, sometimes, both.

By way of an example, suppose your neighbour erects a fence in such a way that it trespasses on your garden. If you choose not to enforce your rights, no official or agency of the state will force you to do so, or do so on your behalf. Suppose, however, that you have chosen to enforce your rights and that the court has made orders in your favour, requiring your neighbour to remove the fence from your garden and pay you damages. Although you have obtained two remedies, you may well decide that all you really want is to have the use of your garden back. If this is so, you may well decide to require your neighbour simply to move the fence, without also requiring the payment of damages. The law leaves this choice entirely up to you.

As a final footnote to the distinction between criminal and civil law, it is worth saying that a single piece of unlawful conduct may be both criminal and civil. For example, suppose A assaults B. A may be successfully prosecuted in a court exercising criminal jurisdiction, where the result may be some kind of penalty such as a fine. Whether or not there is a successful prosecution, B may sue A in a court exercising civil jurisdiction and, if successful, obtain damages.

If you think it strange that a claim for damages may succeed where a prosecution has failed, you may be immediately congratulated on having read the text carefully and critically. However, the answer is quite straightforward. In a *criminal* case the prosecution needs to produce evidence which is convincing enough to prove that the defendant is guilty *beyond a reasonable doubt*. In *civil* cases, on the other hand, claimants can succeed on evidence which is significantly less convincing, because the standard of proof in civil cases is only *the balance of probabilities*. In other words, claimants in civil cases need only show that it is *more likely than not* that what they allege to have happened did actually happen.

● Law and justice

Introduction
The proposition that law is about enabling (or, at least, helping) people to live peaceably in a well-ordered society, is only a starting point. Much depends on how peace and good order are established and maintained. Societies that are based on abuses of fundamental human rights will often use law as an instrument of violence and oppression against their citizens. These societies (so-called *police states*) will undoubtedly be peaceful and well-ordered, but they can scarcely be called *just*. Thus, within a few, short sentences – and taking only one example – we have identified the need to consider not only *law* but also *justice*.

At this stage two further questions arise. First, how do we identify what we mean by *justice*; or, in other words, *what is the content of justice*? Secondly, once we know what we mean by *justice*, we need to ask *what is the relationship between law and justice*?

The content of justice

Introduction
We will begin our consideration of the content of justice with the importance of respecting and protecting fundamental human rights. The difficulty is that, although this can reasonably be considered to be at least one aspect of justice, what it actually requires in any given case may be a great deal less clear.

For example, does it follow that a society which prohibits racial discrimination in the field of employment must prohibit the proprietors of Chinese restaurants from employing only Chinese waiting staff, where they think this form of racial discrimination is necessary in order to provide their establishments with the ambience which their customers enjoy?

Similarly, although admittedly by way of a more extreme example, most people would say that they support freedom of religion and worship. However, suppose a group of people chooses to revive the religious beliefs which formed the foundation of the Central American Aztec civilisation before the European conquest. These beliefs required the offering of human hearts and blood as nourishment for the sun god. Does a commitment to respecting and protecting freedom of religion mean that we must accept the right of this group to practise human sacrifice? When answering this question, is it relevant to ask whether the victims are themselves followers of the faith who are happy to die in the service of their god?

Even leaving aside questions involving fundamental human rights, it is not difficult to imagine situations where the requirements of justice are less than obvious. Suppose a thief (T) steals property from its owner (O) and sells it to a buyer (B), who genuinely and reasonably believes T to be its owner. If the property is traced to B, does justice require that B should be allowed to keep it, or that it should be returned to O? You may argue that the answer to this question is unimportant, because if B is allowed to keep the property, O will have the right to obtain compensation from T. Alternatively, if the property is returned to O, B will have the right to obtain compensation from T. In either case, therefore, it seems that the innocent victim will be protected and that the loss will fall, as it should, on the guilty party. In the real world, however, experience shows that T will either have vanished or lack the means to pay any compensation to anyone. In practice, therefore, in the vast majority of cases, either B or O will have to stand (or, perhaps, share) the loss, even though they are both innocent victims of T's criminal conduct.

As you might expect, the law does, in fact, have answers to all these questions, but we will not pursue them here. What we will do instead is to pick up a methodological point and consider three different ways of identifying the content of justice in specific *types* of cases. Our first approach is based on *economic* considerations, our second on *psychological* considerations, and our third on a more general idea which is commonly labelled *public policy*, and which may appear in a variety of forms.

An economic approach to justice

An economic approach to justice may be illustrated by the problem that arises when a car crash occurs at a junction between a major road and a minor one, where the view of drivers emerging from the minor road is restricted by an overgrown roadside hedge. More particularly, if a car emerging from the minor road collides with a car on the major road, can the driver of the emerging car lay at least part of the blame on the local highway authority, which could have cut back the hedge in such a way as to improve visibility at the junction? Assuming there is no relevant case law or statute, and that the court must, therefore, approach this question at the level of principle, there are likely to be two opposing arguments.

On the one hand, it can be argued that a driver who encounters a particularly dangerous situation on the road should exercise a correspondingly high degree of care. Furthermore, any liability which the court imposes on the driver will, in reality, almost always fall on the driver's insurance company rather than on the driver personally. (For the present purposes, since we are discussing the matter at the level of principle, we can ignore the possibility of the loss of any no-claims bonus which the driver may have earned, as well as any excess which he or she may have to pay.) On the other hand, it can be argued that if the local community at large (acting in this case through the local highway authority) has allowed a dangerous situation either to arise or continue (or both), it is only fair that the local community at large should accept at least some financial liability for accidents which then occur. If it is agreed that such liability is fair in principle, each individual case will simply require the apportionment of liability between the driver and the local highway authority, in the light of all the facts.

If you stop to think about these two arguments for a few moments, it becomes obvious that the problem may be seen in largely economic terms. More particularly, the cost of any liability which falls on the driver will be borne by the driver's insurance company – or, more accurately, by the other policyholders and shareholders of the driver's insurance company, who may suffer, respectively, from increased premiums and reduced dividends. The cost of any liability which falls on the local highway authority will ultimately be borne by the local community at large through the increases in council tax which will be necessary to enable the local authority to pay either insurance premiums or damages. Where insurance cover does exist, the reality of the matter is that the court has to decide how the losses should be allocated between two insurance companies (or, again more accurately, between their respective policyholders and shareholders).

On the basis of a purely economic analysis, therefore, the question requires the economic efficiency of both alternatives to be assessed so that an informed choice can be made between them. On this view, it follows that the interests of justice become the same as the interests of economic efficiency.

You may, of course, object that the judges who decide such cases lack the skills and knowledge which would equip them to undertake the relevant economic analysis with the same expertise that professional economists would bring to the task. While this is no doubt true, those who argue for the requirements of justice to be identified by reference to economic considerations may make two responses. First, expert evidence could be used here, as it is in many other cases involving technical matters. Secondly, and more fundamentally, most people would probably accept that the concept of justice is an ideal that we should strive to attain. This being so, it would be unfortunate if we were to limit our perception of the scope of the concept merely because of the inability of the legal system to attain the ideal in its fullest form.

Finally, if you wish to pursue the arguments in cases such as this, you could usefully read *Stovin v Wise (Norfolk County Council, Third Party)* [1996] AC 923, where the House of Lords, by a majority of three to two, reversed the decision of the Court of Appeal, reported at [1994] 1 WLR 1124.

A psychological approach to justice

Turning to the psychological approach to justice, and taking a single example, before the Coroners and Justice Act 2009, the defence of provocation reduced murder to manslaughter. (The practical significance of this was that murder carried, and still does carry, a mandatory sentence of life imprisonment, while manslaughter carried, and still does carry, only a maximum sentence of life imprisonment, but no minimum whatsoever.)

The essence of provocation was a sudden and temporary loss of self-control caused by the victim's conduct. A court which was considering a plea of provocation had to ask itself whether the defendant's response to the victim's conduct had been reasonable. This raised a particular difficulty where a woman who had been subjected to domestic violence over a period of time finally lost her self-control in response to something which was, when viewed in isolation, relatively trivial. Could the court take account of the history of violence as well as the immediate cause of the loss of self-control? The courts came to accept that the victim's whole course of conduct could be relevant, but before they felt able to come to this conclusion they had had to be persuaded that *battered wife syndrome* is a form of post-traumatic stress disorder, and that, therefore, it could be just to uphold a plea of provocation in these circumstances. (Section 56 of the 2009 Act abolished the whole of the existing defence of provocation and ss. 54 and 55 now contain a statutory re-working of the underlying idea, in terms of loss of control which is triggered by certain specified circumstances. However, it is clear that this reform of the law continues to be based on psychological considerations.)

Finally, if you wish to pursue the way in which the courts came to accept the psychological realities of domestic violence, you could usefully read the decisions of the Court of Appeal in *R v Thornton* [1992] 1 All ER 306 and *R v Ahluwalia* [1992] 4 All ER 889, although you will have to bear in mind that the court was dealing with the old law of provocation in both cases.

A public policy approach to justice

For an example of a situation in which some people would think about the requirements of justice in terms of public policy, suppose A is injured and becomes unfit for work as the result of an accident for which B is responsible. Also suppose that A belongs to an occupational pension scheme which pays out ill-health benefits. A's loss of income will be the difference between the earnings which he or she would have received but for the accident, and the pension which he or she does actually receive as a result of the accident. In other words, to allow A to receive damages based on the total loss of earnings, *as well as receiving the pension*, would result in over-compensation.

On the other hand, if the damages are reduced to take account of the pension, B has to pay less than he or she would have paid if A had not invested in a pension scheme which included ill-health benefits. This would mean that B has become the true beneficiary of A's investment in the pension scheme. While this solution avoids over-compensation, the fact that A receives no benefit from his or her pension contributions is not only intrinsically unfair, but is also contrary to that aspect of public policy which encourages people to take responsibility for their own future needs.

In fact, the law prefers the element of over-compensation and does not, therefore, require the damages to be reduced on account of the pension.

Finally, if you wish to pursue the arguments which arise in cases such as this, you could usefully read *Parry v Cleaver* [1970] AC 1, where the House of Lords, by a majority of three to two, reversed the decision of the Court of Appeal, which is reported at [1968] 1 QB 195.

The relationship between law and justice

Introduction

Having considered the topic of the *content of justice*, we can now turn to the second of our further two questions, namely *what is the relationship between law and justice*? We will approach the topic by considering some broad schools of thought in legal theory.

Legal theory is a very broad area of study and most individual legal theorists have concentrated their efforts on only one or two aspects of the whole subject. Since lawyers love to classify everything, it is not surprising that they classify legal theorists. Traditionally, many theorists have approached the relationship between law and justice in terms of the relationship between morality and law. We will consider both these positions in turn, beginning with the traditional classification which divides legal theorists into two groups, one of which argues for what is known as *natural law*, while the other one argues for what is known as *positivism*.

Natural law
Although all natural law theorists emphasise the role of morality in relation to law, closer consideration reveals that the *natural law* position as a whole can be further subdivided into two.

The first sub-group consists of those theorists who advance a *strong* version of natural law, by arguing that something which appears to be a law (for example, in the English legal system, an Act of Parliament) is nevertheless not truly a law if it is unjust. (In this context, the word *unjust* is normally used to mean something like *violating the moral principles according to which humankind should live*.)

The second sub-group consists of theorists who advance a *weak* version of natural law. These theorists accept that whatever the legal system asserts to be a law is, by definition, truly a law, while nevertheless insisting that the *desirability* of all laws must be assessed by reference to the requirements of natural law.

In very general terms, older versions of natural law theory tend to be of the strong kind, while more modern versions tend to be of the weak kind. However, both versions share a common problem, namely *what are the requirements of natural law*? Or, to put it another way, *what is the content of the moral principles according to which humankind ought to live*? Or, yet again, to link the matter even more clearly to our previous discussion, *what is justice*?

Very broadly speaking, if we go back to the beginning and regard all natural law theorists as a single group (disregarding for the present purposes the distinction between those who advance the strong and the weak versions) they will once again fall into two sub-groups. This time, however, the basis of the division between them will be different.

Members of one sub-group argue that the requirements of natural law (and therefore the content of justice) may be identified by reference to religious beliefs of one kind or another. Members of the other sub-group argue that it is possible to identify the requirements of natural law through the exercise of human reason alone, and that there is no need to introduce religious belief into this process.

All we can safely conclude at this stage, therefore, is that there may be significant disagreements, even between natural law theorists, as to what justice truly requires in a given situation. Similarly, in purely practical terms, each side to a dispute may genuinely believe that it has justice on its side, while disagreeing fundamentally as to what this means in terms of how their dispute should be resolved.

Positivism

The second main group of legal theorists regards the *existence* and the *desirability* of a law as being two quite distinct matters. For these theorists (who are generally known as *positivists* because they emphasise law as it is *posited* or *laid down*), anything is truly a law if it has been laid down as a law according to the formal requirements of the legal system in question. To return to the earlier example, within the English legal system, the provisions of an Act of Parliament are, by definition, law. However, it would be a serious mistake to conclude that the positivists' emphasis on the formal requirements of a legal system means that they are interested only in law and not in justice. The positivists' position is rather that separating the processes of *identifying* and *evaluating* laws is important for a number of reasons.

Among the positivists' reasons for separating questions as to the nature of law from questions as to the nature of justice is that, as we have seen, the nature of justice is such that disagreement as to its requirements will often arise. From the positivist viewpoint, therefore, any definition of law which depends on the concept of justice is bound to lead, in some cases at least, to disagreement as to whether an alleged law is truly a law at all. Since law is an essential element in the fabric of society (because it enables – or at least helps – people to live peaceably in a well-ordered society), it follows that questioning the very existence of something which appears to be a law may amount to undermining, at least to some extent, the basis of society itself.

Before moving on, it is worth repeating that the positivists' insistence on separating questions of the existence of laws from questions of their desirability does not exclude argument as to whether particular laws are just or unjust, or as to what the law on a particular subject ought to be. The positivist position is simply that the two matters should be dealt with separately.

How real is the distinction between natural law and positivism?

At this stage you may well be wondering what, if anything, is the difference between *weak versions of natural law* and *positivism*. The answer lies in the fact that, while many positivists accept that conclusions as to the requirements of justice rest on the moral principles according to which humankind should live (and therefore differ from natural lawyers only as to the point at which this consideration becomes relevant), others rely on matters which would find no place in natural law theory, such as the *economic*, *psychological* and *public policy* considerations which we discussed at pp. 6–9.

Choosing between natural law and positivism
While positivists may challenge natural lawyers on the basis that if natural law were truly natural, it should be possible to formulate a single, universally agreed and coherent account of its requirements, so natural lawyers may challenge positivists on the basis that their concept of law is, in essence, law without values. If you study legal theory (which you may encounter under a variety of names, including *jurisprudence* or *legal philosophy*) in more depth, you may well conclude that there is something in both criticisms.

If your temperament is such that you like clear-cut categories and are therefore uneasy about living with doubt, you will probably align yourself with one or other of the theoretical positions, while persuading yourself that the objections to it are either unsound or relatively unimportant.

On the other hand, if your temperament is such that you can happily accommodate matters of doubt, you may prefer to avoid aligning yourself absolutely with either position. In this case, you will probably be saying (on the basis of your further study of individual legal theorists) that many members of each group have something useful to say about the nature of law, the nature of justice and the relationship between the two. If this is indeed your view, you will probably also conclude that to insist on applying an uncompromising label to yourself (and to other people) is a sign that you attach more importance to labels than to the substance of the theories which those labels describe.

● Some distinctions between the academic study and the practice of law

Some people who become law students never have any intention whatsoever of entering the legal profession. Some others have professional aspirations when they become law students, but change their minds during the course of their studies. Finally, of course, there are those law students who do become practising lawyers (either solicitors or barristers) in due course.

Whichever category you think (or know) you fall into, while you are a law student you will often be dealing with law as it works in practice, but you will be doing so from an academic perspective, with no practical consequences flowing from your analyses, criticisms and conclusions. It follows that you need to be aware of some of the major differences between being a law student and being a member of the practising profession.

Perhaps the central point of distinction is that practitioners have clients who are hoping to achieve certain outcomes. Those outcomes will vary from routine, low-profile matters such as making a valid will, to exceptional, high-profile matters such as bringing, or defending, legal proceedings involving issues of high constitutional principle. Whatever the clients' desired outcomes may be, however, practising lawyers act on their clients' instructions, provided those instructions do not require the doing of anything which is either illegal or contrary to their code of professional conduct.

Of course, lawyers may advise clients as to what outcomes are most likely to be achievable, and perhaps also as to which are most likely to be genuinely in the clients' best interests; and clients may change their minds in the light of such advice. But clients are never obliged to accept advice, no matter how sound that advice may be. Newcomers to the law frequently ask whether a lawyer is bound to accept instructions. The answer is that solicitors are always free to decline to accept instructions, although commercial considerations are such that very few solicitors will turn away work of a kind which they usually undertake. On the other hand, barristers are required by their code of professional conduct to accept any instructions within a field of law in which the individual barrister practises and for which a proper fee is offered.

Law students, on the other hand, in common with their teachers, enjoy greater freedom, being subject to neither commercial reality, clients' instructions nor the rigours of the codes of professional conduct which bind practitioners. Of course, neither law students nor their teachers are entirely free from constraints. Students who wish to succeed must keep their examiners reasonably happy, while teachers who wish to remain employed, and to progress in their careers, must keep both their students and their employers reasonably happy. In reality, however, these constraints are much less limiting than those which apply to practitioners.

An important aspect of the freedom enjoyed by law students is the possibility of *criticising* the law. Although practitioners may, of course, also indulge in the intellectual exercise of criticising the law, in the purely practical world of advising clients, negotiating with other lawyers and appearing before courts, they are almost always limited by what the law on a particular point simply *is*. Admittedly, in cases involving statute law it may be possible to achieve startling results by the imaginative use of creative techniques of interpretation, while those who practise in the highest courts may have the opportunity to influence the development of the law through the doctrine of binding precedent. (Both these points are discussed further in Chapter 7.)

However, the fact remains that, under the British constitution, it is simply impossible for any court to quash an Act of Parliament. Additionally, while it is not impossible for the Supreme Court (and previously was not impossible for the House of Lords) to depart from one of its own previous decisions, in practice it may refuse to do so, in the interests of legal certainty, even if it considers the previous decision to be wrong. (The doctrine of binding precedent is discussed in more detail in Chapter 7.) On the other hand, students may cheerfully write essays, while their teachers may equally cheerfully give lectures and write books and articles, arguing that particular aspects of the law are wrong in terms of legal principle or are unjust and should be changed.

Another important distinction between the worlds of academe and practice is that students are presented with fact situations on which they are asked to advise. You will investigate the techniques involved in answering such questions when you get to Chapter 11, but for the moment the essential point is simply that students are given a set of facts to which they must apply the relevant law. In practice, though, most cases turn entirely on disputes as to the facts, with both parties agreeing about which principles of law will be relevant when the issues of fact have been resolved. Of course, in some cases the process of resolving factual disputes may involve issues of law in the form of the law of evidence, which deals with the way in which disputed facts may be proved. However, in practice, arguments on the law of evidence are relatively rare, with most factual disputes being resolved on the very simple basis of *which witnesses does the court believe*?

● The skills required for success as a law student

Law students require a variety of aptitudes and, to use a more specifically practical word, skills. Reduced to their most basic, what is required is an aptitude for hard work coupled with an analytical mind which enjoys the challenge of expressing difficult ideas clearly. Furthermore, there is no escaping the fact that much of the hard work will involve a great deal of reading and note-taking; and much of this will, at least in the short term, be heavy going and unexciting. However, if undertaken properly, this work will, over a period of time, accumulate into a substantial body of knowledge, which can then be applied to the key tasks of writing essays and solving problems by way of both coursework and examination.

A useful approach to effective reading and note taking is the SQ3R technique, the stages of which are:

- survey;
- question;
- read;
- recall (*or* recite);
- review.

The aim of the SQ3R technique, which was first promoted by the American psychologist Francis Robinson in 1941, is to help you read purposefully in order to create a mental framework of the topic as you read. We will discuss the techniques of researching, planning and answering both essay and problem questions in Chapters 10 and 11. For the moment, however, we shall confine ourselves to showing how the SQ3R technique can help you to study a topic simply in order to understand it, rather than to research, plan and write a piece of written work.

To begin your consideration of a chapter in a book or an article in a law journal, for example, you will *survey* the whole piece by skimming through the pages, paying particular attention to any introductory summary and conclusion, as well as to the headings and subheadings which break up the text. Having understood the structure of the piece as a whole, you will then *question* what value it has for you, by asking whether it reinforces, extends or contradicts your existing knowledge of the topic. Assuming that you wish to proceed further with the piece, you will then *read* it properly, making appropriate notes. If you find yourself copying out any passages word-for-word, be careful to use quotation marks round the relevant passages and to note their precise location. If, at some later stage, you wish to incorporate these passages into pieces of written work, you will then have no difficulty in citing your source accurately, in order to avoid laying yourself open to an allegation of plagiarism. (Plagiarism, which is a form of cheating, is discussed at pp. 167–170 and 173.)

At this stage, and by way of a slight digression from the SQ3R technique itself, it may be worth saying that your notes will become a very personal part of your resources. Some people rely simply on a careful structure of headings and subheadings, while others use graphics (such as boxes, circles, different colours and connecting arrows) to create emphasis, illustrate links and raise questions. There are only three really important things to bear in mind:

- You must be able to understand your notes easily when you come to re-read them.
- They must be structured in such a way that they help you to generate a mental map of the topic.
- Do not take the easy option of simply highlighting or underlining what you see as the key sections of a text, rather than making notes from them, because:
  - note-taking is an important skill which you may well need in the future (for example, when attending meetings or when taking instructions from clients); and it can be acquired and developed only through practice;
  - the act of note-taking makes you decide for yourself how the main points of the material can best be summarised. The crucial point here is that the mental activity which this involves is an invaluable part of the learning process; and
  - your notes will be an important resource when you come to write coursework essays and revise for examinations. In the context of coursework, as we shall see at p. 169, working from notes is a very helpful way of avoiding plagiarism (or cheating), while in the context of examinations, almost everyone finds they can revise most effectively from materials which are in their own handwriting rather than from the printed page (whether or not it is enhanced by highlighting or underlining).

Returning specifically to the SQ3R technique, the *recall* stage is a way of embedding in your mind what you have read. If you are reading a particularly complex chapter or article, you might find it helpful to read just part of the text, take a short break, and then test your ability to recall the basic concepts, arguments or core facts of the material you have just read. For a less complex text, you might do the recall stage a day or two later. Recall should be done without looking at the notes you made during the *reading* stage. One way to consolidate your thoughts is to write a summary of the material while you are *recalling* it; or alternatively you could create a diagram such as a flow chart or algorithm, or simply recite what you know out loud. The method you choose will very much depend on your learning style and temperament. The key thing is to use a method that helps you to instil in your mind what you have read, while also developing your understanding of the material.

Finally, you will *review* what you have been reading, in order to reinforce your understanding and to check that you have not missed anything of importance. The *review* can take place at anytime after the *recall* stage. In most cases (as with the *recall* stage itself) the time when you *review* your material will depend on how difficult you found the reading. Simple material can be quickly noted and then reviewed days later. Complex material may need to be *read* and *recalled* in short sections, and then *reviewed* in longer sections, all on the same day.

Organising yourself to read in this way can take a great deal of self-discipline, but the SQ3R technique remains a popular method of effective reading. While you may find the system laborious at first, it has the advantage of helping you read actively, questioningly and effectively. The pressures of academic life are such that you can never read everything in detail. Learning to read purposefully now will be hard work, but it will save you a great deal of time and effort later on.

It is important to emphasise the need for hard work as an essential part of studying law, because far too many students are tempted to think that they can succeed by relying on what they imagine to be their natural ability, without bothering to add the expenditure of effort. To take an analogy, some people prefer the more or less instant gratification which comes from watching a television adaptation of a classic novel to the rather more laborious process of reading the novel itself. Those who prefer watching television to reading the book are less likely to study law successfully, unless they rapidly acquire a taste for text-based materials.

It is also important to emphasise that studying law is a cumulative process. This means that you must *absorb*, *understand* and *retain* at least the main principles of every subject that you study, so that you will be able to apply them to other subjects later on. For example, you will need a sound grasp of foundation subjects such as contract law and administrative law before you can progress successfully to subjects such as employment law and environmental law.

Incidentally, it is often said that lawyers neither know nor need to know any more law than other people, but that they simply need to know where to look it up. While it is, of course, true that many lawyers do frequently look things up, there are various reasons why it is quite simply untrue to say that they neither know nor need to know any more law than other people do.

The first point is that, in common with members of other learned professions, lawyers are expected to know a lot of material. There are several reasons why this is so.

First, as a matter of psychology, clients are unlikely to have much confidence in lawyers who plainly know no law.

Secondly, lawyers who have to spend time on getting themselves onto an equal footing with their more knowledgeable competitors before they can start spending time on the key task of giving advice or providing other professional services, will have to charge more than their competitors charge. It follows that lawyers who do not know the law will be at a commercial disadvantage against competitors who do know a lot of law, since those who know the least will have to charge the most.

Thirdly, having found the law, you need to be able to understand it. This requires both a good grasp of that area of law known as *legal method* (so that you can understand and apply the sources you have looked up), and a wider knowledge of the law relating to various topics. After all, there is no point in looking up a legal rule which seems to dispose of your case if you are unaware of another and more authoritative rule which will prevail. An example may help.

Suppose your client's widowed mother has died without leaving a will, and that your client is her only child. If you simply look up the Act of Parliament dealing with inheritance of property in situations where there is no will, you will conclude that your client is entitled to inherit the whole of his or her mother's estate. However, suppose that your client killed his or her mother. This may have been by murder or manslaughter, or, perhaps more probably, by being the driver of a car in which the mother was a passenger and which was involved in an accident for which your client was responsible and as a result of which the mother died.

The Act of Parliament which lays down the rules of succession where there is no will makes no mention of the fact that those rules are subject to an additional set of rules which seek to prevent people benefiting from their own wrongdoing. The additional rules, which originated in the courts but have since been developed by another Act of Parliament, may or may not (depending on all the circumstances of the case) prevent your client from inheriting. It follows that a lawyer who merely identifies the first Act of Parliament, but who is unaware of the additional rules contained in both case law and the later Act of Parliament, may give bad advice.

Fourthly, there will be many occasions in professional practice when it is simply impossible to look up the law, and lawyers must, therefore, rely on their legal knowledge. For example, they may be in a meeting with clients, or appearing as advocates in court, when only a few textbooks may be available, and pressure of time may mean that even these can be used only to jog the memory, rather than as sources on which to base research.

Quite apart from a capacity for hard work, law students require good linguistic and analytical skills. Although these may sound like, and in some cases will indeed be, two distinct skills, in practical terms they often merge into one. For example, take an Act of Parliament which, among other things, prohibits the possession of obscene articles for publication for gain, except where publication is

> justified as being for the public good on the ground that it is in the interests of science, literature, art or learning, or of other objects of general concern.

Clearly this exception would apply to the depiction of nudity in classical art and to the publication of photographs of human genitals in medical textbooks. But what about cases involving articles which are plainly obscene on any sensible meaning of the word? Can the defence argue that such articles are nevertheless lawful because they help some people to release their frustrations through sexual fantasies (with a consequent reduction in the number of sexual offences) and that this is plainly an object of general concern?

A linguistically perceptive response to this question would proceed on the following lines. If the exception applies to *any* 'objects of general concern', why did Parliament specify the preceding categories (namely 'science, literature, art or learning')? Is it not reasonable, therefore, to interpret the words 'other objects of general concern' as being limited to other things *of the same kind* as those which are specified? Thus the argument for the defence does not justify the application of the exception.

Furthermore, and quite apart from purely linguistic considerations, when the content of the argument for the defence is analysed, it becomes plain that what is really being claimed is that the availability of obscene articles can be justified simply on the ground that they are obscene. It is difficult to see how anyone could reasonably regard this as a credible interpretation of an Act of Parliament which was passed in order to subject obscene articles to very strict controls.

As a final point on the need for good language skills, it may be useful to consider a classic legal anecdote. The story is told of a judge who, having listened patiently to an advocate who was making a long and learned submission, said: 'Well, Mr Smith, having listened to all you have had to say, I must confess that I am none the wiser'. 'Perhaps not, my Lord', replied the advocate, 'but at least your Lordship is better informed'. Whether or not you find this funny may be a good indicator of whether you are sufficiently sensitive to nuances of meaning to be likely to succeed as a law student.

● Conclusion

Both law and justice are complex subjects which require a great deal of careful analysis if you are going to discuss them sensibly.

Having read this chapter, you may be fired with enthusiasm and impatient to read the rest of this book and pursue your study of law. Alternatively, you may have found it dense, difficult and – to put it bluntly – either boring or incomprehensible, or both. Whichever category *you* fall into is less important than the fact that you will have benefited from reading it.

If you fall into the first category, you are likely to enjoy both the remainder of this book and the rest of your time studying law.

If you fall into the second category, you are likely to find the study of law rather heavy going and unrewarding.

Regardless of these (unless you have found this chapter totally incomprehensible, in which case you might be best advised to try to persuade your college or university to allow you to change your course), you should, at the very least, have developed some insight into the question with which we began: what is law, and the study of law, *about*?

Finally, if you did not find the anecdote about being none the wiser but better informed even slightly amusing, you may be among those who conclude that legal humour is not very funny.

2 The Sources of English Law

There are three domestic sources of English law, namely the common law (which is developed by the courts), statutes (which are enacted by Parliament) and delegated legislation (which is made by people acting under the authority of Parliament). European Union law is also an important source of English law, especially through the doctrines of direct applicability and direct effect. Under the Human Rights Act 1998 (HRA), the European Convention on Human Rights (ECHR) is, strictly speaking, a source of substantive law only in relation to public authorities. Nevertheless, the ECHR is of enormous practical importance because of the way in which the HRA requires English courts to approach the decision-making process in cases involving almost all the rights which the ECHR protects.

● Introduction

For all practical purposes, the sources of English law are the common law, statute law and delegated legislation, and European Union law. We will discuss each of these in turn, but before we do so it is worth commenting that the omission of the European Convention on Human Rights from the sources of English law is intentional. The reason for this omission is that, strictly speaking, under the Human Rights Act 1998, the Convention is a source of English law only to the very limited extent that it is unlawful for public authorities to breach those articles of the Convention which the Act classifies as 'Convention rights'.

However, it would be seriously misleading to suggest that the Convention is unimportant in English law, because in addition to the duty which it imposes on public bodies (and which we have just noted), the Human Rights Act 1998 requires all courts to:

- have regard to the law of the Convention in all cases involving 'Convention rights', and
- to interpret all English legislation in such a way as to give effect to 'Convention rights' wherever it is possible to do so, even if the legislation in question pre-dates the Act itself.

We will return to the Convention and the Human Rights Act in more detail in Chapter 5, but it is never too early to understand that, in many situations, you will have to consider *three legal systems* (namely domestic English law, European Union law, and the law of the European Convention on Human Rights), and the ways in which they interact with each other, if you are going to have a proper understanding of the law as it is administered by the English courts.

● Common law and statute law

Introduction
An initial difficulty with the phrase *common law* is that it has a variety of meanings, with the correct one in any given context depending on that context. Thus it may be contrasted with *statute law*, *equity* and *civil law*. For the moment, we will use the phrase *common law* in its most general sense of *judge-made law*, by way of contrast with *statute law and delegated legislation*. Within our discussion of this meaning of the phrase, we will explain the origins and meaning of *equity*, leaving only the distinction with *civil law* to be dealt with briefly at the end of our discussion. However, as we shall see, the phrase *common law* may also be used in a narrower sense, in which it contrasts with *equity*.

Common law, equity, statute law and delegated legislation
Common law is that part of the law which is contained in the decisions of the courts, rather than being made by Parliament. Of course, an important part of the status of any system of *law* is that it must be *binding*. In the case of the common law, bindingness flows from the doctrine of *binding precedent*, which is one of the main topics discussed in Chapter 7.

Historically, the common law originated in the King's courts. More particularly, it emerged from the practice of the King's judges, who travelled round the country when administering the law, adopting what they considered to be the best legal rules from each area and enforcing them in other areas as well. Thus, at a time when communications were such that there could be wide variations between laws in different localities, the King's judges used their powers to minimise those variations and enforce a single set of laws that were *common* to the whole country. In other words, they created the *common law*.

Although, as we shall see in Chapter 7, the modern version of the doctrine of binding precedent is surprisingly flexible, in earlier times the common law valued uniformity above flexibility. Consequently, there were many situations in which the common law lacked the flexibility to produce fair results in individual cases. It was to counter this tendency of the common law that the doctrines of *equity* emerged.

Equity originated in the office of chancery, whose head was the Lord Chancellor and whose function it was to issue the writs that were the documents used to begin actions at common law. What happened was that the office of chancery began to introduce a more flexible system of rules, which operated alongside the rules of common law but were much more geared to producing results that were consistent with what was thought to be good conscience. This parallel system came to be called *equity*, and in due course its operation and development came into the hands of the Lord Chancellor's court, namely the *court of chancery*.

To take a straightforward example of how the relationship between the common law and equity worked (and, indeed still does work), suppose that you agree to sell me an 'old master' painting, but you then decide not to go through with the deal and refuse to deliver the goods even though I am ready, willing and able to pay the price we have agreed. The only remedy the common law can offer me is damages. However, in cases like this, the subject matter of the contract is unique and therefore no amount of money will enable me to go out and buy an equivalent painting. Equity, on the other hand, has developed a remedy (called *specific performance*) for cases like this. If I obtain an order for specific performance against you, you will be obliged to perform our contract and deliver the goods I have agreed to buy. If you fail to comply with the order, you will be in contempt of court and may be sent to prison.

A moment's thought will show you that, since the whole purpose of having the two systems of common law and equity was to get different answers to the same question, it was inevitable that the courts of common law and chancery would find themselves at loggerheads. Returning to the example we have already considered, if you are ordered to pay me damages at common law, and you comply with the order, that will be an end of the matter. However, if equity also orders you to perform the contract, and you fail to do so, you could be imprisoned for contempt of court.

The rule that emerged to deal with conflicts of this kind was that where the two systems conflicted, equity was to prevail over the common law. Since the Judicature Acts of 1873–75, both common law and equity have been administered by the same courts; but, as this jurisdictional change did nothing to avoid conflict between the two systems, there is still a maxim to the effect that where equity and the [common] law conflict, equity prevails.

Perhaps an even more important aspect of equity's creativity than the invention of additional remedies may be found in its invention of the law of trusts. While it is difficult to produce a totally accurate definition of the word *trust*, the idea which underlies all trusts is simple enough, namely that property is owned by one person (or a group of people) for the benefit of another person (or a group of other people). The person or people who own the property is (or are) called the *trustee* (or *trustees*), while the person or people who have the benefit of the property is (or are) called the *beneficiary* (or *beneficiaries*). Because the beneficiaries have the benefit of the property, they are sometimes said to be the *beneficial owners*, even though the common law regards the trustees as being the *legal owners*.

If trustees use trust property for their own benefit, equity will hold them to account. Indeed, one equitable remedy is known as *account* because it compels defendants to account for – or, in other words, pay back – their wrongful profits.

Strictly speaking, this explanation of the nature of a trust is defective, because trusts need not benefit people, but may exist for the benefit of animals and other things, such as the maintenance of buildings. However, the outer limits of the nature of trusts cannot be pursued here. All that need be said is that, historically, wealthy families found that trusts provided a very important way of managing their property. In the modern world, however, the main importance of trusts is that they provide the legal frameworks for the operation of pension funds and unit trusts.

Having seen how judge-made law as a whole contains the contrasting systems of common law and equity, we can now move on to the distinction between judge-made law as a whole, and law made either by Parliament or by someone else acting under authority conferred by Parliament.

Statute law and delegated legislation
Although the courts are still developing the common law, the main sources of English law are now statutes and delegated legislation.

Statutes, as their alternative name *Acts of Parliament* makes plain, are made by Parliament itself. However, in a modern, fast-moving and complex society, Parliament cannot possibly generate all the legislation that is needed. Therefore many statutes delegate to other people or bodies (typically, but by no means exclusively, Secretaries of State and local authorities) the power to make a great deal of detailed law in order to supplement that which is contained in the statutes themselves. Delegated legislation takes many forms, but the most common are statutory instruments (which are usually made by Secretaries of State) and byelaws and compulsory purchase orders (both of which are usually made by local authorities).

Statutes, along with certain Orders made by the Privy Council when exercising the Royal Prerogative on behalf of the Crown (but not enactments of the Scottish Parliament, the Welsh Assembly and the Northern Ireland Assembly) are called *primary* legislation. Laws made by people or bodies acting under authority conferred on them by Parliament are called, variously and interchangeably, *secondary*, *subordinate* or *delegated* legislation. Only statutes come within the doctrine of the legislative supremacy of Parliament, for the very simple reason that they are the only form of legislation made by Parliament.

Common law and civil law

As we have seen, the phrase *common law* is sometimes used generally to mean judge-made law as distinct from statute law, and sometimes more specifically to mean that part of judge-made law which originated in the King's courts, as distinct from that part of judge-made law known as *equity*.

A fundamentally different contrast may be made between *common law* and *civil law*. The contrast in this context is between the English legal system (together with those countries whose legal systems are derived from it, such as Australia, New Zealand and the United States of America) on the one hand, and the legal systems of the states of continental Europe on the other, whose legal systems are derived from Roman Law.

One of the most important functional distinctions between common law and civil law systems is that the latter have no doctrine of *binding* precedent. (The doctrine of binding precedent is discussed in Chapter 7.)

Finally, it is important to notice that the use of the term *civil law* discussed here has nothing whatsoever to do with the distinction between *civil* law and *criminal* law which is discussed in Chapter 1.

● European Union law

Introduction

Originally, there was only the European Coal and Steel Community (ECSC), which was created by the Treaty of Paris 1951. This community, which came into being in 1953, was established for a fixed term of 50 years. Accordingly, it no longer exists, but its functions were transferred initially to the European Community and subsequently, under the Treaty of Lisbon, to the second incarnation of the European Union.

In 1957 two Treaties of Rome established two further communities, namely:

- the European Economic Community (EEC), as it was originally called before the Treaty on European Union 1992 (the TEU or Maastricht Treaty) renamed it as the *European Community* (EC); and
- the European Atomic Energy Community (also known as Euratom).

As well as renaming the European Economic Community as the European Community, the Treaty on European Union created the first incarnation of the European Union. The Union was a composite construction, which was usually said to consist of three pillars. One pillar consisted of the two remaining communities (taken together as a single entity for the purpose of counting the pillars), alongside two areas of inter-governmental co-operation which, by the time of the Treaty of Lisbon 2007 (ToL), covered a Common Foreign and Security Policy (CFSP) and Police and Judicial Co-operation in Criminal Matters (PJCCM). It is important to notice that, at this stage in its evolution, the European Union was not itself a legal entity, being instead an amalgam of two legal entities and two political collaborations. However, under the Treaty of Lisbon, which came into effect in 2009, all the functions of the Union were transferred to a new *legal* entity which became the second incarnation of the European Union and replaced all three pillars of its original incarnation.

The structure and functioning of the second incarnation of the European Union are governed by the Treaty on the Functioning of the European Union (TFEU) and the Treaty on Union (TEU). In form, these treaties are heavily amended versions of, respectively, the EC Treaty and the TEU as they were immediately before the ToL. The fact that the drafters of the ToL achieved the objectives of that treaty by the technique of amending two existing treaties (including renaming one of them) means that the ToL itself will very seldom be referred to, since what matter are the texts of the TFEU and the TEU in its post-ToL incarnation.

The sources of European Union law

Clearly the TFEU and the TEU are the basic sources of EU law. We will not pursue the detailed content of either of these Treaties here, except where it is necessary to do so in relation to the other sources of EU law or where it is useful to comment that previous amendments to their original versions had resulted in various article numbers being applied at different times to what are, either exactly or in effect, the same provisions. For example, what is now art. 267 of the TFEU had previously been both art. 177 and art. 234 of the EC Treaty. (For the broad effect of art. 267, see p. 110.)

Under art. 288 TFEU there are three other types of EU instruments which are binding (and which are, therefore, sources of law), namely:

- Regulations;
- Directives; and
- Decisions.

We will consider the nature of each of these sources in turn, before considering how they, together with the treaties, impact on the English legal system.

The nature of Regulations

Regulations, which are the form of EU law that most closely resembles statute law within the English legal system, are plainly a source of law.

We will come to the effect of EU Regulations in English law in a few moments, but it is worth noticing at this stage that, despite their similarities, English statutes differ from EU Regulations in one important respect. Under the doctrine of the legislative supremacy of Parliament (see Chapter 3), the English courts have no power to quash Acts of Parliament, because it is Parliament and not the courts which are supreme. On the other hand, the European Court of Justice can quash individual Regulations which it finds to be unlawful.

The nature of Directives

Directives have no equivalent within the English legal system. Directives are instructions from the EU to the member states requiring them to achieve certain legal results within their national legal systems, but leaving it for each member state to decide how this should be done. Each Directive will specify a date by which member states must comply with its terms.

It is clear from the nature of Directives that they are not a source of law in the same way that the Treaties and Regulations are sources of law, because they depend on member states for their implementation. Nevertheless, there is plainly a sense in which they are sources – even if only conditional sources – of law, because they bind member states to produce specific legal consequences.

The nature of Decisions

Decisions are addressed to member states or to individuals and are binding upon those to whom they are addressed. Therefore they are plainly a source of the law which applies to those states or individuals.

● How European Union law enters English law

Introduction

The whole of EC law (as it then was) was received into English law by s. 2(1) and (4) of the European Communities Act 1972. However, in order to understand this statement fully, we must investigate two doctrines of what is now EU law that have no equivalents in English law, namely *direct applicability* and *direct effect*.

- Direct applicability
  A provision of EU law is said to be *directly applicable* if it becomes part of the law of member states *automatically*; or, in other words, without any action on the part of member states.
- Direct effect
  A provision of EU law is said to be *directly effective* if, and only if, it creates rights which are enforceable in the courts of a member state at the instance of people who are aggrieved by breaches of the provision.

Most people's immediate reaction when they first encounter the distinction between *direct applicability* and *direct effect* is one of puzzlement. How can a provision of EU law enter the legal systems of member states without also creating rights which are enforceable in the courts of those states? After all, is it not one of the prime functions of courts to enforce all the law in all cases? Understandable though this puzzlement is, in reality it flows from not thinking the topic through with sufficient rigour.

Even if we limit ourselves entirely to the English legal system, many laws do not give rise to rights that are enforceable in the courts. For example, I have the *power* (or *capacity*) to enter into contracts, such as a contract to buy a book. However, if I choose to exercise that power by buying a book written by author A rather than a competing title written by author B, nobody can argue that I have infringed the rights of author B.

The direct applicability and direct effect of different forms of EU law
Since some forms of EU law are only directly *applicable*, while others are also directly *effective*, we obviously need to know which is which. We will consider the treaties, regulations, directives and decisions in turn, but before doing so we will refine the basic question before adding two further ones.

The refinement involves rephrasing the basic question so that it becomes:

- Which forms of EU law are *capable* of being directly effective?

The first additional question is:

- Supposing we are dealing with a form of EU law that *is capable* of being directly effective, how do we know whether this particular provision *actually is* directly effective?

The second additional question is:

- Supposing the particular provision of EU law actually *is* directly effective, against whom can it be enforced? (If it can be enforced by a private individual or organisation against the state, its direct effect is said to be *vertical*. If it can be enforced by a private individual or organisation against another private individual or organisation, its direct effect is said to be *horizontal*.)

To answer this additional question, we need to understand what is meant by *the criteria for direct effect*.

The criteria for direct effect
It is obvious that people who seek to enforce their legal rights in court must be in a position to say what they claim those rights to be. In terms of EU law, the technical terminology that covers this point is *the criteria for direct effect*. Reduced to their essentials, the criteria for direct effect are basically the commonsense requirements that the provision of EU law in question must be both:

- clear and precise in its expression (so that the court can know what it is being asked to enforce); and
- self-contained (in the sense that its implementation must not depend on the exercise of discretion by the public authorities of member states).

If we decide that a particular provision of EU law is of a type which is *capable of direct effect*, and that it also *satisfies the criteria for direct effect* (so that it is, therefore, *actually directly effective*), we then come to the second additional question posed above:

- is the direct effect:
  - only vertical; or
  - both vertical and horizontal?

A provision's direct effect will be only *vertical* if a private individual or organisation can enforce it only against the state. Its direct effect will also be *horizontal* if a private individual or organisation can also enforce it against another private individual or organisation.

Although this statement may seem rather dense on a first reading, it is, in fact, underpinned by some very clear logic. Both treaty articles and regulations present no difficulties: they are both directly applicable and capable of having direct effect. Furthermore, there is no reason to limit their direct effect; and, therefore, in the interests of making EU law as effective as possible, their direct effect is both vertical and horizontal. However, matters are less obvious when it comes to Directives.

As we have seen, Directives require member states to take some action, and therefore they are not directly applicable. However, where a member state fails to implement a Directive by the due date, the result will be that people within that state will be deprived of rights which they would have had if the state in question had complied with its obligations under EU law.

Where this situation arises, therefore, if a person brings an action against the member state which is in default, that state may well reply: *but you do not have the rights you are seeking because we have not implemented the Directive*. However, such a reply would be a clear violation of the fundamental principle of justice that nobody should be allowed to gain advantage from their own wrongdoing, and therefore the Court of Justice has held that, under these circumstances, the Directive can be enforced against the defaulting member state. (*Grad v Finanzamt Traustein* [1970] ECR 825.) In other words, it will have vertical direct effect.

However, if an action is brought against another private individual or organisation, the same logic will not apply. After all, it is not the fault of any private individual or organisation that the state has not complied with its obligations under EU law, and therefore the argument based on gaining advantage from wrongdoing does not even get off the ground. In other words, the potential direct effect of Directives can only ever be vertical, and not horizontal.

By way of example, suppose a Directive requires employers to provide free annual eyesight tests for all their employees who drive motor vehicles. If a member state fails to implement this Directive by the due date, government employees could enforce the Directive against the state, but employees of private organisations could not enforce it against their employers, because the failure to implement the Directive is not their employers' fault.

The EC Treaty does not make Decisions directly applicable, but it does make them binding on the people to whom they are addressed. As the Court of Justice said in *Grad*, the effectiveness of Decisions would be seriously reduced if the courts of member states could not treat them as part of EU law. In other words, Decisions are both directly applicable and capable of vertical direct effect.

This leaves the question of whether their direct effect is *only* vertical, or both vertical and horizontal. Although the Court of Justice has never been called upon to decide this point (which is, therefore, presumably of little importance in purely practical terms), there is no reason, in principle, to withhold horizontal direct effect from Decisions. For example, where a Decision addressed to a company has the consequence that one of its contracts is void because it is contrary to EU law, the other party to the contract should be able to rely on the voidness in an action against the company. Any other conclusion would mean that the company to whom the Decision is addressed would gain an advantage (in this case, a valid contract) by breaching the Decision which rendered the contract void.

A tabular summary
The whole topic of direct applicability and direct effect is summarised in the two tables overleaf.

Indirect effect
Finally, even where Union law lacks direct effect, it may still have an *indirect effect* on the laws of member states, in the sense that a relevant provision of EU law may influence the interpretation of existing national laws of member states. This proposition is sometimes known as the *von Colson*

principle or the *Marleasing principle* after the leading cases of *von Colson v Land Nordrhein Westfalen* [1986] 2 CMLR 430 and *Marleasing SA v La Comercial Internacional de Alimentacion SA* [1992] 1 CMLR 305.

Table 1

	Directly applicable?	*Capable of direct effect?
Treaty Articles	Yes	Yes
Regulations	Yes	Yes
Directives	No	**Yes
Decisions	Yes	Yes

*A provision which is capable of having direct effect will not actually have direct effect unless it also satisfies the criteria for direct effect.
**Provided the Directive has not been implemented within the time allowed.

Table 2

	Capable of vertical direct effect?	Capable of horizontal direct effect?
Treaty Articles	Yes	Yes
Regulations	Yes	Yes
Directives	Yes	No
Decisions	Yes	Probably

● Resolving conflicts between English law and European Union law

One inevitable consequence of the entry of EU law into English law is that, from time to time, specific provisions of the two systems will conflict with each other. It is clearly established that these conflicts will be resolved in favour of EU law, but we will postpone further discussion of this matter until we come to the topic of the supremacy of EU law in the next chapter (see pp. 45–48).

● European Convention on Human Rights

The European Convention on Human Rights and its effect on the English legal system are discussed in Chapter 5.

● Conclusion

In order to be confident of your ability to understand the way in which English law works, you need a good working knowledge of three legal systems. More particularly, in addition to understanding domestic English law, you need to understand both EU law and the law of the European Convention on Human Rights.

The sources of domestic English law are the common law (using this phrase in its broad sense to mean all judge-made law, including equity), together with statute law and delegated legislation.

The principal sources of European EU law are the TFEU and the TEU, together with Regulations, Directives and Decisions. The doctrines of direct applicability and direct effect govern the ways in which EU law impacts upon the domestic English law.

The law of the European Convention on Human Rights, and the operation of the Human Rights Act 1998, are discussed in Chapter 5.

3 The Constitutional Context of English Law

A constitution provides the legal structure for the governance of a state. The British constitution is underpinned by the doctrines of the legislative supremacy of Parliament, the rule of law and the separation of powers. However, it is practically unique in not being contained in a single written document. Membership of the European Community involves a voluntary limitation on the legislative supremacy of Parliament; but the Human Rights Act 1998 does not try to limit the legislative supremacy of Parliament in any way.

● Introduction

In this chapter we will pick up and develop the point (which we introduced briefly at p. 2) that constitutional law is concerned with the allocation of public (or governmental) power between different institutions and people. We will begin by considering the nature of constitutions generally, before looking more closely at the British constitution.

● What is a constitution?

Introduction

Every state must have a constitution in the sense of a body of legal rules (usually supplemented by a collection of informal practices which are called *constitutional conventions*), both of which will reflect certain underlying political doctrines and will provide a framework for the governance of that state. While it is obvious that both the underlying doctrines and the content of the rules and practices will vary from one state to another, it is also true, if less obvious, that the way in which those doctrines, rules and practices are presented will also vary from one state to another.

Written and unwritten constitutions

Almost all countries have what are called *written constitutions*, in the sense that there is a single document containing at least the most important formal rules, which may be expressed in varying degrees of detail. In the context of this meaning of the phrase *written constitution*, the British constitution is usually described as being *unwritten*. However, it is important to note that this is a technical usage of the word *unwritten*. More particularly, it does not mean that the rules are not written down anywhere, but simply that they are not written down in one place. In fact, almost all the formal rules of the British constitution are written down, either in the judgments of the courts or in Acts of Parliament, while the underlying doctrines and almost all the informal practices are described in sources ranging from textbooks on constitutional law and political science to the memoirs of politicians. From time to time, the doctrines and informal practices may also be recognised by the courts.

The factual inaccuracy of the term *unwritten constitution* leads some people to reject the *written/unwritten* terminology altogether, preferring to use the terms *codified* and *uncodified* instead. Since *codified* means *brought together in a single document* (or at least in a small number of documents), while *uncodified* means *not brought together in this way*, there is much to be said for this usage. However, this does not exhaust the possible variations of terminology, since some people prefer to speak in terms of *formal* and *informal* constitutions. From your point of view, however, all that really matters is that you are able to understand whatever usage you may come across.

The relationship between *constitutions* and *law*

Since the constitution validates the exercise of power by governments, two questions arise, namely:

- what validates the constitution? and
- what is the relationship between government and the constitution?

One of the best brief answers to these questions, at least from the viewpoint of the political tradition which is usually known as *liberal democracy*, may be found in the words of Tom Paine, the 18th century English radical:

A constitution is not the act of a government, but of a people
constituting a government, and *a government without a constitution
is power without a right ... A constitution is a thing antecedent to a
government; and a government is only the creature of a constitution*.
(*The Rights of Man*, 1790; emphasis added.)

In short, therefore, the constitution comes before, and validates, the
government, rather than the government coming first and then validating
the constitution. It follows that, since law is the product of *governmental
processes* (using that phrase loosely for the moment), we can adapt Paine's
words and say that the *constitution is a thing antecedent to the law*.

One crucial function of any constitution is to identify the person who, or the
body which, exercises supreme power within the state. Different constitutions
take different views of this matter, with variations in constitutional histories between different states usually providing the explanation for how the matter has
been resolved in each case. Some states, such as the United States of America,
place this ultimate power in the Supreme Court. On the other hand, perhaps the
most important doctrine of the British Constitution is that this ultimate power
lies with Parliament. At this stage, therefore, it is appropriate to turn our attention to the underlying doctrines of the British Constitution generally.

● The underlying doctrines of the British constitution

Introduction
There are three underlying doctrines of the British constitution, namely:

- the *legislative supremacy of Parliament*;
- the *rule of law*; and
- the *separation of powers*.

If your course includes a more detailed study of the British constitution,
you will consider each of these doctrines in some detail at that stage, but
whether or not this is so, it will be useful for us to consider each of them
briefly here.

The legislative supremacy of Parliament
The *legislative supremacy* (or, as it is sometimes called, the *sovereignty*) *of
Parliament*, has been at the heart of British constitutional law for over three

centuries, since the Glorious Revolution of 1688. The idea of the *legislative supremacy of Parliament* is simply that:

- Parliament can pass any legislation it wishes to pass; and
- only Parliament can repeal legislation which Parliament has passed.

However, three points must be made if this statement is not to be seriously misleading.

First, it is essential to grasp that *Parliament* is *not* the same thing as the *House of Commons*. More particularly, for something to be an *Act of Parliament*, it must normally have been passed by both the House of Commons and the House of Lords and must always have received the Royal Assent from the monarch. The exceptional situation lurking behind the word *normally* in the previous sentence arises where a special procedure, which is contained in the Parliament Acts 1911 and 1949, is invoked. The details of this procedure are complicated, but its effect is simple: the House of Lords may delay legislation for one year, but cannot veto it. The only exceptions are Bills which the Speaker of the House of Commons certifies as being *money bills* – which are exempt even from the one year delaying power – and bills to prolong the life of Parliament, which are exempt from the provisions of the Parliament Acts altogether, and which can, therefore, still be vetoed by the House of Lords. The Parliament Acts procedure is very seldom invoked, although notable examples of its use include:

- the Parliament Act 1949, which was itself passed under the provisions of the 1911 Act and which reduced the Lords' delaying power from two years to one;
- the War Crimes Act 1991, which permits United Kingdom courts to try people charged with certain war crimes, provided they were, on 8 March 1990, or have subsequently become, British citizens or residents of the United Kingdom, the Channel Islands or the Isle of Man; and
- the Hunting Act 2004 which creates an offence of hunting wild mammals with dogs.

Secondly, the fact that something – in this case the legislative power of Parliament – is *legally* uncontrolled does not necessarily mean that it is *totally* uncontrolled. More particularly, in a liberal democracy, it is extremely unlikely that Parliament would use its powers in a way which would be universally viewed as being oppressive or unjust in any other way. Furthermore, there are two relevant constitutional conventions, namely that *the*

House of Lords usually defers to the House of Commons, and that *the monarch does not withhold the Royal Assent*. The combined effect of these conventions is that, in purely practical terms, the political party that dominates the House of Commons will also very largely dominate the whole of the legislative process.

Thirdly, in *Factortame Ltd v Secretary of State for Transport (No 2)* [1991] 1 AC 603, the House of Lords accepted that when Parliament passed the European Communities Act 1972, it effectively surrendered part of its sovereignty, to the extent that whenever English law and what is now European Union law conflict, European Union law prevails.

By way of contrast to this third point, and although we will not pursue the protection of fundamental rights until we come to Chapter 5, it may be worth noting here that the Human Rights Act 1998 contains nothing which limits the continuing legislative supremacy of Parliament. More particularly, s. 4(5) of the 1998 Act expressly provides that where a United Kingdom statute is found to be in breach of a *Convention right* (as defined by s. 1(1) of the Act), neither the outcome of the case, nor – more importantly in the present context – the continuing validity of the offending statute, will be affected.

Two further, but unconnected, points may usefully be made by way of conclusion.

First, the doctrine of *the legislative supremacy of Parliament* is limited, as the phrase itself indicates, to Acts of *Parliament*, and therefore the doctrine does not apply to *delegated legislation*, which can be – and frequently is – quashed by the courts. (We have already considered the topic of delegated legislation in Chapter 2; but, very briefly, you will recall that it is legislation made by some person or body other than Parliament, to whom Parliament has delegated the power to legislate.)

Secondly, Parliament's power to repeal Acts of Parliament may be exercised either expressly or impliedly. The idea of express repeal requires no comment, but it is worth noticing that implied repeal occurs where two statutory provisions are so fundamentally incompatible that one must give way to the other. In this situation, Parliament is presumed to have been aware of the earlier provision, and therefore is also presumed to have intended that the later one should repeal it.

The rule of law

Introduction

The doctrine of the rule of law states what is essentially a *political* ideal, namely that government should be conducted according to law, rather than discretion. It comes in two versions, namely *formal* and *substantive*. We will consider each in turn.

Formal versions of the rule of law
One of the most famous statements of a formal version of the rule of law comes from AV Dicey, a leading Victorian commentator, who said that it requires

> the absolute supremacy or predominance of regular law as opposed to the influence of arbitrary power, [with the resulting exclusion of] the existence of arbitrariness ... or even of wide discretionary authority on the part of the government. (*The Law of the Constitution*, first published in 1885.)

While Dicey's version has an obvious and immediate appeal, on reflection it can be seen to be a substantial overstatement: the process of government inevitably requires the exercise of discretionary – and sometimes wide discretionary – authority. Nevertheless, Dicey was right to identify the dangers of discretionary powers, even though it would be impossible, in practical terms, to eliminate them. What really matters, therefore, is not that discretionary powers should be eliminated, but that:

- whatever the limits which are imposed upon discretionary governmental powers, they must be identified by law;
- there must be legal mechanisms for deciding whether government has exceeded those limits; and
- the courts must be able to provide remedies when government has been shown to have exceeded those limits.

Furthermore, and even before the question of the extent and control of discretion arises,

- laws must be made in accordance with the procedures laid down by the constitution.

Of course, it is implicit in what has just been said that those who advance purely formal versions of the rule of law exclude from the scope of the doctrine any concern with the *content* of the law, provided that any relevant formalities and restrictions have been observed. Thus an absolute dictatorship whose laws systematically differentiate between the rights of its subjects on the grounds of their race, sex, sexual orientation or religious beliefs could easily comply with the rule of law in a purely formal sense, while at the same time the content of its law could be seriously lacking (at any rate according to the generally prevailing standards of contemporary western democracies). It is this aspect of the matter which leads many political and legal theorists to prefer *substantive* versions of the doctrine.

Substantive versions of the rule of law
By way of contrast with their *formal* counterparts, *substantive* versions of the rule of law require more than mere compliance with the relevant formal criteria: they rely upon the idea of the rule of law for the additional purpose of providing the basis for certain substantive rights.

Obviously, substantive versions of the doctrine present problems which their formal counterparts do not encounter, since there may be sincere, legitimate and reasonable disagreements as to which substantive rights the law should recognise and uphold. For example, does allowing same-sex marriage represent a proper respect for individual autonomy by allowing people to make up their own minds as to what constitutes the good life? Or does it represent an insidious undermining of the traditional view of marriage as the union of one man and one woman, and thus indirectly undermine society itself by undermining one of its most important building blocks, namely the family?

While arguments such as these may be both interesting and important, once the doctrine of the rule of law becomes inextricably linked with the content of the law, there is clearly a danger that those who lose such arguments on particular issues will feel that the rule of law has let them down; and they may, therefore, become alienated from society as a whole. Where this happens, those who prefer the formal versions of the doctrine will argue that the substantive versions have not only failed to deliver on their own terms, but – even more seriously – have undermined the whole enterprise of law as an agent of social cohesion. In other words, the formal argument will be that the substantive argument has helped to destroy that which it appeared to be advocating.

How strict is the formal/substantive distinction?
Although the distinction between formal and substantive versions of the rule of law, as outlined above, appears to present a straightforward choice between two alternatives, it can be argued that a formal version may require rather more than mere compliance with formalities, without forfeiting its status as a formal version. The argument to this effect is that law must,

in its very nature, be capable of guiding conduct; and therefore it follows that *any* version of the rule of law must have *some* substantive content. As a bare minimum, for example, legal acts performed by public bodies and officials should be guided by rules which are open, stable, clear and general, because laws which do not satisfy these criteria do not enable the people who are affected by them to know what they can and cannot do. (In other words, the nature of law itself means that even the most strictly formal version of the rule of law must implicitly contain some qualitative criteria and this means that they are not truly and exclusively formal in nature.)

On this view of the matter, therefore, the distinction between formal and substantive versions of the rule of law is more a matter of degree than a straight choice between two alternatives.

By way of an aside, this last comment illustrates a very important aspect of the way in which lawyers very often think. Many questions which appear to be capable of being asked (and answered) on a straightforward *either/or* basis cannot truly be dealt with on this basis because closer and more critical consideration reveals a spectrum of possibilities consisting of two extreme – and often very simple – positions, between which there is a range of much more subtle possibilities. It is, therefore, the task of the law – and, therefore, of lawyers – to classify these more subtle possibilities into categories which both reflect the realities of life in terms which can be proved, so that people – and, ultimately, the courts – can know how the law applies to specific cases.

The separation of powers

The doctrine of the separation of powers is usually attributed to the 18th century French political philosopher Montesquieu, and more particularly to his book *L'Ésprit des Lois*, although the origins of the idea can actually be traced back to classical antiquity.

The doctrine divides all forms of power exercised by the state into three categories, namely *legislative*, *executive* and *judicial*, with the nature of each being as follows:

- legislative power involves *making* law;
- executive power involves *administering* the law, in the sense in which governmental agencies and officials administer it; and
- judicial power involves *interpreting and applying* the law in the sense in which the courts interpret and apply it.

Having identified these three types of power, the doctrine then requires that no more than one type should be exercised by a single body or official.

So, for example, the legislature that makes the law should not also interpret it and apply it in individual cases. Similarly, executive bodies and officials who administer the law should not have the power to make authoritative decisions as to what the law means and how it is to be applied in individual cases. Furthermore, the courts which interpret and apply the law should not also make it.

Although it is important to note that the British constitution has never reflected this strict version of the doctrine, the basic idea of the separation of powers retains considerable practical importance in several ways. One of the most obvious examples of this importance lies in the field of judicial review (which, as we will see at p. 52, is the process that requires the court to decide whether a *decision-making process* is *lawful*, but without asking whether the *decision itself* is *right*). The case of *R v Birmingham City Council ex parte Sheptonhurst Ltd* [1990] 1 All ER 1026 provides a useful example of judicial review in action.

The case was one of several similar ones in which the court was concerned with the refusal of local authorities to renew expiring sex shop licences that had been granted under statutory powers. In each case, the local authority had concluded that the appropriate number of sex shops in the relevant area was nil, and therefore all applications for licences would be refused, even though, on the facts of each of the cases which were before the court on this occasion, there had been no change of circumstances since the previous licences had been granted.

The court held that when considering an application for renewal of a sex shop licence, a local authority must *have regard to* the fact that a licence had previously been granted. However, provided it does have regard to this fact, its decision to refuse to renew a licence will *not* be perverse simply because there has been no change in the character of the relevant locality or in the use to which any premises in the vicinity are put.

The crucial point in the court's approach to cases such as this is that the legislature is not only supreme but must also be taken to know that a local authority is a democratically elected body, whose membership changes from time to time in line with the changing views of the local electorate. It is not surprising, therefore, that what is 'appropriate' may be perceived differently by different elected representatives at different times. Equally, it is not surprising that the court, being aware of the doctrine of the separation of powers, should decide not to intervene.

Although the constitutional basis of the *Birmingham* case is readily apparent, the courts are also clearly aware that there are cases where the doctrine of the rule of law does require them to intervene. As Farwell

LJ said, in *R v Shoreditch Assessment Committee ex parte Morgan* [1910] 2 KB 859, 880:

> It is a contradiction in terms to create a [decision-maker] with limited jurisdiction and unlimited power to determine such limit at its own will and pleasure – such a [decision-maker] would be autocratic, not limited ...

Nevertheless, the court remains conscious that its constitutional role is limited. For example, in *R v Hillingdon London Borough Council ex parte Puhlhofer* [1986] AC 484, which arose in the context of local authorities' statutory duties in cases of homelessness, Lord Brightman said (at p. 518):

> My Lords, I am troubled at the prolific use of judicial review for the purposes of challenging the performance by local authorities of their functions under the Act ... Where the existence or non-existence of a fact is left to the judgment and discretion of a public body and that fact involves a broad spectrum, ranging from the obvious to the debatable to the just conceivable, it is the duty of the court to leave the decision of that fact to the public body, save in a case where it is obvious that the public body, consciously or unconsciously, are acting perversely.

Perhaps the most important thing for you to take away from the discussion so far is that, when it comes to real cases, there is often a degree of tension between the basic doctrines underlying the British constitution. When should the courts be primarily conscious of their limited status according to the doctrines of the legislative supremacy of Parliament and the separation of powers, and therefore refuse to intervene in a particular case? Alternatively, when should they assert themselves as the guardians of the rule of law? Finally, to what extent is it relevant – as will often be the case – that the decision-maker, whose conduct has resulted in the case being brought to court, is democratically accountable? (In other words, when should the court take the view that the existence of a *political* mechanism of control is sufficient to justify the court in refusing a *legal* remedy?)

The limited nature of the separation of powers in the British constitution
So far we have mentioned only in passing that the British constitution does not reflect a strict version of the doctrine of the separation of powers. Until recently, the most complete breach of the doctrine lay

in the status of the Lord Chancellor as a member of the legislature (as Speaker of the House of Lords), the executive (as a government minister) and the judiciary (as a member of the Appellate Committee of the House of Lords). However, the ancient office of Lord Chancellor is now held together with the new office of Secretary of State for Justice and its holder does not sit as a judge, so we will not dwell on this former oddity. On the other hand, we will consider one other, less total but more important (albeit also recently defunct) way in which the British constitution has historically failed to reflect the doctrine, together with two ways in which it continues to do so. These are:

- the status of the Appellate Committee of the House of Lords as the highest court of appeal in the English legal system;
- the domination of the legislature by the executive; and
- the power of the courts to make law through the doctrine of binding precedent.

Secondly, we can develop a point that we made when discussing the meaning of the word *Parliament* (see p. 37). As a matter of political reality, all members of the government (or, to use the terminology which better fits the separation of powers, the *executive*) will sit in Parliament (or, again to use the terminology which better fits the separation of powers, the *legislature*). Furthermore, the vast majority of them will sit in the House of Commons. In other words, the political party which forms the government will usually dominate the House of Commons, and will, therefore, also effectively dominate the legislative process. The only exception to this proposition is that a government with only a very small (or perhaps even non-existent) majority in the House of Commons will be very dependent on the loyalty of its back-benchers. Since this may limit the range of legislative proposals which the government chooses to bring forward, it is not wholly fanciful to say that, in this situation at least, the legislature is exercising some control over the executive. However, this situation is relatively unusual.

Starting with the Appellate Committee of the House of Lords, no strict version of the doctrine of the separation of powers could have tolerated the degree of overlap between the *legislative* and *judicial* functions which inevitably flowed from having a committee of one of the Houses of Parliament also functioning as a court. With the coming of the Supreme Court this is, of course, no longer an issue, but the enduring authority of the House of Lords' decision makes it worthy of notice nevertheless.

Thirdly, the courts (that is to say, the *judiciary*) make law (that is to say, they *legislate*) through the doctrine of binding precedent. However, as we shall be considering this doctrine more closely in Chapter 7, we will say no more about it at this stage.

Clearly, therefore, there are various ways in which the functioning of the separation of powers as an underlying doctrine of the British Constitution is not as straightforward as it may appear to be at first sight. However, all those bodies and officials who perform public decision-making functions are aware of the terms of the doctrine, and will, despite its qualified nature in the British context, treat it as constraining their freedom of action in at least some contexts.

● Devolution to Scotland, Wales and Northern Ireland

The Scotland Act 1998 created the *Scottish Parliament*, the Government of Wales Act 1998 created the *National Assembly for Wales* (which is commonly known simply as *the Welsh Assembly*), and the Northern Ireland Act 1998 created the *Northern Ireland Assembly*. All three statutes devolve certain legislative powers to the bodies which they create, with the powers of the Welsh Assembly having been extended by the Government of Wales Act 2006. The mass of detail in each of these devolutionary schemes need not be pursued here.

● The European Union dimension

Introduction
We have dealt with the sources of EU law, and its reception into English law, in the previous chapter (see pp. 28–32). However, the fact that we are now discussing the constitutional context of the English legal system makes it appropriate to deal here with the basic question of the supremacy of EU law over the laws of the member states; and, more particularly, its supremacy over English law.

The supremacy of Union law over the laws of the member states
From a very early stage in the development of the European Economic Community (as it then was), the Court of Justice established the supremacy of what is now EU law over the laws of the member states. As the Court put it, in the leading case of *van Gend en Loos* [1963] CMLR 105, 129:

The Community constitutes a new legal order ... for whose benefit the states have limited their sovereign rights.

Very shortly afterwards, in *Costa v ENEL* [1964] CMLR 425, the Court said (at pp. 455–456):

The reception within the laws of each member State, of provisions having a Community source, and more particularly of the terms and of the spirit of the Treaty, has as a corollary the impossibility, for the member State, to give preference to a unilateral and *subsequent* measure against a legal order accepted by them on the basis of reciprocity ...

The transfer, by member States, from their national orders in favour of the Community order of the rights and obligations arising from the Treaty, carries with it a clear limitation of their sovereign right upon which a *subsequent* unilateral law, incompatible with the aims of the Community, cannot prevail. (Emphasis added.)

The justification for the supremacy of EU law over national law lies in the Court's insistence that EU law must apply uniformly in all member states.

In accordance with the principle of the precedence of Community law, the relationship between provisions of the Treaty and direct applicable measures of the institutions on the one hand and the national law of the member states on the other is such that those provisions and measures not only by their entry into force render automatically inapplicable any conflicting provision of current national law but – in so far as they are an integral part of, and take precedence in, the legal order applicable in the territory of each of the member states – also preclude the valid adoption of new national legislative measures to the extent to which they would be incompatible with Community provisions.

Indeed any recognition that national legislative measures which encroach upon the field within which the Community exercises its legislative power or which are otherwise incompatible with the provisions of Community law had any legal effect would amount to a corresponding denial of the effectiveness of obligations undertaken unconditionally and irrevocably by member states pursuant to the Treaty and would thus imperil the very foundations of the Community.

(Emphasis added. *Italian Finance Administration v Simmenthal*
[1978] 3 CMLR 263, 283.)

Furthermore, it is clear from *Internationale Handelsgessellschaft mbH*
[1972] CMLR 255, that EU law prevails even over a fundamental doctrine
of a member state's constitution. The facts were that a German company argued that a Community Regulation was invalid because it infringed
the principle of proportionality, which was a fundamental principle of the
German Constitution, and the Constitution contained nothing which would
give supremacy to Community law. Although the Court of Justice decided,
on the facts, that there had been no breach of the principle of proportionality, the Court took the opportunity (at p. 283) to re-emphasise the supremacy
of Community law:

> The law born from the Treaty [cannot] have the courts opposing to
> it rules of national law *of any nature whatsoever* ... the validity of a
> Community instrument or its effect within a member state cannot
> be affected by allegations that it strikes at either the fundamental
> rights as formulated in that state's constitution or the principles of a
> national constitutional structure. (Emphasis added.)

The EU doctrine of the supremacy of EU law clearly raises a difficulty in
relation to the United Kingdom. One side of the argument may be outlined
thus:

- The United Kingdom courts should not uphold United Kingdom legislation which is inconsistent with EU law, because (at least in the case
  of legislation passed after the European Communities Act 1972), the
  doctrine of *implied repeal* will operate to repeal, at least as far as
  is necessary for the instant case, that part of the 1972 Act which
  provided for the law of the EU to prevail over the law of the United
  Kingdom. (The doctrine of *implied repeal* is explained at p. 38.)

The other side of the argument may be outlined thus:

- when passing the 1972 Act, Parliament made what is now EU law
  part of English law; and
- it is a basic doctrine of EU law that it shall prevail over any inconsistent laws of member states; and

- *Internationale Handelsgessellschaft mbH* (see above) shows that this basic doctrine prevails over even the most basic constitutional doctrines of member states.

The House of Lords resolved the matter in *Factortame Ltd v Secretary of State for Transport (No 2)* [1991] AC 603. In the context of a decision that came down in favour of the second argument, Lord Bridge said (at pp. 658–659):

> If the supremacy within the European Community of Community law over the national law of member States was not always inherent in the EEC Treaty, it was certainly well established in the jurisprudence of the Court of Justice long before the United Kingdom joined the Community. Thus, whatever limitation of its sovereignty Parliament accepted when it enacted the European Communities Act 1972 was entirely voluntary. Under the terms of the 1972 Act it has always been clear that it was the duty of a United Kingdom court, when delivering final judgment, to override any rule of national law found to be in conflict with any directly enforceable rule of Community law. Similarly, when decisions of the Court of Justice have exposed areas of United Kingdom law which failed to implement Council Directives, Parliament has always loyally accepted the obligation to make appropriate and prompt amendments.

Finally, the case of *Thoburn v Sunderland City Council* [2002] EWHC 195 Admin [2003], QB 151 must be noted. In the context of an appeal by way of case stated to the High Court, Laws LJ expressly rejected the possibility of relying on the doctrine of implied repeal where a later statute conflicts with the European Communities Act 1972. The basis of his decision was that there is a category of 'constitutional statutes' (including Magna Carta, the Bill of Rights 1689, the Human Rights Act 1998, and – crucially in the present case – the European Communities Act 1972) which '*by force of the common law* cannot be impliedly repealed'. (Emphasis added.) In passing, it may be worth noting that, while this decision may well be correct in relation to the narrow point of the inapplicability of the doctrine of implied repeal in relation to the European Communities Act 1972, the House of Lords subsequently doubted whether there is a category of statutes which can properly be described as 'constitutional'. (*Watkins v Secretary of State for the Home Department* [2006] UKHL 17, [2006] 2 AC 395.)

● The European Convention on Human Rights

The status of the European Convention on Human Rights within the British constitution is discussed in Chapter 5. All that need be said here is that no issues concerning the legislative supremacy of Parliament arise from the way in which the Human Rights Act 1998 makes the Convention relevant to the English legal system.

● Conclusion

The word *constitution* is used in two senses. In one sense it means the body of rules and informal practices which provide for, and control, the governance of the state. In another sense, it means a single document which sets out at least the most important of those rules. Every state must have a constitution in the first sense. In practice, almost all states also have a constitution in the second sense. However, there is no single document containing the British constitution, which is, therefore, described variously as being *unwritten*, *uncodified* and *informal*.

Despite the informal way in which the British Constitution is presented, it clearly functions within a framework provided by the three doctrines of the legislative supremacy of Parliament, the rule of law and the separation of powers.

The European Communities Act 1972 has added the doctrine of the supremacy of what is now EU law to the doctrinal basis of the British constitution. By way of contrast, the Human Rights Act 1998 does not affect the legislative supremacy of parliament.

The law of the European Convention on Human Rights, and the operation of the Human Rights Act 1998, are discussed in Chapter 5.

4 The Jurisdictions of the Principal Courts

Most of the principal English courts exercise both criminal and civil jurisdictions and do so both at first instance and on appeal. The High Court also exercises a supervisory jurisdiction by way of judicial review. Questions of European Union law raised in domestic courts may be referred to the European Court of Justice under the preliminary ruling procedure. The European Court of Human Rights may order a state to pay compensation where there has been a breach of the Convention, but it can neither enforce that order nor compel the state to change its law in order to make it comply with the Convention.

● Introduction

In order to understand some of the material in this book, you will need also to understand, at least in outline, the jurisdictions of the principal English courts as well as the EU's courts and the European Court of Human Rights. (In this context, *jurisdiction* simply means *the power to hear a case*. In other contexts – see, for example, p. 88 – it means *the geographical area which is subject to the court's power*.) To begin with, you will simply have to *learn* some of the detail, which will no doubt seem tedious. However, as you become immersed in the study of law, you will find that you rapidly acquire the ability to refer to the right court in the right way.

The principal statutes governing the jurisdictions of the English courts include the Magistrates' Courts Act 1980, the Senior Courts Act 1981 (renamed from being the Supreme Court Act 1981 by the Constitutional Reform Act 2005), the County Courts Act 1984, the Courts and Legal Services Act 1990, the Civil Procedure Act 1997 and the Constitutional Reform Act 2005.

(Other statutes deal with the sentencing powers of criminal courts and the administration of various courts, but these topics are beyond the scope of this book.)

One complication which is worth noting at this stage is that the Supreme Court Act 1981 constituted the Supreme Court as consisting of the Crown Court, the High Court and the Court of Appeal (omitting the Appellate Committee of the House of Lords which, although often referred to as a court – as indeed it is in this book – was technically not a court at all, being rather a committee of one of the Houses of Parliament). The Constitutional Reform Act 2005 created what is now the Supreme Court, to which it transferred the jurisdiction previously exercised by the Appellate Committee of the House of Lords and – as we saw in the previous paragraph, renamed the 1981 Act as the Senior Courts Act, to reflect the fact that the Crown Court, the High Court and the Court of Appeal were subsequently to be known as the *Senior Courts* rather than as the *Supreme Court*. The consequence of this is that whenever you see the expression *the Supreme Court* used in the context of the English legal system, you need to ask yourself when that expression was being used, so that you know which one of its two meanings was intended. Admittedly, the answer to this question will usually – and increasingly – be obvious, since the expression will almost always mean the current Supreme Court. However, it is easy to become complacent when ambiguous terms almost always bear the same one of their two meanings, and therefore to overlook the possibility that you have encountered one of the occasional instances in which they bear the other meaning.

● The three types of jurisdiction

Introduction
The courts exercise three types of jurisdiction, namely *at first instance, on appeal*, and *supervisory*, where the proceedings are by way of *judicial review*.

Jurisdiction at first instance
Cases which are being heard for the first time are said to be *at first instance*. In these cases the court will have to identify those facts which are agreed and make findings of those facts which are not agreed, before deciding what the relevant law is and applying that law to the facts in order to reach a decision.

Jurisdiction on appeal

A challenge to a decision reached at first instance will be by way of *appeal*. The court which hears the appeal is said to have *appellate jurisdiction*. An appellate court which upholds an appeal will normally be able to substitute its own decision for the one that was reached at first instance. The exception to this proposition is that in appeals *by way of case stated* (see below), the appellate court will usually be limited to sending the case back to the lower court for further consideration in the light of the appellate court's judgment. However, in some circumstances, even where an appeal is by way of case stated, the appellate court can direct the lower court to reach a specific decision.

Supervisory jurisdiction

The High Court has, for many centuries, *supervised* the way in which some lower courts and administrative decision-makers exercise their decision-making powers. This jurisdiction is called *judicial review*. Although a claim for judicial review may, at first glance, seem to be much the same as an appeal, closer examination reveals a crucial difference. In judicial review, the court will be considering the *legality of the decision-making process* that produced the earlier decision, rather than the *correctness of the decision* itself. One consequence of this is that, even if the court upholds a claim for judicial review, its most extensive power will usually be limited to quashing the decision and requiring the decision-maker to reconsider the decision on a lawful basis. The exception to this proposition is that where a lawful decision-making process could result in only one possible decision, the court that upholds the claim for judicial review may simply make that decision itself, without involving the original decision-maker.

Although the essence of the distinction between *appeal* and *judicial review* is quite clear, it will be apparent from what has been said that there is some overlap between *appeal by way of case stated* and *judicial review*. The explanation for this is complex and involves delving into legal history. We will simply note it and pass on.

● The hierarchy of the courts

Introduction

The hierarchy of the courts, including for these purposes tribunals and inquiries, is best represented as a diagram.

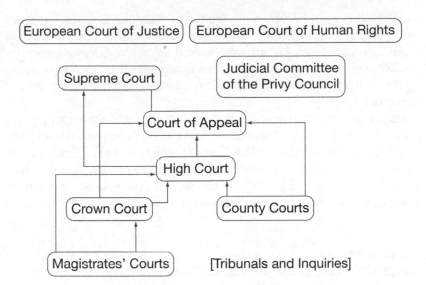

Magistrates' courts

The jurisdiction of the magistrates' courts includes both civil and criminal elements. It is almost entirely exercisable only at first instance, but some very limited elements of civil jurisdiction involve hearing appeals.

The magistrates' civil jurisdiction at first instance does not include either contract or tort, but does include a very mixed bag of aspects of administrative law. These relate especially (but not exclusively) to the topics of highways and public health, and are largely left over from the time when the magistrates exercised many of the functions that are now exercised by elected local authorities.

Similarly, the appellate jurisdiction of the magistrates is almost entirely limited to administrative law, with a particular focus on appeals against certain decisions of local authorities in matters such as public health, highways and licensing.

When sitting as family proceedings courts, the magistrates' civil jurisdiction is at first instance only, and includes a variety of aspects of child welfare and family law, but does not include divorce.

The magistrates' criminal jurisdiction includes both trials (including guilty pleas) and sending people to the Crown Court, either for trial or for sentence. When sitting as youth courts, the magistrates' criminal jurisdiction involves defendants who are under the age of 18.

Most magistrates are not legally qualified (or, to use the more formal vocabulary, and putting it the other way round, they are *lay*) and are not paid for their services. However, some are both legally qualified and employed on a full-time, salaried basis. The latter were known for many years as *stipendiary magistrates*, but are now known as *District Judges (Magistrates' Courts)*. In practice, lay magistrates tend to rely heavily on their legal advisers for advice on the law, although technically they decide both the law and the facts.

Magistrates have no particular style and title as such, although they may put *JP* after their names. (*JP* stands for *Justice of the Peace*, which is an alternative, somewhat more formal and ancient, synonym for *magistrate*.) When addressing a bench of magistrates, the formal mode of address is *Your Worships*, but in practice many advocates address the entire bench through the chair, in which case the form of address is *Sir* or *Madam*, as the case may be.

The Crown Court

The Crown Court's jurisdiction includes both civil and criminal elements, and is exercisable both at first instance and on appeal.

The Crown Court's civil jurisdiction at first instance does not include either contract or tort. It is principally concerned with residual aspects of administrative law, particularly in relation to highways, and dates very largely from the time when the magistrates, sitting either in Petty Sessions (which are now known as magistrates' courts) or at Quarter Sessions, performed many of the functions which are now performed by local authorities. (Quarter Sessions were abolished and replaced with the Crown Court by the Courts Act 1971.)

The Crown Court's criminal jurisdiction at first instance covers those cases which have been transferred from the magistrates' courts and is exercised by trying those defendants who plead not guilty and sentencing those who plead guilty. It also includes dealing with people whom the magistrates have committed for sentence. A Crown Court trial is conducted by a judge and a jury, while sentencing on a guilty plea is done by a judge sitting with magistrates.

The Crown Court's appellate jurisdiction in both civil and criminal cases consists almost entirely of hearing appeals against decisions of the magistrates; and therefore, once again, the civil side does not include contracts and tort. In criminal cases, appeals may be against either conviction or sentence. Appeals against conviction are by way of re-hearing, which means that there is a full trial, with the witnesses giving their evidence again, as they did in the magistrates' court. Appeals against sentence are heard on the basis of the prosecution explaining the facts of the offence and the advocate for the defendant explaining the basis on which it is submitted that the sentence was excessive. Both types of appeal are heard by a judge sitting with magistrates rather than with a jury. The prosecution cannot appeal to the Crown Court against an acquittal by the magistrates.

Judges of the Crown Court are known as *circuit judges*. Their formal style is *His* (or *Her*) *Honour Judge Blank*, which may be abbreviated in writing to *HHJ Blank*, or *HH Mary Blank*. More informally, but very commonly, a circuit judge may be described as *Judge Blank*. Circuit judges are addressed as *Your Honour*.

County Courts

The County Courts' jurisdiction is entirely civil, and is exercisable almost entirely at first instance. However, it does have a very limited appellate jurisdiction, arising especially (but not exclusively) in relation to a range of decisions made by local authorities concerning certain aspects of housing law.

In contrast to the civil jurisdiction of both the magistrates' courts and the Crown Court, the County Courts' jurisdiction includes contract, tort and divorce.

Circuit judges are also County Court judges, and therefore the details given above, in relation to style and mode of address, need not be repeated here.

The High Court

Although the High Court is nominally one court, it functions as three separate units, namely the Queen's Bench Division, the Chancery Division and the Family Division.

Its jurisdiction includes both civil and criminal elements, with some elements being exercisable at first instance and some being exercisable on appeal. The Queen's Bench Division's jurisdiction at first instance is entirely civil, and includes cases in contract and tort. The Queen's Bench Division's appellate jurisdiction (which is by far the largest part of the appellate jurisdiction of the High Court as a whole) takes the form of appeals by way of case stated from magistrates' courts, and from the Crown Court when that court is exercising its appellate jurisdiction. Appeals by way of case stated can raise points of law only. In procedural terms, the court whose decision is being appealed sends the Queen's Bench Division a written statement of the facts of the case, as they were either agreed by the parties or found by the court, together with the court's understanding of the relevant law, and the way in which that law applied to those facts. The Queen's Bench Division then says whether the lower court got the law, and its application to the facts, right or wrong. It will then usually send the case back to the court from which it came, telling it either what decision it should make, or leaving it to come to its own decision in the light of the law as it was found to be on the appeal. Sometimes, particularly in minor cases where a substantial period of time has elapsed in waiting for the appeal to be heard, the High Court may content itself by giving judgment on the relevant point of law, without sending the case back at all. The Queen's Bench Division also has a *supervisory* jurisdiction, which, as we saw at p. 52, is simply another way of saying it has jurisdiction by way of *judicial review*. This jurisdiction, which in practice almost always involves cases decided by a magistrates' court (but can also arise from decisions of a Crown Court exercising its appellate jurisdiction) covers both civil and criminal cases.

The Chancery Division has only civil jurisdiction, and deals with cases involving company law, property, inheritance disputes and similar matters. It is almost entirely at first instance, although it does include a few types of appeal from the County Courts.

The essence of the Family Division's jurisdiction is self-evident from its title, and includes divorce.

High Court judges are technically known as *puisne judges.* (*Puisne*, pronounced *puny*, does not indicate lack of power but is simply an old word for *junior*.) Their formal style is always written as *Blank J* but is always spoken as *Mr* (or *Mrs*) *Justice Blank*. Describing a High Court judge as *Judge Blank*, or even as *Justice Blank* (without the *Mr* or *Mrs*) is the sort of error which marks you out either as someone who is uneducated in the law or as someone who cannot be bothered with detailed accuracy. You would be foolish to project either of these images of yourself into the mind of whoever is marking your work. (We will explain how to deal with the titles of judges in Chapter 12, in the context of mooting.)

The Court of Appeal

Although the Court of Appeal is nominally one court, it is divided into a Criminal Division and a Civil Division. The principal jurisdiction of both Divisions is – perhaps obviously – appellate.

The Criminal Division hears appeals from the Crown Court against either conviction or sentence or both. It also has a limited quasi-appellate jurisdiction, hearing certain types of cases which are referred to it by the Attorney-General or the Criminal Cases Review Commission. These cases arise from acquittals by juries, sentences passed by the Crown Court which the prosecution consider to be too lenient, and convictions which are alleged to have been miscarriages of justice.

The Civil Division hears appeals from both the County Courts and the High Court.

The Lord Chief Justice, who is also the Head of the Judiciary, presides over the Criminal Division of the Court of Appeal, while the Master of the Rolls presides over the Civil Division. The other judges of the Court of Appeal are formally known as *Lord Justices of Appeal*. The written styles of the Lord Chief Justice and the Master of the Rolls are, respectively, Lord (or Baroness) Green, CJ and Lord (or Baroness) Grey, MR; or, where the Master of the Rolls has not yet been granted a peerage, Sir John (or Lady Mary) Grey, MR, but the spoken usage is to give the title in full: for example Lord Green, Lord Chief Justice. The other judges of the Court of Appeal have the written style of Blank LJ, which is spoken as *Lord* (or *Lady*) *Justice Blank*.

The Supreme Court and the House of Lords

For many years the House of Lords was the highest court of appeal within the English legal system, but this came to an end in October 2009 when the new Supreme Court came into operation. On the basis that the House of Lords no longer exercises judicial functions, you may wonder why it is mentioned in this chapter. The answer is partly that the new Supreme Court inherited its judicial functions and partly that its decisions will continue to be cited for very many years to come (so you need to know something about the way it functioned).

Although it is usual to speak simply of the *House of Lords*, it is more accurate to speak of the *Appellate Committee of the House of Lords*. The appeals which this committee heard came from the Court of Appeal in both civil and criminal cases, as well as from the High Court in civil cases where permission was given to bypass the Court of Appeal (and go straight to the House of Lords) and in criminal cases. (Civil appeals which bypass the Court of Appeal are known, for the obvious reason as *leapfrog appeals*.)

Members of the Appellate Committee were, in practice, specifically appointed to that position, although, strictly speaking, peers who held or had held high judicial office were also eligible to sit. Those who were specifically appointed were formally known as *Lords of Appeal in Ordinary*. The only female Law 'Lord' to be appointed was Baroness Hale of Richmond. Lords of Appeal in Ordinary were known by their titles (for example, Lord Grey and Baroness – or Lady – Green) with no distinction between the written and spoken forms. One senior Supreme Court Justice is designated as the President of the Supreme Court, while another is designated as the Deputy President. These justices have the designatory letters P and DP after their names, while the others have SCJ.

Law Lords received life peerages when they were appointed, but it was decided that new appointees would not continue to do so. Initially this caused no difficulty since the Law Lords were simply transferred to the new court and became Justices of the Supreme Court. However, subsequent appointees will almost never have peerages. The difficulty which this causes was highlighted by the appointment of Dyson LJ as a Supreme Court Justice, who then had to sit as Sir John Dyson when all his colleagues were peers. Although there was no doubt that Sir John was a worthy appointment, there remained the fact that there was the possibility of embarrassment arising from a perception of inequality of esteem. In due course, therefore, it was decided to give Sir John the courtesy title of Lord Dyson, but not a peerage. (Although this was a novelty in terms of the English legal system, there is a long-established practice of giving the courtesy title *Lord* to senior judges in the Scottish legal system.)

Finally, by way of a footnote, it is worth noting the distinction between the *Appellate Committee* (which we have just been discussing) and the *Appeals Committee*, which also consisted of Lords of Appeal in Ordinary, but the function of which was to deal with petitions for permission to appeal to the House of Lords, rather than with the appeals themselves. Although this terminology is obviously inappropriate in the context of the Supreme Court, the practice of applications for permission to appeal being determined by three-judge panels continues, whereas appeals themselves are always held by at least five-judge panels (with seven-judge or even nine-judge panels being possible).

The Judicial Committee of the Privy Council

The Judicial Committee of the Privy Council is principally concerned with both civil and criminal appeals from certain Commonwealth countries, although the number of countries preserving this avenue of appeal has diminished over the years.

Additionally, it has jurisdiction in appeals relating to the disciplinary procedures of certain professional bodies. The Judicial Committee's former jurisdiction in respect of certain constitutional disputes arising out of devolution to Northern Ireland, Scotland and Wales has been transferred to the Supreme Court.

The principal members of the Judicial Committee of the Privy Council are the Supreme Court Justices (having previously been the Law Lords), together with senior judges from those overseas countries which still retain the right of appeal to the Privy Council.

Oral usage is the same as in the High Court, the Court of Appeal and the House of Lords, so the detail given above need not be repeated here; and, once again, the examples given in the context of High Court judges may be easily adapted.

Rights of appeal and permission to appeal in the English courts

Whether there is any right of appeal in a given situation will always depend on the relevant statutory provisions. These provisions contain a mass of practical detail which need not concern you in your early days as a law student.

However, in very general terms, there will often be one appeal on either (or both) the facts and the law, with the possibility of a further appeal on the law only.

Many rights of appeal may be exercised only where permission to appeal is granted. Depending on the context, permission may be granted either by the court whose decision is being challenged or by the court that will hear the appeal if permission is granted.

Tribunals and inquiries

Historically, tribunals and inquiries have often been dealt with together by way of appendages to any description of the hierarchy of the courts. Describing them as *appendages* carries the point that they are not part of that hierarchy but are nevertheless connected to it. The connections are two-fold. First, tribunals and inquiries both conduct hearings in order to resolve disputes, and this constitutes an obvious parallel with the courts. Secondly, the conduct of those hearings, and the content of their outcomes are often subject to control by the courts, by way of either appeal or review. (See page 52 for the distinction between *appeal* and *review*.) However, recent developments in relation to tribunals mean that they are now gaining something which is at least akin to the status of courts in their own right, and while it has always been possible for a tribunal to be given the status of a court, the recently created Upper Tier Tribunal (which has very wide-ranging jurisdiction) is (as we shall shortly see) a court. Inquiries, however, remain very much an appendage to any account of the hierarchy of the courts.

What all this means, for our purposes, is that we must distinguish between tribunals and inquiries and indicate the kind of business which comes before each of them.

Tribunals are, and always have been, independent of government. Inquiries, on the other hand, are, and always have been, an integral part of the machinery of governmental decision-making. So, for example, a typical tribunal will deal with disputes between landlords and tenants as to the appropriate rent for a particular property, or between employers and employees as to whether a particular dismissal had been unfair.

Typically, a tribunal will consist of a legally qualified chair and two 'wing members' (so called because they sit on either side of the chair) who will not be legally qualified but will have relevant practical experience. On the other hand, a typical inquiry will be concerned with a matter such as whether a local planning authority's refusal of planning permission is justified, or whether a compulsory purchase order made by a local authority (or some other public body) should be confirmed by or on behalf of the appropriate Secretary of State and thus become effective. Originally, the officials who conducted inquiries (who were – and still are – usually called *inspectors*) would typically write reports which would then be considered by relatively senior civil servants who would make the actual decisions on behalf of the relevant Secretary of State. For many years, however, in all but the most important inquiries, the inspectors themselves have actually made the decisions,and in doing so they apply government policies to the facts of each case. In other words, the inquiry process is – and always has been – an integral part of governmental decision-making, rather than being independent from it.

Despite the fact that tribunals and inquiries differ very significantly from each other, they have one crucial thing in common, namely the fact that they are composed of people with special knowledge of the kind of matters which come before them. So, for example, one of the wing members in a tribunal dealing with an employment dispute will be drawn from the employers' side of industry and the other will be dawn from the union side. Inspectors dealing with the kind of matters mentioned above will hold appropriate professional qualifications relating to the built environment.

The European Court of Justice and the General Court

The Court of Justice of the European Coal and Steel Community was established in 1954, and renamed as the Court of Justice of the European Communities in 1958. It was renamed again as the Court of Justice of the European Union in 2009 when the Treaty of Lisbon came into effect. From 1989 until 2009 there was also the Court of First Instance, although this title is somewhat misleading if it is understood to suggest that all cases started there, since some cases began in the Court of Justice. In any event, when the Treaty of Lisbon came into effect the CFI became the General Court. Detailed rules identify the court in which a particular case will begin but the essence of the scheme lies in distinguishing between cases according to their significance and complexity.

The mass of detail surrounding the jurisdiction of these courts need not be pursued here. Suffice it to say the bulk of the jurisdiction involves two categories of cases. First, either one of the institutions or a member state may allege that one of the other institutions or member states is in breach of Union law. Secondly, where a point of Union Law arises in a case before a court of a member state, that court may (and sometimes must) seek the opinion of one of the Union's courts, in order to enable it to give its own judgment. This is known as the *preliminary ruling procedure*. The procedure in the Court of Justice, is governed by art. 267 of the Treaty on the Functioning of the European Union (which was originally art. 177 and then art. 234 of the EC Treaty), while the procedure in the General Court is governed by art. 225 of the Treaty.

Although any of the parties to the proceedings before the court of the member state may ask the court to seek a ruling on a question of EU law, no party ever has any right to insist that a request for a ruling shall be made. Furthermore, once a case has been considered by one of the EU's courts, it will return to the national court that requested the ruling, which will then give its judgment in the light of the ruling. It is, therefore, wrong to describe the preliminary ruling procedure as an *appeal.*

Individuals, and organisations such as companies and local authorities, have only very limited rights of access to the Court of Justice, although they do have somewhat wider access to the General Court.

Judges of both Courts have the style of *judge* and are described and addressed accordingly.

● The European Court of Human Rights

Although the protection of fundamental rights is discussed in Chapter 5, it is convenient to note here that the European Court of Human Rights, which sits at Strasbourg, hears complaints alleging infringements of the European Convention on Human Rights. A party who is dissatisfied with a decision of an English court may complain to the European Court of Human Rights, but this will involve entirely new proceedings and is not an appeal against the English decision.

The principal remedy available in the European Court of Human Rights is merely a declaratory judgment that a breach of the Convention has occurred. Additionally, however, the court may award compensation, but there is no mechanism to enable such an award to be enforced if the state against which the order is made fails to comply.

Judges of the European Court of Human Rights have the style *judge*, and are described and addressed accordingly.

● **Conclusion**

The system of courts within the English legal system is hierarchical, with each court exercising one or more of three jurisdictions, namely first instance, appellate and supervisory.

In addition to the courts of the domestic English legal system, the European Court of Justice (together with the General Court) and the European Court of Human Rights must also be taken into account.

5 The Protection of Human Rights and Fundamental Freedoms

The importance of protecting human rights and fundamental freedoms is now taken for granted in the liberal democracies of the western world. The Human Rights Act 1998 (HRA) gives special status in English law to most of the rights and freedoms which the European Convention of Human Rights protects, and calls these 'Convention rights'. The HRA has therefore greatly reduced the need to rely on the common law for such protection. The HRA does not affect the legislative supremacy of Parliament, but it does allow the higher courts to make declarations of incompatibility in respect of statutes which breach 'Convention rights' and to quash almost all delegated legislation.

● Introduction

This chapter considers the way in which English law protects, or fails to protect, *human rights and fundamental freedoms* (a phrase which is usually abbreviated simply to *human rights*). It will consider both the common law and statute law, with the emphasis in the latter context being on the Human Rights Act 1998.

● Protection of human rights by the common law

Although there is no doubt that the common law is capable of protecting human rights, there is equally no doubt that it cannot be relied upon to do so, as the following three cases will show.

The first case is *R v Lord Chancellor ex parte Witham* [1998] QB 575, where the Lord Chancellor (acting with the concurrence of the Lord Chief Justice, the Master of the Rolls, the Vice-Chancellor and the President of the Family Division) had exercised a statutory power to increase court fees quite substantially, and to remove an exemption from fees for people on income support. Even though the new rules contained a power for the Lord Chancellor to reduce or remit the fees in individual cases on the ground of undue financial hardship, the High Court granted a declaration that he had exceeded his statutory powers. The basis of this decision was simply that the effect of the increases would be to exclude many people from access to the courts.

The second case is *Malone v Metropolitan Police Commissioner (No 2)* [1979] Ch 344, where a man who had been convicted of handling stolen goods complained that the police had tapped his telephone during their investigation. Sir Robert Megarry V-C held that the telephone tap had been lawful because the law did not restrict this kind of activity by the police. Although he could have done so, he was unwilling to find that Malone had a right not to have his telephone tapped, simply so that he could then hold that that right had been infringed. The creation of such rights, according to the judge, is a matter for Parliament, not the courts.

The third case, *R v Secretary of State for Social Security ex parte B and Another* [1997] 1 WLR 275, shows that the judges may disagree among themselves on matters of human rights even within a single case. The Secretary of State had made certain regulations under the Social Security (Contributions and Benefits) Act 1992. The content of the regulations was such that some asylum seekers, who would previously have been eligible for benefits while their applications for asylum were being assessed, would, in the words of Simon Brown LJ (at p. 292), be reduced to 'a life so destitute that to my mind no civilised nation can tolerate it'. However, Neill LJ dissented, on the basis that the regulations had been aimed primarily at, and would principally affect, people who were not genuine asylum-seekers. Furthermore, although the regulations would 'also have a very serious effect on a considerable number of genuine asylum-seekers and those who might be hoping to obtain exceptional leave to remain', the Secretary of State had not crossed 'the threshold of illegality', bearing in mind not only the 'objects to be achieved by the legislation and its results' but also the need 'to strike a balance' in 'the allocation of the resources made available to him'. (See p. 283.)

● Statute law other than the Human Rights Act 1998

Of course, the common law is not the only – or even the main – vehicle for developing the law. However, statutory intervention in relation to specific areas of human rights law (such as discrimination on the grounds of race and sex) has been haphazard, and appears to have resulted more from perceived political need than from any fundamental concern with the principle of equality.

● The European Convention on Human Rights

Introduction

The European Convention for the Protection of Human Rights and Fundamental Freedoms (which is commonly referred to simply as the *European Convention on Human Rights*, which in turn is commonly abbreviated to *ECHR*) was agreed in 1950 by the states of Western Europe.

The ECHR is a product of the *Council of Europe* (rather than the *European Union*) and is enforced by the *European Court of Human Rights*, which sits at *Strasbourg* (rather than the *European Court of Justice*, which sits at *Luxembourg*). Despite the obvious importance of the provisions of the ECHR, successive British governments, of both major political persuasions, consistently refused to introduce legislation giving its provisions any status in English law, on the basis that English law was perfectly capable of protecting human rights anyway. However, in 1997 the newly elected Labour government put an end to this consensus by introducing the Bill that became the Human Rights Act 1998 (HRA).

Some key concepts under the European Convention on Human Rights

It is important to notice that, with the exception of the prohibition of torture or inhuman or degrading treatment or punishment by art. 3, all the rights and freedoms guaranteed by the Convention are subject to some kind of limitation or qualification. Of particular interest in this respect are arts 8 to 11, which may all be restricted by law to such extent as is 'necessary in a democratic society' for the reasons set out in each of the articles. (For the full text of the articles, see Appendix 1, at pp. 221–226.) It is useful to notice, therefore, that in a case concerning homosexual relationships, the Court of Human Rights identified 'tolerance and broad-mindedness' as two of the 'hallmarks' of a democratic society. (*Dudgeon v United Kingdom* (1982) 4 EHRR 149, [53].)

Turning to the phrase 'necessary in a democratic society', in *Handyside v United Kingdom* (1976) 1 EHRR 737, [48], while upholding the law relating to the forfeiture of obscene publications, the Court said that 'while the adjective "necessary" ... is not synonymous with "indispensable", neither has it the flexibility of such expressions as "admissible", "ordinary", "useful", "reasonable" or "desirable"'. More positively, in *Olsson v Sweden* (1989) 11 EHRR 259, [67], while finding that the then current state of Swedish law provided no basis for the practice of social workers of restricting parental access to children who were in public care, the Court said:

> According to the court's established case-law, the notion of *necessity* implies that an interference corresponds with a *pressing social need* and, in particular, that it is *proportionate* to the legitimate aim pursued. (Emphasis added.)

These cases provide a useful introduction to two of the Strasbourg court's key concepts, namely the *margin of appreciation* and the doctrine of *proportionality*. Taking these in turn, the *margin of appreciation* is the area for the exercise of discretion that the Strasbourg court accepts must remain with national legal systems. In *Handyside* (above) the Court said (at [48]–[49]):

> By reason of their direct and continuous contact with the vital forces of their countries, state authorities are in principle in a better position than the international judge to give an opinion on the ... "necessity" of a "restriction" or "penalty" .... It is for the national authorities to make the initial assessment of the reality of the pressing social need
> ...
> Consequently art. 10(2) leaves to the contracting states a margin of appreciation. This margin is given both to the domestic legislator ("prescribed by law") and to the bodies, judicial amongst others, that are called upon to interpret and apply the laws in force.
> Nevertheless, [the Convention] does not give the contracting states an unlimited power of appreciation. The court, which ... is responsible for ensuring those states' engagements, is empowered to give the final ruling on whether a "restriction" or "penalty" is reconcilable with [a Convention right or freedom] .... The domestic margin of appreciation thus goes hand in hand with a European supervision. Such supervision concerns both the aim of the measure challenged and its "necessity"; it covers not only the basic legislation but also the decision applying it, even one given by an independent court.

Secondly, the doctrine of *proportionality* requires that the *means* which are used must be proportionate to the *ends* which are to be achieved, because, in the words of the Court in *Soering v United Kingdom* (1989) 11 EHRR 439, [89]:

> Inherent in the whole of the Convention is a search for a fair balance between the demands of the general interest of the community and the requirements of the protection of the individual's fundamental rights.

● The Human Rights Act 1998

The scheme of the Act

The scheme of the Human Rights Act depends on the core concept of *Convention rights*. However it is important to understand that, under s. 1(1) of the HRA, the phrase *Convention rights* does not include all the rights guaranteed by the Convention, but only:

> the rights and fundamental freedoms set out in –
> (a) articles 2 to 12 and 14 of the Convention, and
> (b) articles 1 to 3 of the First Protocol, and
> (c) articles 1 and 2 of the Sixth Protocol,
> as read with articles 16 to 18 of the Convention.

More particularly, the concept of Convention rights does not extend to arts 1 and 13, which deal, respectively, with securing Convention rights to everyone within the courts of the contracting state and providing effective remedies in national courts.

Articles 16 to 18 of the Convention respectively:

- permit restrictions on the political activities of aliens;
- prohibit any interpretation of the Convention that would permit the destruction or limitation of the rights and freedoms guaranteed by the Convention; and
- require that the restrictions permitted by the Convention shall be applied only for the purposes for which they were created.

A summary of Convention rights

The full text of the articles and protocols which guarantee Convention rights within the terms of the HRA is set out in Appendix 1 (see pp. 221–226), but may be summarised as follows:

art. 2   the right to life;
art. 3   prohibition of torture or inhuman or degrading treatment or punishment;
art. 4   prohibition of slavery and forced labour;
art. 5   the right to liberty and security of the person;
art. 6   the right to a fair trial;
art. 7   freedom from the imposition of retrospective criminal liability and punishment;
art. 8   the right to respect for private and family life;
art. 9   freedom of religion;
art. 10 freedom of expression;
art. 11 freedom of assembly and association;
art. 12 the right to marry and found a family;
art. 14 prohibition of discrimination in enjoyment of rights under the Convention.

First Protocol
art. 1   the right to property;
art. 2   the right to education;
art. 3   the right to free elections.

Sixth Protocol
arts 1 & 2   prohibition of the death penalty.

Section 1(2) makes the operation of these articles subject to *derogations* and *reservations*. Schedule 3 contains *derogations* relating to terrorist activity and a *reservation* relating to preserving efficient instruction and training, and avoiding unreasonable public expenditure when seeking to satisfy the right of parents to ensure that their children are educated 'in conformity with their own religious and philosophical convictions'.

The status of Convention rights in English law

Introduction
The starting point, and one which cannot be emphasised too strongly, especially because it is repeatedly misrepresented in the media, is that, in the words of Lord Clyde in *R v Lambert* [2001] UKHL 37, [2002] 2 AC 545, [135], 'the Act did not incorporate the rights set out in the Convention into the domestic laws of the United Kingdom'. What the Act does do, however, is to identify most of those rights, which it then labels 'Convention rights'

and upon which it then confers a special status which has a variety of consequences. It is that status and those consequences which we will now examine.

Section 2 of the Act provides that any court or tribunal which has to determine any question in relation to a Convention right 'must take into account' the case-law of the European Court of Human Rights. Strictly speaking, as Laws LJ and Poole J pointed out in *Gough and Another v Chief Constable of Derbyshire* [2001] EWHC Admin 554, [2002] QB 459, [32], s. 2 means what it says, and therefore the duty of the court is 'to take account of Strasbourg jurisprudence, not necessarily to apply it'. However, cases in which the courts refuse to apply Strasbourg jurisprudence are likely to be few and far between, bearing in mind the view of Lord Slynn in *R (Alconbury Developments Ltd) v Secretary of State for the Environment, Transport and the Regions* [2001] UKHL 23, [2003] AC 295, [26]:

> In the absence of some special circumstances it seems to me that the court should follow any clear and constant jurisprudence of the European Court of Human Rights. If it does not do so, there is at least a possibility that the case will go to that court, which is likely in the ordinary case to follow its own constant jurisprudence.

Interpretation and validity of English legislation
Section 3(1) of the Act provides that

> so far as it is possible to do so, primary and subordinate legislation must be read and given effect in a way which is compatible with the Convention rights.

As a result of s. 3(2) of the Act, s. 3(1) applies to all legislation, whatever its date of enactment, including legislation which was passed before the 1998 Act. However, also as a result of s. 3(2), the court's inability to find a compatible interpretation under s. 3(1) does not affect the *validity* of any *primary* legislation, nor of *delegated* legislation where the terms of the Act under which it is made are such that the incompatibility is inevitable. (In practice, *primary* legislation almost always means Acts of Parliament, although occasionally it may also mean certain instruments made by the exercise of the royal prerogative.) As we saw at p. 25, *subordinate legislation* is simply another form of words for *delegated legislation*. On the assumption that both primary legislation made in exercise of the royal prerogative and Acts protecting delegated legislation made under them will both be very rarely encountered in practice, the effect of these provisions is therefore to introduce a new principle of interpretation of general (but not quite universal) application. This principle of interpretation preserves the legislative supremacy of Parliament, while making practically all delegated legislation quashable on the ground of incompatibility with Convention rights.

The duty imposed on public authorities
Section 6 of the Act makes it unlawful for a public authority to act in a way that is incompatible with Convention rights. For these purposes, the expression *public authority* is defined as *excluding* both Houses of Parliament but as *including* courts and tribunals, as well as 'any person certain of whose functions are functions of a public nature'. The effect of s. 7 of the Act is that a person who wishes to establish that there has been a breach of the duty under s. 6 may do so either proactively by claiming judicial review, or reactively by way of defence to proceedings brought by, or at the instigation of, a public authority.

Declarations of incompatibility
Although the Act contains nothing to diminish the legislative supremacy of Parliament, s. 4 does give a court at (or above) the level of the High Court the power to make declarations of incompatibility where primary legislation conflicts with Convention rights. Such declarations have no effect on the parties to the cases in which they are made, nor on the continuing operation or validity of the provisions in respect of which they are given. However, under s. 10 of the Act, they may result in the provisions being amended or repealed by remedial orders. (These remedial orders will typically take the form of delegated legislation, in order to avoid the pressures on time which beset the government's legislative programme. However, where the declaration of incompatibility relates to an Order in Council made in exercise of the royal prerogative, the remedial order may be in the form of a further Order in Council.) Section 10 also provides that remedial orders may be made following adverse findings by the European Court of Human Rights.

Statements of compatibility
All Bills are scrutinised by a Joint Committee of both Houses of Parliament, to check whether they contain any provisions which would, if enacted, breach any Convention rights. Furthermore, Ministers who are in charge of Bills in either House of Parliament must, before the Second

Reading of the Bill, do one of two things. The first, and overwhelmingly more common possibility, is a statement of compatibility, to the effect that the Bill contains nothing that is incompatible with Convention rights. The second possibility is that, even though the Minister is unable to make a statement of compatibility, the House is nevertheless being invited to proceed with the Bill. The latter alternative does not arise very often, but the Bill which became the Communications Act 2003 was one particularly interesting exception. The issue was whether political advertising should be banned from the broadcast media. Although such a ban could appear to breach the right to freedom of expression under art. 10 of the European Convention on Human Rights, as interpreted by the European Court of Human Rights in *Vgt Verein Gegeng Tierfabriken v Switzerland* (2002) 34 EHRR 4, the government took the view that the ban was nevertheless justified. The government's reasoning was that, in the absence of a ban on all political advertising, the wealthiest political interests would dominate the advertising carried by the broadcast media. When viewed in this way, a degree of interference with freedom of expression could be seen as the lesser of two evils.

● European Union law and the protection of human rights

Introduction

In *Nold v Commission* [1974] 2 CMLR 338, the European Court of Justice emphasised that 'fundamental rights form an integral part of the general principles of law, the observance of which it ensures'. By way of an example of how this statement has been implemented in practice, *Stauder v City of Ulm* [1969] ECR 419 arose from the Community's plan to reduce surplus stocks of butter by selling it cheaply to certain groups within the population. One individual objected to the way in which the German authorities implemented the scheme, because he was required to disclose his name to the retailer of the butter, as a result of which the retailer would know that he was receiving certain welfare benefits.

The Court of Justice acknowledged that this infringed the principle of equality, and was therefore a breach of the individual's fundamental rights. (In the event, however, the Court of Justice avoided the problem by saying that the Commission's decision, which formed the basis of the scheme, should be interpreted so that such disclosure by individuals was not a precondition to their obtaining cheap butter.)

From the Treaty of Maastricht to the European Charter of Fundamental Rights

The first treaty article to contain a general statement of the importance of fundamental rights was art. F(2) of the Treaty of Maastricht (the original TEU), which provided that

> the Union shall respect fundamental rights, as guaranteed by the European Convention for the Protection of Human Rights and Fundamental Freedoms ... and as they result from the constitutional traditions common to the member states, as general principles of Community law.

Although the European Union Charter of Fundamental Rights (the *EUCFR* or, simply, the *Charter*) was published at the Nice Conference in December 2000, it was not included in the resulting Treaty of Nice 2001 and so was not incorporated into EC law (as it then was). The Treaty of Lisbon subsequently took a rather roundabout approach to the Charter by amending the TEU which now states:

> The Union recognizes the rights, freedoms, and principles set out in the Charter of Fundamental Rights ... which shall have the same legal value as the Treaties. (Art. 6(1) TEU.)

At a purely practical level, therefore, the Charter has the same status as it would have had if it had been expressly incorporated into EU law. However, two points must immediately be made.

First, the Charter is not intended to create any new rights, being merely declaratory of a range of existing personal, civil, political, economic and social rights which already existed in a variety of legislative instruments, including the legal systems of both the EU itself and its members states, as well as in international conventions from the Council of Europe, the United Nations and the International Labour Organization.

Secondly, the United Kingdom has negotiated an opt-out from the Charter (as have Poland and the Czech Republic – see below), to the effect that neither national courts nor the Court of Justice can declare domestic law to be incompatible with the Charter. However, this opt-out is expressed in terms of preventing judicial declarations of incompatibility, rather than preventing reliance on the substance of the pre-existing rights which the Charter is designed to recognise. Its significance, therefore, appears to be more as a political gesture than as a legal provision. Furthermore, judgments of the ECJ which apply the Charter will become (in effect) sources of EU law in the same way that other judgments do, so the developing body of EU law will apply to the states which have opted out, irrespective of their opt-outs in relation to declarations of incompatibility. Further discussion may be found in specialist textbooks on EU law, but for the present purposes it is sufficient to identify the fact of the United Kingdom's opt-out, with no further need to explore it in detail. Nevertheless, a brief summary of the content and scope of the Charter (which is taken entirely from http://europa. eu/) may be useful as an indicator of the scope of EU law generally in relation to the protection of rights.

- Chapter I: dignity (human dignity, the right to life, the right to the integrity of the person, prohibition of torture and inhuman or degrading treatment or punishment, prohibition of slavery and forced labour);
- Chapter II: freedoms (the right to liberty and security, respect for private and family life, protection of personal data, the right to marry and found a family, freedom of thought, conscience and religion, freedom of expression and information, freedom of assembly and association, freedom of the arts and sciences, the right to education, freedom to choose an occupation and the right to engage in work, freedom to conduct a business, the right to property, the right to asylum, protection in the event of removal, expulsion or extradition);
- Chapter III: equality (equality before the law, non-discrimination, cultural, religious and linguistic diversity, equality between men and women, the rights of the child, the rights of the elderly, integration of persons with disabilities);
- Chapter IV: solidarity (workers' right to information and consultation within the undertaking the right of collective bargaining and action, the right of access to placement services, protection in the event of unjustified dismissal, fair and just working conditions, prohibition of child labour and protection of young people at work, family and professional life, social security and social assistance, health care, access to services of general economic interest, environmental protection, consumer protection);
- Chapter V: citizens' rights (the right to vote and stand as a candidate at elections to the European Parliament and at municipal elections, the right to good administration, the right of access to

documents, European Ombudsman, the right to petition, freedom of movement and residence, diplomatic and consular protection);
- Chapter VI: justice (the right to an effective remedy and a fair trial, presumption of innocence and the right of defence, principles of legality and proportionality of criminal offences and penalties, the right not to be tried or punished twice in criminal proceedings for the same criminal offence);
- Chapter VII: general provisions.

Scope

The Charter applies to the European institutions, subject to the principle of subsidiarity, and may under no circumstances extend the powers and tasks conferred on them by the Treaties. The Charter also applies to EU countries when they implement EU law. If any of the rights correspond to rights guaranteed by the European Convention on Human Rights, the meaning and scope of those rights is to be the same as defined by the Convention, though EU law may provide for more extensive protection. Any of the rights derived from the common constitutional traditions of EU countries must be interpreted in accordance to those traditions.

Protocol (No) 30 to the Treaties on the application of the Charter to Poland and the United Kingdom restricts the interpretation of the Charter by the Court of Justice and the national courts of these two countries, in particular regarding rights relating to solidarity.

The omission of any mention of the Czech Republic's opt-out is due entirely to the fact that it was negotiated to late to be included in the text of the protocol.

● Conclusion

English law has always been capable of protecting human rights but has not always shown that it can be relied upon to do so.

The European Convention for the Protection of Human Rights and Fundamental Freedoms, which came into force in 1953 and is usually known simply as the *European Convention on Human Rights* or *ECHR*) has never been incorporated into English law by Act of Parliament. However, the Human Rights Act 1998 creates and defines an English law concept of *Convention rights*, and provides that in cases where Convention rights are relevant, English courts must take into account the law as developed by the Court of Human Rights (which sits at Strasbourg and interprets and applies the ECHR); and, wherever it is possible to so, must also interpret Acts of Parliament in such a way as to make them compatible with Convention rights. The Act also provides that it is unlawful for public bodies to act in ways which are incompatible with Convention rights.

The European Court of Human Rights applies a number of concepts, including *restrictions which are necessary in a democratic society*, the *margin of appreciation* and *proportionality*.

6 Finding and Citing the Sources of Law

The law can change frequently. In the English legal system, the courts develop the common law on a case-by-case basis, with Parliament using statutes to make more comprehensive changes. Textbooks, journals, casebooks and statute books are, at best, aids to understanding the primary sources of cases, statutes and European materials, but they are never replacements for reading those primary sources. Developing the research skills to find and use both paper-based and electronic resources will help you keep up to date, while citing your sources in accordance with the standard conventions will help you to communicate this information to others.

● Introduction

As a student, you will have to consult many books, journals, law reports, statutes and European materials in order to find the law. You will not always have a great deal of time to search for the law you need. Knowing, therefore, where to find the relevant law, and how to search for it, is a skill well worth learning at an early stage of your law studies.

We will examine the materials you are most likely to use in your studies, including both paper-based and electronic materials. Increasingly, the electronic resources available are Internet-based, although you may also still encounter some sources on CDs and DVDs. All modern students of law must, therefore, have at least basic IT skills which they can develop, if necessary, while acquiring knowledge of the specialist legal sources.

● Libraries and learning resource centres

In many institutions, the current trend is for *libraries* to be part of *Learning Resource Centres*, or *Integrated Learning Resource Centres*, in order to emphasise the fact that sources of knowledge are no longer exclusively paper-based. However, for convenience and brevity, this chapter will refer only to *libraries*, leaving readers to translate the terminology to fit the style of their own institutions.

While different libraries may use different systems to organise their stock of books and other materials, most libraries arrange their stock according to a classification system, with books usually being grouped together according to their subject matter. (Some books may be housed on open access shelves, with others being retained in short-loan, reference-only or reserve sections, to which only the librarians have access.) It is also common for books to be located separately from journals, law reports and other media, such as CDs, DVDs and microfiche.

When searching for material, your first port of call should be the *library catalogue*. Although some specialist collections still use card-based and microfiche catalogues, in most modern libraries the catalogue will be electronic. Electronic catalogues can always be accessed from dedicated computer terminals in the library itself, but may in many cases also be accessed via the Internet.

Using the library catalogue to search for materials is a better way of identifying whether the library has the resources you need than physically browsing the shelves. This is because much of the library's stock will, at any given time, be in use by other readers, either within the library or on loan. Online catalogues usually allow you to reserve books which are currently out on loan, and this will often be the easiest (and sometimes the only) way to get hold of a popular text during term time.

If you are living away from home during term time, it is worth checking what arrangements for vacation access your college or university library has with other colleges and universities. In each case, of course, if you are to make good use of any other libraries to which you have access, you will need to spend some time familiarising yourself with the way they are organised.

● Textbooks, casebooks, statute books and journals

Introduction

Textbooks will usually be your basic learning resource. For most subjects, your lecturers will specify a textbook or a choice of textbooks, and you will be expected to buy one of these. You may also be expected to buy a casebook and a statute book, and to supplement all your books by reading articles in a variety of journals.

Textbooks and casebooks

The idea of a textbook is very straightforward. Most textbooks cover conventional subjects (such as criminal law or land law), but some are wider in their scope. The most extreme version of width of scope is *Halsbury's Laws of England*, which is an encyclopaedic work running to more than 50 volumes, including a comprehensive updating service.

The distinction between textbooks and casebooks is that textbooks contain the authors' statements, explanations and criticisms of the law, while casebooks contain extracts from the judgments of the courts and, where relevant, statutes and other materials, together with linking commentary and criticism. While casebooks are, on the whole, very useful aids, because the editor has done the work of sifting through the cases in order to decide which ones to include, as well as sifting through each individual case to decide which are the key passages in the judgments, they have two major limitations.

First, if a case is fundamental to your understanding of a particular area of law, you should not simply rely on what someone else thinks are the key points in the case, but you should read the whole case before deciding for yourself what it is really about. For example, the editor of a casebook may simply note that there was a dissenting judgment, without reproducing any of it. In practice, however, it is not uncommon for dissenting judgments to be adopted as *ratio* either by an appellate court in the same case, or by another later court which is free to depart from the earlier decision within the limits set by the doctrine of binding precedent.

Secondly, if you progress to practising the law professionally, you will often have to read entire cases for yourself in order to identify precisely those propositions for which they are – and are not – authority. This kind of analysis requires legal skills of a high order, which can be gained only by extensive experience and repeated practice. It is never too early to start acquiring and developing these skills.

Statute books

In addition to textbooks and casebooks, there are various series of statute books aimed specifically at students. These contain statutes relating to particular topics, such as criminal law, land law or employment law, and contain those statutory excerpts which the editors consider to contain the key legislative provisions relating to the topic. It is always worth checking at the start of your course whether you can take statute books (or photocopies of the statutes themselves) into your examinations. You will often find that you are permitted to do so, provided that the text is clean in the sense of being free from notes of any kind. If this is so in your college or university, it will obviously be in your own financial interest to avoid making notes in your statute books while you are studying. Otherwise, you will have to make the unpalatable choice between not taking your statute books into the examination, or buying new copies for that purpose. (Even if you are not permitted to take annotated statute books or statutes into your examinations, you may be permitted to underline and highlight, and put edge markers on the pages. It is important that you should clarify at a very early stage whether your college or university permits any – or all – of these devices.)

Choosing books

You will be expected to buy your own copies of any books which are prescribed as essential reading. Student numbers are such that no library will be able to afford to stock sufficient copies of these basic books for every student to be able to borrow a copy.

When your lecturers recommend one specific book (whether it is a textbook, a casebook or a statute book), your wisest course of action is to buy that particular book rather than an alternative. This is because the lecturer will almost certainly have tailored the content of the course with the basic readings in mind, and if you buy a different book it is highly unlikely that it will cover the material in exactly the same way and in the same order as the recommended text. This means that you could waste a lot of time working out if (and where) the material in the designated text is covered in the alternative you have bought. Of course, none of this means that you should not *read* other books. You will often find that reading more than one book enhances your understanding of a topic, as well as giving you the opportunity of impressing your examiners by saying that 'while author X argues such and such, it is worth noticing that author Y takes the contrary view and argues so and so'. However, the realities of students' finances are such that *buying* multiple texts is, quite simply, not usually an option

Finally, if your lecturers recommend books which they have written, do not assume that they are simply feathering their own nests at your expense. The economics of academic authorship simply do not work that way. In terms of pounds-per-hour, most academics would be better off spending their evenings and weekends stacking shelves in supermarkets rather than writing textbooks. The real reason why most academics write textbooks is that – rightly or wrongly – they feel frustrated by the quality of the existing books at the appropriate level in their subject areas.

Journals

To supplement your textbooks, you are likely to be referred to articles in legal journals. Most of these will deal with particular topics, such as criminal law or property law (such as the *Criminal Law Review* and the *Conveyancer*) in greater detail than is possible within textbooks. Some journals, however, such as the *New Law Journal* and the *Solicitors Journal* provide wider (if necessarily more superficial) coverage of the contemporary legal scene. Perhaps the most important quality of all journals, whatever their scope may be, is that they can be more up-to-date than textbooks, casebooks and statute books.

One particularly useful section of many journals contains short case notes. Even in the most academically heavyweight journals, these are seldom more than three or four pages long, and often run to no more than a page or two. These case notes can be an excellent introduction to some of the more complex recent developments in the law. Additionally, by referring to back numbers, you can see how cases which are now accepted as leading authorities were viewed at the time when they were decided.

Online resources

Some student texts are now available as electronic books (ebooks) which can be downloaded and read on computers and other electronic devices. Companion websites providing updating services between editions, online access to individual or sample chapters of books and study advice are increasingly common and are a good starting point for exploring the style and contents of a particular book before buying it.

Most of the journals held by college and university libraries are also accessible online as subscription services. You are likely to have access to some of these *via* intranet or Internet portals (also known as *gateways*), but since the range of relevant journals will vary from one institution to another, all that can usefully be said here is that you should familiarise yourself with what is available to you.

Additionally, there are some online journals and information resources which are freely accessible to anyone with access to an Internet connection, as we will now demonstrate. However, we can do no more that give a brief taste of what the Internet has to offer. With this mind, and also having regard to the fact that the content of the Internet is rapidly changing, we will focus on websites and portals which are part of established academic projects, and are therefore likely to be available for some time.

One useful starting point is the Lawlinks website (available at http://kent.ac.uk/lawlinks/), maintained by the University of Kent at Canterbury. This site is organised by subject headings and provides an annotated list of websites.

Although very few full-text journals are available free online, the Electronic Law Journals Project based at the University of Warwick does provide free access to two current titles. These are *Law, Social Justice and Global Development Journal* (available at http://www2.warwick.ac.uk/fac/soc/law/elj/lgd/) and the *Entertainment and Sports Law Journal* (available at http://www2.warwick.ac.uk/fac/soc/law/elj/eslj/). Both journals are peer-reviewed and full-text versions of articles published in them are available free to download and print. The *European Journal of Law and Technology* (available at http://ejlt.org//index) is part of the Open Journal System but at the time of writing it is the only journal available. Other journals, including all the journals published by the Oxford University Press (available at http://www.oxfordjournals.org/) provide searchable online indexes, together with tables of contents and abstracts of some articles, while restricting access to full-text articles to subscribers. Although searching for an article in this way will not produce the full-text version, it is nevertheless much quicker than browsing through volumes of journals on library shelves (assuming both that your library takes the journal in question and that it happens to be on the shelf when you are browsing).

Finally, two general points might be usefully made. First, one consequence of the fact that the best online resources are regularly updated is that links and URLs do not always endure in the same way as paper-based materials. Secondly, the accuracy of a great deal of information posted online is questionable. Taking these points together, you need, therefore, to consider keeping copies of valuable resources you discover online (in case they are gone when you next visit the site); and to develop a critical approach to using online sources. A useful resource for developing an effective and evaluative approach to online research is the set of interactive tutorials for legal research on the Intute website (available at http://www.vts.intute.ac.uk/he/tutorial/lawyers).

The status of textbooks and journals

The textbooks you will read are likely to have been written specifically for students; and the material they cover, and the limited detail into which they go, will reflect this. If you go on to practise law, you will encounter rather grander tomes designed especially for practitioners. Whatever the breadth and depth of a textbook, and however impressive it is in terms of size, you must always remember that no modern court will ever regard any textbook as being an authoritative source of law in the same way that cases and statutes are authoritative sources of law. The same is true of journal articles.

This modern view of the non-authoritative status of learned authors may be contrasted with the attitude taken in some cases by judges in earlier centuries, when statements made by authors such as Glanvill in the 12th century through to Blackstone in the 18th century were often treated as being binding statements of law. Of course, the modern approach does not disqualify the courts from seeking assistance from the best available scholarship: it merely preserves the constitutional position (which is explained in Chapter 2) as to what does, and does not, count as a source of law.

Applying this principle to your activities as a student, it follows that you may treat the views of authors as being persuasive when you are presenting a piece of coursework or an examination answer. However, you should be careful to use those views as supplements to your legal arguments, rather than as substitutes for the careful citation of judicial decisions and statutes. Similarly, when citing from casebooks, you must cite the report of the case itself, rather than the extract from the casebook, because it is the views of the judges, and not the views of the casebook editor, which carry weight. (You will remember that the nature of casebooks is that they contain extracts from judgments. The original reports, on the other hand, may also contain passages casting doubt on the extracts selected by the casebook's editor.)

Law reports

Introduction
The effective operation of the system of binding precedent (which we mentioned briefly in Chapter 2 and will consider more fully in Chapter 7) depends on the availability of reliable reports of the courts' decisions. However, before giving any further consideration to law reports, it will be useful to consider how cases are named.

Conventions in case names
The usual convention when naming a case is that the name of the party who is initiating the current stage of the proceedings will be placed first. So if Smith is suing Jones for breach of contract, the case will be *Smith v Jones*. If Smith loses

and appeals, the case will still be *Smith v Jones* on appeal, but if Jones loses and appeals, the case will become *Jones v Smith* on appeal. However, this statement of the usual convention must be qualified in two ways.

First, in the Supreme Court (following the House of Lords), the case name reverts to whatever form it had at first instance, irrespective of who is the appellant.

Secondly, case names in criminal law are usually given in the form of *R v Smith*, whether at first instance or on appeal. The *R* stands for either *Rex* or *Regina* (meaning *King* or *Queen*) depending upon the sex of the monarch who was reigning at the time of the case.

Thirdly, some proceedings give rise to case names in special forms. One of the most common examples is judicial review, where historically the application to the court was made by the Crown on behalf of the real applicant. Although this is now pure fiction, the case names continue to reflect the original practice. For many years, the form was, for example, *R v Secretary of State for Whatever ex parte Smith*. However, the current usage, pursuing the same example, is *R (on the application of Smith) v Secretary of State for Whatever*, or, more briefly, *R (Smith) v Secretary of State for Whatever*.

Other exceptional usages include cases involving the estate of someone who has died, which are often given the name of the deceased, preceded by the word '*Re*', which means 'in the matter of'. So if Smith has died, a case dealing with the estate may be reported as *Re Smith*. A similar form is often used when cases deal with the welfare of children, except that the convention there is to use only initials, as, for example, in *Re SA (A Minor)* (where SA are the initials of the person concerned) in order to preserve anonymity. Another exception can arise in cases involving ships, which are sometimes named after the ship or ships involved. (See, for example, the alternative name for *Ellerman Lines Ltd v Murray*, which is given in the next paragraph.)

Sometimes a case may appear in two series of law reports under two different names. References to such a case may give both names, linked by the abbreviation *sub nom* (meaning *sub nomine*, or *under the name of*). For example, you may encounter the following: *Ellerman Lines Ltd v Murray* [1930] All ER Rep 503, *sub nom The Croxteth Hall, The Celtic* 47 TLR 147. In this example, the editor of one series has used the names of the parties, while another has used the names of the ships involved in the case.

The range of law reports

Introduction
Strictly speaking there is no 'official' series of law reports, but in practice the reports published by the Incorporated Council of Law Reporting for England

and Wales, a non-profit-making body founded and run by the legal profession, are often referred to as the 'official' reports.

The leading series of law reports
The law reports published by the Incorporated Council are predominantly general series in terms of their subject matter, and include *Appeal Cases* (AC), *Chancery Division* (Ch), *Family Division* (Fam) and *Queen's Bench Division* (QBD). The Appeal Cases cover the decisions of the House of Lords and the Judicial Committee of the Privy Council. The reports named after the three divisions of the High Court cover not only cases heard in those divisions but also appeals arising from them which go to the Court of Appeal. (As we saw in Chapter 4, criminal appeals from the Queen's Bench Division go straight to the Supreme Court, and are therefore reported in the Appeal Cases.) Additionally, the Incorporated Council publishes the *Weekly Law Reports* (WLR). This is a general series which, as its name implies, is published weekly, before being bound as three volumes for each year. Those cases which the editor considers to be least important appear in volume 1, while the rest appear in volumes 2 and 3. In due course, the cases from volumes 2 and 3 appear again in the *Appeal Cases*, *Chancery*, *Family* and *Queen's Bench* series, where they benefit from the inclusion of outlines of the advocates' arguments.

The Incorporated Council's three specialist series are the *Industrial Cases Reports* (ICR) which contain only cases involving employment law, the *Business Law Reports* (Bus LR) which cover a wide range of topics such as banking law and intellectual property law under the broad heading of business law and the *Public and Third Sector Law Reports* (PSTR) which cover a diverse array of matters of interest to charity and public service lawyers. The Incorporated Council's website, http://www.lawreports.co.uk/, contains some useful resources, including *WLR Daily*, which provides brief summaries of important cases within 24 hours of judgment being given.

As well as the law reports published by the Incorporated Council, there are many commercially published series of law reports. The commercially published series you are most likely to encounter is the *All England Law Reports* (All ER) which was traditionally a general series appearing in weekly parts, before being bound as four volumes for each year. (Unlike the *Weekly Law Reports*, no significance attaches to the placing of a case in any particular volume.) After many years as an entirely general series, the *All England Law Reports* embarked on a modest programme of diversification which has produced two sub-series. These cover European Community cases and commercial law cases, and are cited as All ER (EC) and All ER (Comm) respectively. However, most of the commercially published series of law reports are whole-heartedly specialist, with many covering quite small areas of law, such as *Housing Law Reports* (HLR) and *Road Traffic Reports* (RTR).

The headnotes in some law reports refer you to other relevant sources of law. The leading series of law reports which contains this kind of material is the *All England Law Reports*, which give any relevant references to other works published by the same company, principally *Halsbury's Laws of England* and *Halsbury's Statutes of England*.

The headnotes in most series of law reports do not contain summaries of the advocates' arguments, but the principal series of the Incorporated Council for Law Reporting for England and Wales (namely the *Appeal Cases* (AC), *Chancery Division* (Ch), *Family Division* (Fam) and *Queen's Bench Division* (QB) reports) do so. (See p. 84 for the contents of each of these series.) Summaries of the advocates' arguments do not appear in the other series published by the Incorporated Council, namely the *Weekly Law Reports* (WLR), the *Industrial Cases Reports* (ICR) and the *Business Law Reports* (Bus LR), nor in the commercially published full-transcript law reports (the leading example of which is the *All England Law Reports* (All ER)), nor in any of the series of short reports. (For the distinction between full-transcript and short reports, see pp. 86–87.)

The fact that most series of law reports do not include summaries of the advocates' arguments may be taken as an indication that they are less than essential. However, you may find them useful if you are mooting (and especially if you know that you are likely to lose on a point of law), because they may suggest lines of argument that you could adopt and, where necessary, adapt. If this tactic succeeds, you will at least have arguments of truly professional quality, which may help you to succeed as the best mooter. You will also find that moot judges will intervene at least once in respect of each advocate, as a means of testing each individual's ability to deviate from a set script. (Mooting is dealt with in more detail at pp. 214–220.)

The headnotes in some series of law reports list the cases cited in the judgment, together with a separate list of those cited in argument by the advocates but not referred to in the judgments. These case lists have two purposes.

First, they provide a research list of cases on similar subject matter which may lead you to more appropriate authorities for a legal problem or issue which you need to solve. However, the availability of electronic databases has reduced the importance of case lists for this purpose.

Secondly, knowing which of the cases that do not appear in the judgment were nonetheless cited to the court can be particularly useful if you already have a detailed knowledge of the relevant area of law and you are surprised to see that a particular case is not mentioned in the judgment. Knowing the case was cited in argument means that you can reasonably assume that the court considered the case to be irrelevant. If, on the other hand, you know that a case was not cited in argument (or if you do not know whether it was cited in argument) you may have an uneasy suspicion that the ensuing decision may not be of the highest quality. In itself, of course, the fact that the court was unaware of a case may mean nothing. For example, if a particular case had been cited, the court might have been able to distinguish it. (For an explanation of distinguishing, see p. 101–104.)

You will find a list of some of the most common abbreviations for series of law reports (together with abbreviations of the titles of many journals) in Appendix 2, but a more comprehensive index of abbreviations, which can be searched by abbreviation or title, is maintained by the University of Cardiff. It is available at http://www.legalabbrevs.cardiff.ac.uk/.

Full transcript and short reports
It is important to notice the distinction between *full transcript* and *short* reports. Full transcript reports, such as the *All England Law Reports*, together with all the series published by the Incorporated Council for Law Reporting and many other series, consist of the full transcripts of the courts' judgments, together with a headnote. We shall return to a more detailed analysis of full transcript law reports in Chapter 8, where we explain how to read a law report, but for the moment it is sufficient to comment briefly on the nature and status of headnotes.

The most important part of the headnote is the law reporter's summary of the case. However, it is essential to notice that, while headnotes are generally accurate, they are only an individual's summary and have no legal status whatsoever. It follows that you rely on them at your peril. The headnotes of some series of full transcript law reports contain only the law reporter's summary, but others contain a variety of other material, such as outlines of the advocates' arguments, including lists of the cases on which the arguments were based, in argument and in the judgment, together with references to extraneous material which the law reporter thinks may be relevant. The summary part of a headnote can take one of three forms.

First, it may be *fully propositional*, consisting only of the reporter's version of the proposition (or propositions) of law which the court formulated in order to dispose of the case, without any attempt to summarise the facts. This kind of headnote is appropriate where the facts are very detailed, but a full grasp of them is not necessary to gain an understanding of the law established by the case.

Secondly, it may be *fully narrative*, which means it tells the story of what happened (thus providing a statement of the relevant facts), before stating the court's ruling as to the relevant law, and then, finally, applying the law to the facts, in order to produce a decision. (The headnote to the report of *Henthorn v Fraser* [1892] 2 Ch 27 (CA), which we will analyse in Chapter 8, takes this form.)

Thirdly, it may be a compromise between the first two styles, consisting of a brief statement of context, followed by a statement of law on which the decision was based. A headnote of this kind would read something like:

> In a dispute as to whether a contractual offer can be revoked after an acceptance has been posted but before it has been received, the court held ...

This style of headnote may be called *semi-propositional*.

Unlike a full transcript report, a short report consists only of the reporter's summary. Again, these are generally accurate, but without the full transcript immediately to hand, you have no easy way of checking whether this is so in individual cases; and, in any event, no summary can ever do justice to all the subtleties of the full judgment. It follows that, as with the headnotes to full transcript reports, you rely on short reports at your peril. However, some short reports (for example, those which appear in the *Criminal Law Review*) do have the advantage that they are accompanied by commentaries which criticise the decisions, or assess their significance, or both. These commentaries are particularly useful in relation to recent decisions, which are unlikely to be discussed in the current edition of the textbook you have been advised to buy.

Citing law reports

Both the High Court and Court of Appeal have indicated, in the *Practice Direction (Judgments Form and Citation)* [2001] 1 WLR 194, that where 'a case has been reported in the official (*sic*) Law Reports published by the Incorporated Council ... it must be cited from that source'. Although in this respect the *Practice Direction* was merely repeating a long established principle, it also broke new ground for the Administrative Court and the Court of Appeal by introducing what are called *neutral citations* of, together with *paragraph numbering* within, judgments, in order to facilitate reference to their published versions on the Internet. Neutral citation has since been extended throughout the High Court by the *Practice Direction (Judgments: Neutral Citation)* [2002] 1 WLR 346, and it was also adopted by the House of Lords and, now, the Supreme Court. Where a neutral citation exists it should be cited first followed by a citation of the best available law report. The following examples show how neutral citations work:

Gregg v Scott [2005] UKHL 2
Austin v Southwark London Borough Council [2010] UKSC 28
Awberry v Marley Building Materials [2005] EWCA Civ 16
Gill v Sandhu [2005] EWHC 43 (Ch)

The number in each citation indicates the number of the judgment in each court in the relevant year. The *UK* element of the House of Lords and Supreme Court citations indicate that the courts were exercising their United Kingdom-wide jurisdictions (final appeals in Scottish criminal cases having always been heard by the Scottish courts). The courts in the other examples have jurisdiction only in England and Wales – hence the *EW* element of their citations.

The convention when citing law reports in print is to *italicise* the name of the case and to provide the full citation at least once. You should apply the *italicising* convention to any word-processed work that you are required to submit. In examinations, which will, of course, be handwritten, the whole script will be in a form of italics. The convention here is that you should un<u>derline</u> case names. In coursework, you should apply the convention of providing a full citation at least once for each case. In examinations, however, no one will expect you to have memorised case references. Beyond this, it is difficult to be dogmatic, since some lecturers will expect you to know the year of the case, while others will regard even this as being an unnecessary burden on your memory.

Sometimes you may wish to be more specific in your citation by providing what are called *pinpoint citations* or *pinpoints*. The pinpoint will be a paragraph number (which is cited using square brackets) or a page number. For example, if you needed to cite the fifteenth paragraph from *Gregg v Scott* (above) and had not cited the case previously, you would write: *Gregg v Scott* [2005] UKHL 2, [2005] 2 AC 176 [15]. If you had already fully cited the case you would simply write: *Gregg v Scott* [15]. In judgments delivered before the introduction of neutral citations which lack paragraph numbers, you will have to cite the case as published in the law report you consulted; the pinpoint will be the page number. So, for example, if you wanted to cite Lord Atkin's famous 'neighbour test' in

Donoghue v Stevenson, instead of simply citing the report and expecting the reader to work through all sixty pages, you would write: *Donoghue v Stevenson* [1932] AC 562 (HL) 566. Where you quote from a judgment and need to identify the judge, this detail can be added in round brackets as in, *Donoghue v Stevenson* [1932] AC 562 (HL) 566 (Lord Atkin). In these examples we have followed the *Oxford Standard for the Citation of Legal Authorities* (known as OSCOLA and available at http://www.law.ox.ac.uk/publications/oscola.php) and included the abbreviation for the court in which the case was decided in round brackets.

A point of general importance when citing law reports is the distinction between square brackets and round brackets. Sometimes a date in a reference is in square brackets, as in [2004] 3 WLR 113, and sometimes it is in round ones, as in (2004) 39 EHRR 15. Where the date is in square brackets, it is an essential part of the reference: the reference 3 WLR 113 is useless, because the *Weekly Law Reports* have been published since 1953, and each year has a volume 3 with a page 113. A date in round brackets, however, is not an essential element of the reference. Therefore, although it is usual practice to include the year, as in (2004) 39 EHRR 15, the reference 39 EHRR 15 would be completely adequate to locate a case since each annual volume of the *European Human Rights Reports* is numbered, so there will only ever be one volume bearing the number 39.

Other jurisdictions follow their own conventions; the full version of OSCOLA provides comprehensive guidance on citing international materials. Because of their impact on English law, the decisions of the European Court of Justice (ECJ) and the European Court of Human Rights require particular mention here. Judgments of the ECJ should be cited using the assigned case number followed by the case name and (where it is reported) the case reference in the official *European Court Reports* (ECR). Since 1989, following the creation of the Court of First Instance, cases are numbered and prefixed by court, with 'C' indicating the ECJ and 'T' indicating the Court of First Instance (now the General Court). The *European Court Reports* are similarly divided, with ECR I indicating a decision of the ECJ and ECR II indicating a judgment of the Court of First Instance (or now the General Court). Thus, a citation such as C-98/01 *EC Commission v United Kingdom* [2003] ECR I-4641 indicates (from the 'C' prefix to the case number and the 'I' following ECR) a decision of the ECJ.

Citing decisions of the European Court of Human Rights is more problematic. The guidance and usage of the court is that cases are cited by name, application number, the abbreviation ECHR and the year and volume number of the relevant official report. Where a paragraph number within a judgment is cited, it is preceded by the '§' symbol. Thus, *Pretty v United Kingdom* no. 2346/02, § 61, ECHR 2002-III would be a reference to paragraph 61 of application number 2346/02 reported in volume 3 of the official reports for 2002. In practice, however, you are likely to find that if a case is reported in the *European Human Rights Reports* (EHRR) that citation is given, and where the case is not reported in the EHRR the application number is cited. The *Pretty* case would therefore be cited as *Pretty v United Kingdom* (2002) 35 EHRR 1 or (if it were not reported in EHRR) Application 2346/02 *Pretty v United Kingdom*.

Online resources

Some series of law reports are now available online as subscription services, and many colleges and universities subscribe to services such as LexisNexis, Westlaw and Justis either as an intranet service (available on your college's or university's networked computers) or via password-protected portals, allowing students to have access from any Internet connection. Since the resources available are constantly increasing, and the methods of accessing them will vary from one institution to another, you will need to check the position in your own college or university.

The fundamental advantage of these electronic databases is that they are searchable by citation, by party names and by keywords, which makes the process of locating a case a great deal quicker than finding the right pages in volumes of law reports. Furthermore, some online databases provide additional features such as case summaries and annotations indicating whether a particular case has been applied, approved, overruled or doubted in later cases; and some even allow educational users to download cases.

The number of free online resources has increased significantly over recent years. The judgments of the Supreme Court, following the practice of the House of Lords since 1996, are posted online within hours of being delivered (available at: http://www.supremecourt.gov.uk/decided-cases/index.html). The archived judgments of the House of Lords are available (at http://www.publications.parliament.uk/pa/ld/ldjudgmt.htm), where they are grouped in years, and within each year they are organised alphabetically. (Incidentally, on the same site you will also find the official report of proceedings in Parliament, known as *Hansard*.) Most of the decisions of the Court of Appeal and an increasing number of High Court judgments as well as decisions of the European Court of Justice and the European Court of Human Rights are available on the British and Irish Legal Information Institute (BAILII) website (http://www.bailii.org/).

Generally speaking, however, the weakness of the databases with free access lies in their search facilities. For example, the House of Lords archive site has only limited search facilities (available through the *advanced search* on the Parliament site: http://www.parliament.uk/), although BAILII is somewhat more sophisticated. As far as the European sites are concerned, the entire case law of the European Court of Justice and the General Court, including its predecessor, the Court of First Instance (available at http://curia.eu.int/en/content/juris/index.htm) is searchable online as are the decisions of the European Court of Human Rights (available at http://www.echr.coe.int/echr/).

● Statutes

Introduction
Although the early development of English law depended to a great extent on the common law, there is no doubt now that statutes – a word which is interchangeable with the phrase *Acts of Parliament*, or, simply *Acts* – are now the principal source of English law.

Citing statutes
There are three ways of citing statutes.

First, there is citation by year and chapter number. In the case of the Energy Act 2004, for example, this form of citation is '2004, c.20', which indicates that it was the twentieth statute to receive the Royal Assent in 2004. The year and chapter number will be found in the heading of the statute.

Secondly, there is citation by the long title. The long title appears at the start of a statute and may be quite substantial. For example, the long title of the Energy Act 2004 is:

An Act to make provision for the decommissioning and cleaning up of installations and sites used for, or contaminated by, nuclear activities; to make provision relating to the civil nuclear industry; to make provision about radioactive waste; to make provision for the development, regulation and encouragement of the use of renewable energy sources; to make further provision in connection with the regulation of the gas and electricity industries; to make provision for the imposition of charges in connection with the carrying out of the Secretary of State's functions relating to energy matters; to make provision for giving effect to international agreements relating to pipelines and offshore installations; and for connected purposes.

Thirdly, there is citation by the short title – for example, the Energy Act 2004.

Although citation by year and chapter number is the most formal method, followed by citation by long title, in practice citation by short title is far and away the most common method. There are two reasons why this should be so. First, compared with citation by year and chapter number, short titles have the advantage that they provide at least some indication of the statute's subject matter. Secondly, compared with citation by the long title, short titles have the advantage that they involve the use of only one short phrase.

Finding statutes

The authoritative version of any statute is the Queen's Printer's copy published by Her Majesty's Stationery Office. Individual statutes are available from the Stationery Office and all statutes are published annually as Public and General Acts and Measures. The real problem with the Queen's Printer's copy of a statute is that it will not be updated in the light of any amending legislation which Parliament may subsequently pass. It follows that the text of the Queen's Printer's copy of an Act may no longer be accurate when you refer to it.

Two commercially published series, namely *Current Law Statutes Annotated* and *Halsbury's Statutes of England*, provide annotations to the text, explaining the effect of the statute and its relationship to other relevant areas of Law. *Halsbury's Statutes* also provides an updating service.

The most recently introduced means of accessing statutes is the UK Statute Law Database, which is mentioned under the next heading.

Online resources

Bills currently before Parliament, and details of their progress through Parliament, can be accessed through http://www.parliament.uk/business/bills-and-legislation/. The texts of Public General Acts (from 1801), Local Acts (from 1852) and UK Statutory Instruments (from 1948) are available at http://www.legislation.gov.uk/ (which also includes Explanatory Notes for statutes resulting from Bills introduced into Parliament from November 1998). This site also includes legislation passed by the Scottish Parliament, the National Assembly for Wales and the Northern Ireland Assembly. Its contents are updated to incorporate the effect of repeals and other amendments. However, the editorial process results in delays, which may cause the texts, as published, to be less than totally accurate. Several online subscription services, such as the LexisNexis Butterworths *Legislation Direct* and Westlaw UK's *United Kingdom Law in Force*, also provide amended and annotated statutes.

● Conclusion

The common law is constantly changing and developing; Acts of Parliament frequently amend other Acts of Parliament in various ways; and the European Community and the European Court of Human Rights are both active. Keeping up-to-date with legal developments is, therefore, essential. New electronic resources are likely to be developed, and the scope of existing ones is likely to change. The resources we have examined here, both electronic and paper-based, do not by any means cover all that is available, but they do direct you towards some solid, and hopefully enduring, starting points.

7 Legal Method

Law, like anything else expressed in language, requires interpretation. Once interpreted, the law then has to be applied to the facts of a particular case. In the English common law, this process of legal reasoning requires an understanding of the doctrine of binding precedent, including the concepts of *ratio decidendi* and *obiter dicta*, and the way in which the courts approach the task of legislative interpretation.

● Introduction

People often begin studying the law with the belief that a lawyer simply has to find the right page of the right book in order to discover the answer to any question of law. However, as this chapter will show, there are two reasons why this view is fundamentally misconceived. First, the sources of law need to be *interpreted* and then *applied to the facts* of the case. Secondly, many lawyers are argumentative by nature, and this tendency often comes to the fore when they are representing their clients. Therefore, it is not altogether surprising that they frequently disagree either as to the interpretation of the law, or as to the correct legal principle to be applied to a given set of facts, or as to both interpretation and application. Some people see this as bending, or attempting to bend, the rules. In reality, however, it is more accurately seen as an indication of the intrinsic flexibility of many legal rules. The truth of the matter is that there are many situations in which it is totally misleading to regard the law as consisting of a set of essentially rigid 'rules' which, unless the court decides to 'bend' them, will always dictate the outcome of any dispute to which they apply.

The scope for alternative answers to the same question, and the willingness of lawyers to argue for any of them, may be illustrated by the old story of someone who wants to know the result of adding 1.1111 to 2.8888. When put to a mathematician, the question receives an unqualified answer: '3.9999'. When put to an engineer, it receives a rather lengthier reply: 'strictly speaking, the answer is 3.9999; but engineering is a practical subject, and for all practical purposes the answer can be said to be 4, so I will say 4'. When the question is finally put to a lawyer, it receives the following reply: 'What do you want it to be?' In other words, if the issue arose in a legal context, the lawyer would be able and willing to argue for whichever answer advanced the client's case.

Turning to the law itself, we saw in Chapter 2 that the principal sources of English law are:

- the common law which is contained in the decisions of the courts, and which has developed through the doctrine of binding precedent;
- statutes which are made by Parliament, and delegated legislation which is made by other people acting under authority given to them by Parliament;
- and European Union law;

with the European Convention on Human Rights, as made applicable to English Law by both the common law and the Human Rights Act 1998, also providing some significant influence, even though it is, strictly speaking, a source of law only in relation to public authorities.

The bulk of this chapter will consider the techniques of legal method which are applicable to each of these sources, but before doing so it will be helpful to outline the nature of legal reasoning generally. This requires an explanation of the form of reasoning which professional philosophers call *syllogistic* (because it takes the form of a *syllogism*). Strictly speaking, legal reasoning is not truly syllogistic, but lawyers always speak as if it is, so it is best to follow their standard usage.

● Syllogistic reasoning

The form of syllogistic reasoning in law is best explained by a simple example:

If $A = B$
And if $B = C$
Then $A = C$.

The first line of this syllogism is called the *major premise*, the second line is called the *minor premise*, and the third line is called the *conclusion*.

Putting this into a specifically legal context, the major premise will be a proposition of *law*; the minor premise will be a proposition of *fact*, and the conclusion will be the *decision* in the case. For example:

> It is an offence to exceed the speed limit in a motor vehicle on a public highway (*major premise/proposition of law*)
> Exceeding the speed limit in a motor vehicle on a public highway is what the defendant did (*minor premise/proposition of fact*)

therefore

> It is an offence to do what the defendant did – or, in other words, the defendant is guilty (*conclusion/decision*).

In reality, of course, simply being able to identify the form of reasoning as syllogistic tells us very little. What we really need to know is how we can identify and formulate:

- the correct proposition of law (the *major premise*); and
- the facts to which the proposition of law must be applied (the *minor premise*).

The answer to the first question is:

- by applying the techniques of legal method.

The answer to the second question is:

- by evidence establishing the facts which are in dispute.

As it is only the first question which falls within the scope of this book, it is to this that we will now turn.

● The common law and the doctrine of binding precedent

Introduction

As we saw in Chapter 1, there are various ways of thinking about *justice*, but at a very basic level most people would probably accept that justice requires similar cases to be dealt with in a similar way. So there is nothing surprising in the fact that judges in developed legal systems tend to follow each other's decisions. What is unusual about the common law system is that, theoretically at least and in certain circumstances, judges are *bound* to follow decisions made in earlier cases.

A system which guarantees consistency between decisions in similar cases will also meet another important requirement of any fair legal system, namely making it possible for lawyers to advise their clients with reasonable confidence as to the legal position. However, a strict system of *binding* precedent also has the disadvantage of causing excessive rigidity, which may not only make it impossible for the courts to respond sympathetically to the particular subtleties of an individual case, but may also prevent the courts from introducing desirable developments into the law.

Although the conflict between the advantages and disadvantages of the system of binding precedent are often presented in the form of a conflict between certainty and predictability on the one hand and flexibility and justice on the other, such an analysis is too superficial to be genuinely helpful. More particularly, as we have seen, sufficient certainty to enable reasonable predictability is itself a part of, rather than being opposed to, justice. The problem, therefore, is not one of resolving a conflict between certainty and predictability on the one hand, and flexibility and justice on the other. It is about striking a broadly acceptable balance which will normally require the courts to follow earlier decisions, while allowing a degree of flexibility in cases where the courts consider this to be appropriate.

We will now consider how the doctrine of binding precedent (which is sometimes still known by the Latin tag *stare decisis*), attempts to strike this balance. (*Stare decisis* may be roughly translated as *to stand by decisions*.) As we will see, there are two elements to the doctrine. One requires us to analyse the hierarchy of the courts, while the other requires us to analyse individual judgments into their component parts. We will begin with the hierarchy of the courts.

The hierarchy of the courts and the doctrine of binding precedent
A working statement of the doctrine of binding precedent could be:

> All courts bind all lower courts, and the Court of Appeal also binds itself, as does the Supreme Court (and as did the House of Lords) although the self-bindingness element of this statement requires some qualification.

The hierarchical structure to which, broadly speaking, this statement refers may be illustrated by repeating the diagram which you first encountered at p. 53. However, when reading the text, you will see that those bodies whose names appear in brackets do not fit neatly into the mainstream of the doctrine of binding precedent.

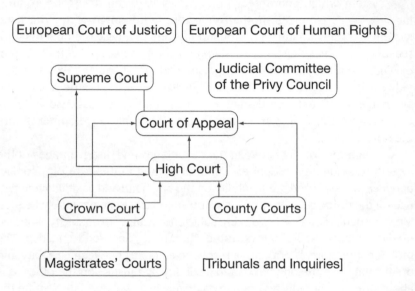

Decisions of the European Court of Justice are binding on English courts. Strictly speaking, however, as we shall see below, the Court is not bound by its own decisions, although in practice it does tend to follow them.

The status of decisions of the European Court of Human Rights within the English legal system is complex and can only be fully understood in the light of the Human Rights Act 1998. Very briefly, however, and at the risk of some over-simplification:

- at common law the English courts have always been willing to have regard to the provisions of the European Convention on Human Rights, but without feeling themselves bound by an instrument which is not actually part of English Law;
- under the Human Rights Act 1998, English courts:
  - must *take into account* any relevant decisions of the European Court of Human Rights; but
  - are not bound to follow them.

Decisions of the Judicial Committee of the Privy Council are never, strictly speaking, binding on any court. However, the fact that there is a very substantial overlap between the Supreme Court Justices (and, previously, the Law Lords) on the one hand, and the Judicial Committee of the Privy Council on the other, means that many Privy Council decisions are usually treated for all practical purposes as having the same status as House of Lords or Supreme Court authorities. The Court of Appeal may even choose to follow a decision of the Judicial Committee of the Privy Council sitting with more than its usual tally of five members and consisting entirely of Law Lords or Supreme Court Justices, rather than following a decision of the House of Lords or the Supreme Court. (See *Attorney-General for Jersey v Holley* [2005] UKPC 23, [2005] 2 AC 580.)

The Privy Council tends to follow its own decisions but is not bound to do so.

The Court of Appeal is basically bound to follow its own decisions, but there are exceptional situations in which it is free to depart from them. The authorities are not altogether clear, but the exceptions may be more flexible in the Criminal Division than in the Civil Division.

The self-bindingness of the High Court depends on which jurisdiction it is exercising:

- when dealing with appeals (i.e. where the correctness of a decision made by another court or other decision-maker is being challenged) it binds itself; but
- at both first instance (that is, when dealing with trials) and in judicial review (that is, when dealing with challenges to the legality of the decision-making processes of another court or other decision-maker, as distinct from challenging the correctness of the resulting decision) its own decisions are only persuasive (which means that it may choose to follow an earlier decision but is not bound to do so).

The Crown Court, county courts and magistrates' courts are not bound by their own previous decisions.

Tribunals (or administrative tribunals as they were traditionally known) are, of course, bound by the decisions of the courts. Increasingly, they also regard themselves as being bound by their own decisions, but the lack of a system of reporting on the scale of the law reports means that it is unwise to rely too heavily on this proposition.

Similarly, inquiries are bound by the decisions of the courts, but the fact that they are very heavily concerned with finding the facts on which a final decision is to be based means that there is practically no scope for any internal system of precedent (because the doctrine of binding precedent is concerned only with statements of law rather than of fact).

The elements of a judgment: *ratio decidendi* and *obiter dictum*

Having dealt with the hierarchy of the courts, the idea of bindingness must be explored in a little more detail. As a preliminary, however, it is worth emphasising that the doctrine of binding precedent is not concerned with the position between the parties to the case which creates the precedent, but is concerned with the provision of rules of law which can then be applied by all later courts; and, more particularly, will actually be *binding* on some of them.

The first point is that not every part of a judgment will be binding. To identify the binding part, a judgment must be analysed into two constituent elements: *ratio decidendi* and *obiter dicta*. The binding part is the *ratio decidendi*, which may be translated as *the reason for the decision*. The remainder of the judgment will be *obiter dicta*, which may be translated as *sayings by the way*, which are not binding but may be persuasive – see p. 104.

The plural of *ratio decidendi* is either *ratios decidendi* or (sticking more faithfully to the original Latin) *rationes decidendi*, according to personal preference. The sentence in the previous paragraph which used the phrase *obiter dicta* required it to be given in its plural form: the singular is *obiter dictum*. It is conventional to speak of *ratio* and *dictum* – and their respective plurals – without using the other part of each phrase. The word *obiter* may be used on its own as either an adjective or an adverb, but should never be used as a noun. In other words, a statement by a judge may be said to be *obiter* (using the word as an adjective) or to be made *obiter* (using the word as an adverb) but never to be *an obiter* (because this would be using the word as a noun).

Identifying the *ratio*

It follows from what has been said that one of the main tasks facing you whenever you read a case is to identify its *ratio*. The first point to be made is – at the risk of stating the obvious – that where there is only one judgment, the *ratio* of that judgment will be the *ratio* of the case, while if a multi-judge court divides into a majority and a minority, the *ratio* of the majority will be the *ratio* of the case. However, these propositions take us nowhere in relation to the key task of identifying the *ratio* of a judgment in the first place.

The difficulty of identifying the *ratio* of a judgment arises from the fact that judges who are deciding cases are usually going to be principally concerned with resolving the issues between the parties. Therefore, any statements of the law which judges make in the course of their judgments will be conditioned by the circumstances of the cases they are deciding, and the fact that their decisions will be subjected to detailed analysis in later cases will usually be of secondary importance to them. The point was well made by Lord Halsbury LC, when he said:

> The generality of the expressions which may be found ... are not intended to be expositions of the whole law but govern and are qualified by the particular facts of the case. (*Quinn v Leathem* [1901] AC 495, 506.)

However, it is not all the facts that will be relevant when interpreting a judgment, but only the *material* facts. Or, putting this another way, when looking for the *ratio* of a case, it is necessary to identify the *material facts* which influenced the formulation of the legal rule on which the decision is based. A useful way of testing the materiality of a fact is to ask: *if this fact had either not been present or had been present but different, would the decision still have been the same*? If the answer to this question is *No*, it follows that that fact must be material. Ultimately, the materiality (or non-materiality) of a fact can only be determined in the light of all the circumstances of a real case. However, in general terms it can be said that facts as to the time and place where things happened, the identity of people and things, and the amount of property involved (including sums of money) will be presumed to be *not* material unless all the circumstances of the case are such that they justify the opposite conclusion. For example, there may be a crucial distinction in some cases between things which happened in a public place and things which happened in a private place. (But even here, the question of precisely *which* public – or private – place is unlikely to be material.)

If the judge in a later case decides that the facts of an earlier case were *materially different* from the facts of the case before him, he can perfectly properly *distinguish* the earlier case. This is not a question of interfering with the authority of the earlier case in any subsequent cases which may be genuinely similar. It is simply a question of deciding that the earlier case is not relevant to the case which is currently being decided, and is not, therefore, a binding authority.

The importance of the technique of distinguishing cases must be stressed, since it is an important way in which judges seek to achieve results which they feel to be appropriate to the cases which they decide. No totally reliable formula for the identification of material facts exists, but an example may help to show how distinguishing can work in practice.

The case of *Burgess v McCracken* (1986) 150 JP 529, arose from the commercial activities of a professional photographer in a public park. His method of business was to get people to agree to have their photographs taken. He then took their photographs, noted their names and addresses, and received a deposit. He subsequently sent them the photographs through the post, and they sent him the balance of his fee. It was important to know whether what he did amounted to *trading in the park*, because if it did he was committing an offence. A magistrates' court acquitted him on the basis that an earlier case (*Newman v Lipman* [1951] 1 KB 333) had decided that exactly the same conduct in a street did not amount to the offence of *trading in the street*.

However, in *Burgess* the prosecution appealed to the High Court, where it was held that there was a legally relevant distinction between streets and parks. The court said that the offence in relation to streets was intended to prevent obstructions of the kind that can arise when traders set up stalls to display their goods. Street photographers do not do this; therefore they do not commit an offence. On the other hand, people go into parks for relaxation and recreation, therefore the offence in relation to parks has a wider purpose, which includes protecting people from annoyance. In the context of a park, therefore, the mere absence of obstruction did not justify an acquittal. (This pair of cases also provides a neat illustration of the truth of the proposition that a decision on the meaning of a word for the purposes of one statute will not be binding as to the meaning of the same word for the purposes of another statute. As we have just seen, in reality, this proposition is simply an example of distinguishing.)

As a means of avoiding a consequence which they feel to be wrong, judges may be tempted to distinguish earlier cases on artificial grounds. Indeed, some people may feel that *Burgess* itself is an example of artificial distinguishing. However, leaving aside the merits of individual examples, the fact that artificial distinguishing does take place must be recognised. Similarly, it must also be recognised that this undermines the predictability of the legal system, because judges vary in their willingness to resort to artificiality. The responsibility of the judges when considering whether to distinguish an earlier case is well explained by Robert Goff LJ, in *Elliott v C* [1983] 1 WLR 939, 947:

> In my opinion, although of course the courts of this country are
> bound by the doctrine of precedent, sensibly interpreted, nevertheless

it would be irresponsible for judges to act as automata, rigidly applying authorities without regard to consequences. Where therefore it appears at first sight that authority compels a judge to reach a conclusion which he senses to be unjust or inappropriate, he is, I consider, under a positive duty to examine the relevant authorities with scrupulous care to ascertain whether he can, within the limits imposed by the doctrine of precedent (always sensibly interpreted), legitimately interpret or qualify the principle expressed in the authorities to achieve the result which he perceives to be just or appropriate in the particular case. I do not disguise the fact that I have sought to perform this function in the present case.

At first sight this attitude may seem to amount to a total denial of the doctrine of binding precedent. However, you will have noticed that Robert Goff LJ did indicate that there are 'limits imposed by the doctrine', and that in the result, he actually felt unable to achieve the outcome which he perceived to be just or appropriate, saying he was 'constrained ... by authority' to reach a conclusion which caused him 'unhappiness'.

A litigant who is disappointed, either by artificial distinguishing or by a failure to undertake real distinguishing, will be in the same position as any other disappointed litigant, and will have no remedy other than pursuing any avenues, whether by way of appeal or judicial review, that the legal system may offer.

It should be apparent by this stage that legal method can be a great deal more flexible than many people assume it to be. One of the classic textbooks on jurisprudence expresses the dynamism of the concept of *ratio* in literally graphic terms:

> If we think of the rule of law as a line on a graph, then the case itself is like a point through which that line is drawn. (Fitzgerald, P. J., *Salmond on Jurisprudence*, 12th edn, 1966, p. 170.)

This flexibility of binding precedent leads to a very important conclusion, namely that it can be seriously misleading to talk simply of the *ratio* of a case. In reality, there are two *ratios*. The first in time is the *descriptive ratio*, which describes the reasoning leading to the decision in the earlier case. This *ratio* can, of course, be identified immediately after that judgment is given. The second *ratio* is the *prescriptive ratio*, which is formulated by a court in the process of making a later decision, and is then developed by a series of subsequent cases. This *ratio* is called *prescriptive* because it *prescribes* the principle of law which is binding on the later court. (You may find it puzzling that it is the later court which decides what it is going to be bound by, since this seems to go against the essential idea of being bound. However, as you progress through your study of law you will see that – puzzling or not – this is, in fact, how the doctrine of binding precedent operates.)

Having established that the flexibility of precedent is, in practice, largely due to the technique of distinguishing previous cases so that they can then be disregarded, coupled with the possibility of interpreting and applying their *ratios* in such a way as to produce just outcomes, we can now turn to the concept of *dictum*.

Assessing the weight of *obiter dicta*

Although, as a matter of definition, *dicta* are not binding, it does not follow that they are entirely irrelevant. They can be said to have *persuasive authority*, meaning that a later court may choose to follow them, even though it is not obliged to do so. An important point here is that the degree of persuasiveness varies greatly. In fact the stage may be reached where there is little practical distinction between *ratio* and *dicta*. The explanation of this will be found in a consideration of the reasons why, in strict theory, *dicta* are not binding.

Two factors are relevant. First, where a point is not central to the case, the advocates who appear will usually not argue the law, or if they do argue it, they will do so with less thoroughness than they would give to the main issues. Secondly, a judge who says something *obiter* will usually not have given the matter the same consideration as he would have done if it were more central to the decision. It follows from these two factors that, if a point has been fully argued, and the court did give it very careful attention, there is no real reason why the court's views should not be treated as being authoritative. An example may be useful.

In *Hedley Byrne & Co Ltd v Heller & Partners Ltd* [1964] AC 465, the facts were that the defendants had made an incorrect statement to the plaintiffs about the creditworthiness of a third party. The plaintiff relied on this statement and lost money as a result. The question was whether the defendants were liable to pay damages to the plaintiff. One complicating factor was that the defendants had expressly stated that they were giving the advice 'without responsibility'. In other words, they were making it clear that they would not consider themselves liable for any loss which resulted from their advice.

The House of Lords said that, in principle, the defendants ought to be liable. On the facts, however, the defendants had disclaimed liability, and therefore the plaintiffs failed to recover damages. If this is analysed into *ratio* and *dictum*, it will be apparent that the *ratio* was that the defendants had disclaimed liability. Since this was all that was necessary for the decision, all the rest of it must have been *obiter*. Nevertheless, the decision on the point of principle has been both generally accepted, and subsequently developed. The attitude of later courts faced with this kind of *dictum* may be found in the words of Cairns J:

> Where five members of the House of Lords have all said, after close examination of the authorities, that a certain type of tort exists, I think that a judge of first instance should proceed on the basis that it does exist, without pausing to embark on an investigation whether what was said was necessary to the ultimate decision. (*WB Anderson & Sons Ltd v Rhodes* [1967] 2 All ER 850, 857.) This comment must, of course, now be read as including statements made by the Supreme Court.

The fact that *dicta* are of varying degrees of authority, from the almost worthless to the very strongly persuasive, leads some people to adopt a sub-classification into *gratis dicta* and *judicial dicta*, with the former being much less weighty than the latter. There is no harm in this terminology, provided you do not allow it to lead you into the trap of thinking that all *dicta* fall fairly and squarely into one category or the other. The truth of the matter is that there is a spectrum of possibilities, from the mere throwaway comment which is worth practically nothing in terms of precedent to the fully argued and carefully considered opinion, the weight of which is indistinguishable from the weight of a *ratio decidendi*; and, in reality, most *dicta* fall somewhere in the middle ground between these extremes.

● Legislation and legislative interpretation

Introduction

Since the Industrial Revolution, social and economic changes have occurred at such a rate that the common law, whose development is dependent on the random process of suitable cases coming before the courts, has been unable to keep pace with the needs of the society it serves. As a result, statutes (which are also known as primary legislation) and delegated legislation have become the major source of English law.

As we saw in Chapter 3, it is a matter of fundamental English constitutional doctrine that Parliament is legislatively supreme. In other words, Parliament can enact any statute it wishes and only Parliament can repeal whatever Parliament has enacted. There may be significant debate over the extent of the power (if any) of one Parliament to bind its successors, and over the relationship between European Union law and English law, but neither of these matters need be pursued for the present purposes.

What does need to be considered is the interpretation or construction of statutes and delegated legislation. In passing, it is worth noticing that judges use the terms *interpretation* and *construction* interchangeably on most occasions, and they can generally be taken to mean the same thing.

Communication and interpretation

Essentially the drafting and interpretation of statutes and delegated legislation is simply an exercise in communication. Having decided what it wants to do, Parliament, or those whom Parliament has authorised to make delegated legislation, communicates the result to the world at large, including the courts which have to enforce it. However, the processes of legislative drafting and interpretation create more than usually acute problems of communication because they involve a vital question of the balance of constitutional power between the courts and the legislators.

A particularly useful collection of insights into the drafting process is provided by a DVD made in 2010 by the Statute Law Society, in conjunction with Oxford University. This explains the legislative process from the political beginnings of a policy proposal through to the conclusion of the Parliamentary stage. The explanations are provided by a former Lord Chancellor (who deals with the political realities surrounding the creation and delivery of the government's legislative programme); a departmental lawyer (who deals with the process by which policy ideas are developed into legislative proposals); First Parliamentary Counsel (who deals with the process of drafting the Bills which, in due course, become Acts of Parliament; clerks from both Houses of Parliament (who deal with the practicalities of Parliamentary procedure); the legal adviser to the Joint Committee on Human Rights (who deals with the work of that committee – which is called *Joint* because its members are drawn from both Houses of Parliament – in scrutinising legislative proposals from a human rights perspective); and a former chair of the Law Commission (that is to say, the official body with responsibility for keeping the law under review and making proposals for reform). There is also a lecture on *How Statute Law Is Made*, given by First Parliamentary Counsel, which provides an overview of the entire topic. On its release, copies of the DVD were distributed to all English and Welsh Law Schools and its content, which may be used for any non-commercial purposes, is freely downloadable from http://itunes.apple.com/itunes-u/statute-law-making-legislation/id407263684/. In more conventional form, *Principles of Legislative and Regulatory Drafting* (McLeod, 2009) provides an accessible introduction to the challenges and techniques of drafting.

The evolution of the current approach to legislative interpretation

There are, and always have been, several principles which the courts use to guide themselves in the task of legislative interpretation. For example, where a statute which creates a criminal offence is open to two or more meanings, there is a presumption that Parliament intended the courts to apply the meaning which is most favourable to the defendant. (*Dickenson v Fletcher* (1873) LR 9 CP 1.) Similarly, there is a presumption that Parliament did not intend legislation to operate retrospectively. (*L'Office Cherifien des Phosphates and Another v Yamasita-Shinnihon Steamship Co Ltd: The Boucraa* [1994] AC 486.) However, principles such as these will, in their nature, apply to relatively few cases, so we shall now turn our interpretation to the evolution of what is currently the single most important guide to legislative interpretation, namely the *purposive approach*.

Historically, when statutes were a relatively minor source of English law, the predominant principle of interpretation was the *mischief rule*, or the *rule in Heydon's Case* (1584) 76 ER 637, which may be stated as follows:

> For the sure and true interpretation of all statutes ... four things are to be discerned and considered:
>
> 1st   What was the Common Law before the making of the Act?
>
> 2nd   What was the mischief and defect for which the Common Law did not provide?
>
> 3rd   What remedy the Parliament hath resolved and appointed to cure the disease of the Commonwealth?
>
> 4th   The true reason of the remedy; and then the office of all the judges is always to make such construction as shall suppress the mischief and advance the remedy, and to suppress continuance of the mischief ... according to the true intent of the makers of the Act.

However, as statutes became increasingly important sources of law, and as Parliament became increasingly democratically validated during the 19th century, the courts relegated the mischief rule to the status of a long-stop, to be invoked only when all else failed. Instead, they started to rely primarily on the so-called *literal rule* of interpretation, which, in the words of Lord Blackburn, required them to give statutory words their *literal* or *plain* meanings, except where these led to

> an inconsistency or an absurdity or inconvenience so great as to convince the court that the intention could not have been to use them in their ordinary signification,

in which case the courts could invoke the so-called *golden rule*, which would

> justify the court putting on them some other signification, which though less proper, is one which the court thinks the words will bear. (*River Wear Commissioners v Adamson* (1877) 2 App Cas 743, 764.)

While this approach may sound perfectly reasonable in the abstract, it is in fact deeply flawed, because it assumes that words have *literal* or *plain* meanings. While there are, no doubt, instances where this is so, there are also very many instances where it is simply not true; and it is these cases which, naturally, are most likely to come before the appellate courts.

Take two examples. First, imagine a poster in a shop window which reads: *Last Week – Everything Half Price*. On a purely linguistic basis, this could mean that the sale finished at the end of the previous week (and that, therefore, everything has now gone back to being full price). But commonsense tells you this is not what the poster means, and that the message it is seeking to convey is that this is the *final* week of the sale. The second example requires you to name the last King of England. On a purely linguistic basis, you could reply that no answer is possible because, being unable to foretell the future, you cannot possibly know who will be the last (in the sense of *final*) King of England. But this response would never occur to most people, who would assume they were being required to name the *most recent* King of England (and would, therefore, say George VI).

While this pair of examples may seem trivial, it does show that the simple, everyday word *last* can mean either *final* or *most recent*, and – crucially – that the correct choice of meaning is *not to be found in the word itself, but in the context in which it is used*. Thus, any approach to interpretation in terms of *literal* or *plain* meanings is based on a fundamental misunderstanding of the nature of words and their meanings.

Eventually, the courts came to appreciate the importance of context when interpreting words. As Stamp J said, in *Bourne v Norwich Crematorium Ltd* [1967] 1 WLR 691, 696:

> English words derive colour from those which surround them.
> Sentences are not mere collections of words to be taken out of the
> sentence, defined separately by reference to the dictionary or decided
> cases, and then put back again into the sentence with the meaning
> which one has assigned to them as separate words so as to give
> the sentence or phrase a meaning which as a sentence or phrase it
> cannot bear without distortion of the English language.

More particularly, the courts came to appreciate that the *purpose* under-lying the legislation is an essential element in the context of the statutory words:

> If one looks back to the actual decisions of [the House of Lords]
> over the last thirty years one cannot fail to be struck by the
> evidence of a trend ... towards the purposive construction of
> statutory provisions. (Lord Diplock, in *Carter v Bradbeer* [1975] 1
> WLR 1204, 1206-1207.)

An example of the power of purposivism may be useful. In *R v Pigg* [1983] 1 WLR 6, the point at issue was whether the defendant's conviction for rape should be upheld or quashed. He had been convicted on a majority verdict, under a statutory provision in the following terms:

> A court shall not accept a majority verdict of guilty unless the
> foreman of the jury has stated in open court the number of jurors
> who respectively agreed to and dissented from the verdict. (Section
> 17(2), Juries Act 1974.)

What actually happened in *Pigg* was that the foreman merely said that ten jurors had agreed to convict the defendant. The clerk of the court then said: 'ten agreed to two of you'. The foreman made no reply. Holding that the proceedings had complied with the statutory requirement, Lord Brandon, with the agreement of the other Law Lords, said (at p. 13):

> the precise form of words by which such compliance is achieved, so
> long as the effect is clear, is not material.

The conviction was, therefore, upheld. Lord Brandon appears not to have been concerned that his interpretation resulted in the upholding of the conviction, even though this ran counter to the basic proposition that criminal statutes should be interpreted strictly in favour of the defendant. Perhaps Lord Brandon's abhorrence of the offence weighed more heavily with him than did any traditional ideas of fair play for the defendant.

● European Union law

Precedent in the European Court of Justice

Although European Union law lies within the civil law tradition, and therefore has no doctrine of binding precedent, it does exhibit a strong tendency to follow its own previous decisions. For example, in *Da Costa* [1963] CMLR 224, when dealing with a preliminary reference from a Dutch court, under what was then art. 177 of the Treaty of Rome (see now art. 267 TFEU), the court said (at p. 238):

> The questions of interpretation posed in this case are identical with those settled ... [in the earlier case of *van Gend en Loos* [1963] CMLR 105] ... and no new factor has been presented to the court.
>
> In these circumstances the [national court] must be referred to the previous judgment.

Legislative interpretation in the European Court of Justice

The civil law tradition has always been purposivist (or to use the word which that tradition itself generally uses, *teleological*) in its approach to legislative interpretation. It has never fallen into the trap of literalism. Two passages from *van Gend en Loos v Nederlandse Administratie der Belastingen* [1963] CMLR 105, which is one of the most important cases in the whole of EU law, indicate the approach of the European Court of Justice.

> The objective of the EEC Treaty, which is to establish a common market, the functioning of which is of direct concern to interested parties in the Community, implies that this Treaty is more than an agreement which merely creates mutual obligations between the contracting states. This view is confirmed by the preamble to the Treaty which refers not only to governments but to peoples. It is also confirmed more specifically by the establishment of institutions

endowed with sovereign rights, the exercise of which affects member states and also their citizens. ((1963) CMLR 105, 129.)

On the basis of this, together with a detailed consideration of the case itself, the court concluded:

It follows ... that, according to the spirit, the general scheme and the wording of the Treaty, art. 12 [of the Treaty of Rome] must be interpreted as producing direct effects and creating individual rights which national courts must protect. ((1963) CMLR 105, 130.)

● The European Court of Human Rights

Precedent in the European Court of Human Rights
As with the European Court of Justice, the European Court of Human Rights is firmly located within the Civil Law tradition. However, and again as with the European Court of Justice, although it has no doctrine of *binding* precedent, the Court of Human Rights 'usually follows and applies its own precedents, such a course being in the interests of legal certainty and the orderly development of the Convention case-law', while being ready to depart from its own previous decisions where there are 'cogent reasons' for doing so, including the need to 'ensure that the interpretation of the Convention reflects societal changes and remains in line with present day conditions'. (*Cossey v United Kingdom* (1991) 13 EHRR 622, 639, in which the Court refused to depart from its decision in *Rees v United Kingdom* (1987) 9 EHRR 56, where it had held that the United Kingdom was entitled to refuse to allow transsexuals to have their birth certificates amended in order to show their acquired sex.)

Legislative interpretation in the European Court of Human Rights
It is a well-established principle of international law, currently contained in the Vienna Convention on the Law of Treaties 1969, that treaties 'shall be interpreted in good faith in accordance with the ordinary meaning to be given to the terms of the treaty in their context and *in the light of its object and purposes*'. (Emphasis added.)

The preamble to the European Convention on Human Rights makes it plain that its object and purpose are 'the maintenance and further realisation of Human Rights and Fundamental Freedoms'. Furthermore, the Court's decision in *Wemhoff v Federal Republic of Germany* (1979-80) 1 EHRR

55, shows that where the wording of the official texts of the Convention cannot be reconciled with each other, the 'object and purpose' of the Convention will be decisive.

● Conclusion

Legal method is much more flexible than many students think when they first approach the law. Good lawyers examine the relevant sources of law with a view to trying to construct an argument which will favour their clients' interests.

When dealing with the common law, a great deal of flexibility arises from the concepts of *ratio decidendi* and *obiter dictum* and the status of each in terms of bindingness and persuasiveness.

Both the European Court of Justice and the European Court of Human Rights come from the civil law tradition, which means that neither of them has a doctrine of binding precedent.

When dealing with legislation, a great deal of flexibility arises from the fact that many words have a variety of meanings, and that even apparently plain words can be interpreted in unexpected ways when regard is had to their purpose. More particularly, the English courts no longer approach the task of legislative interpretation in a literal way, preferring to give greater importance to the purpose of the legislation.

Another consequence of the fact that both the European Court of Justice and the European Court of Human Rights come from the civil law tradition is that they both approach legislative interpretation in a purposive way.

8 Reading Law Reports and Statutes

Cases and statutes are the principal building blocks of English law. You must, therefore, be able to read them both confidently. In relation to both sources, you must be familiar with the way the text is likely to be laid out. In relation to law reports, you must be able to identify the *ratio decidendi* of a case and assess the weight of *obiter dicta*. In relation to statutes, you must always try to identify the purpose of the Act, and be aware that (almost always) some words and phrases will be defined by the Act itself, while others will be left open for interpretation by the courts.

● Introduction

We noted in Chapter 2 that the English legal system is a common law system, which means that a great deal of the law has been created, and some of it continues to be developed, by the courts when deciding individual cases. Indeed, there are still some significant areas of law – such as the tort of negligence – which remain relatively untouched by statute and which are, therefore, largely dependent on the courts for their continuing development on a case-by-case basis.

Nevertheless, despite the continuing importance of the common law, statutes now create a far greater volume of law than judicial decisions do. It follows, therefore, that you must rapidly acquire the ability to read both cases and statutes. Quite apart from anything else, statutes have to be interpreted by the courts. This point divides into two sub-points. First, the principles of statutory interpretation are themselves part of the common law rather than having been enacted by Parliament. Secondly, under the doctrine of the separation of powers (which is explained at pp. 41–45) it falls to the courts to decide the definitive meanings of individual statutes, and these decisions may then bind other courts in later cases arising from the same statutes.

Of course, you may be tempted to rely on the few lines in a textbook which purport to tell you what a case decides or what a statute means; and there is no doubt that textbooks can be very useful as a means of gaining a bird's-eye view of a topic. However, when it comes to more detailed study, whether by way of preparation for tutorials or essays, or when assembling a body of notes from which you will be able to revise for examinations, there is no effective substitute for reading the cases and statutes themselves.

In this chapter we are going to do two things. First, we shall take a substantial extract from the report of the Court of Appeal decision in *Henthorn v Fraser* [1892] 2 Ch 27 (which is a leading case in the law of contract) and explain how you can get the maximum value from the time and energy you will invest in reading it. More particularly, there are two aspects to this part of the chapter. Our first aim is to help you find your way around a typical law report in terms of identifying its elements and understanding its structure. Our second aim is to illustrate how the *ratio decidendi* of a judgment can be identified and how the weight of *obiter dicta* can be assessed. Of course – and recalling the distinction between the *descriptive* and *prescriptive* meanings of the word *ratio*, which is explained at p. 103 – all we can do at this stage is to identify the *descriptive ratio*, since it is only the judges in later cases in which this one has been cited who can identify the *prescriptive ratio*.

Secondly, we shall take the Dealing in Cultural Objects (Offences) Act 2003, which is a very short, modern statute, in order to illustrate both the basic structure of a simple statute and some points of statutory interpretation.

● Reading Law Reports

Introduction

You will very shortly come to an extract of a report of the case of *Henthorn v Fraser*, where the issue was whether a person who has offered to sell certain property to another person can withdraw (or, to use the technical term, *revoke*) that offer after the other person has put his acceptance of the offer in the post but before the prospective seller has received it.

We have taken the report from The Law Reports, where it appears in one of the volumes which contain decisions of the Chancery Division of the High Court and decisions of the Court of Appeal arising from appeals against those decisions. (In fact, as you will see when you read the report carefully, this particular case was heard at first instance by the Vice-Chancellor of the County Palatine of Lancaster. This court of chancery no longer exists but it was the local equivalent of the High Court – to which its jurisdiction passed when it was abolished – so nothing turns on this particular historical oddity.)

We have reproduced the report in substantially the same form as that in which it was originally published, subject to the following alterations.

First, it has been sufficient for our purposes to reproduce only the headnote and the judgment of Lord Herschell. However, if you read the original report you will see that both the other judges concurred. More particularly, Kay LJ delivered a fully reasoned judgment, while Lindley LJ simply delivered a short statement of his concurrence.

Secondly, as well as being selective in relation to the text, we have also edited it in three other ways. The first, and most obvious, aspect of our editing is that we have inserted text boxes at various points in order to provide a commentary on either what has just been said, or what is about to be said, in the text. Additionally, we have modernised some of the typography. Finally, we have expanded the footnotes by including explanations of the case references.

Reading the case for the first time

Since you cannot realistically hope to absorb all the details on your first reading of a case, at this stage you should read the text fairly quickly in order to acquire an overview of what the case is about and how the court approached its decision. *However, you should not, at this stage, slow yourself down by reading the text boxes.* On your second and subsequent readings, when you know roughly what the case is about, you will be in a better position to understand both the text and the text boxes. Even on your first reading, however, there is one detail you should make a point of noticing. It is only from the point (on p. 30 of the report) where you find '1892. March 26. LORD HERSCHELL', that you are reading the actual words of the judgment (all the previous text having been provided by the law reporter). This is significant because it is only the judgment which contains the definitive version of the facts and the authoritative statement of the law.

The report and the boxed commentary

| 2 Ch | CHANCERY DIVISION | 27 |

HENTHORN v FRASER

> On the top line is the page heading. Here it tells you the volume (2), report series (Chancery Division) and page number (27) of the Law Report you are reading. It does not, however, tell you that it is a decision of the Court of Appeal, since Chancery Division reports include first instance decisions of the High Court (Chancery Division) as well as appeals which arise from those decisions.
>
> Below the page heading is the name of the case. The topic of case names is discussed more fully at p. 82, but since this case involves an appeal, it is reasonable to assume that the appellant's name comes first, followed by the respondent's. One odd aspect of this particular case-name is that the respondent is given as *Fraser* (who, according to the report, was the secretary of the building society) rather than as being the building society itself. The report does not explain this, but since nothing turns on this detail we can safely ignore it.

1892 March 3, 26

> These are the dates on which the court dealt with the case. The fact that two dates are given (March 3 and 26) suggest that the case was heard on the earlier date but the court did not give its judgment immediately, preferring to give careful consideration to the arguments which it had just heard. This is confirmed at the start of Lord Herschell's judgment (towards the foot of p. 30 of the report) where the law reporter expressly identifies March 26 as the date of the judgment. The technical way of describing what is happening when this kind of delay occurs is to say that the court reserves judgment. Headnotes sometimes indicate that judgment was reserved by including the abbreviation *cur adv vult*. This represents the Latin phrase *curia advisari vult*, which translates literally as the court wishes to be advised, although, in reality, the court will be advising itself rather than seeking any outside assistance.

Lord Herschell, Lindley and Kay, LJJ

These are the names of the judges who decided the case. (The abbreviations of judicial titles are explained in Chapter 4.)

Contract by Letters – Acceptance of Offer by Post – Time of Acceptance – Withdrawal of Offer.

These are the catchwords (which are sometimes known as the keywords). They provide a very general idea of what the case is about. They seldom extend beyond three or four lines, and they always appear in italics.

The reporter's summary of the case comes next and is the part of the headnote which you will find most useful. In this case, the headnote is fully narrative. (The three possible styles of headnote are explained at p. 86.) This headnote is unusual because it contains two summaries of the facts, with the second being a little more detailed than the first. It is much more usual for the law reporter to decide which facts are worth including and then include them in a single summary.

H, who lived at Birkenhead, called at the office of a land society in Liverpool, to negotiate for the purchase of some houses belonging to them. The secretary signed and handed to him a note giving him the option of purchase for fourteen days at £750. On the next day the secretary posted to H a withdrawal of the offer. This withdrawal was posted between 12 and 1 o'clock, and did not reach Birkenhead till after 5 p.m. In the meantime H had, at 3.50 p.m., posted to the secretary an unconditional acceptance of the offer, which was delivered in Liverpool after the society's office had closed, and was opened by the secretary on the following morning:

Held, that where the circumstances under which an offer is made are such that it must have been within the contemplation of the parties that, according to the ordinary usages of mankind, the post might be used as a means of communicating the acceptance of it, the acceptance is complete as soon as it is posted.

Held, that in the present case, as the parties lived in different towns, an acceptance by post must have been within their contemplation, although the offer was not made by post.

Held, that a revocation of an offer is of no effect until brought to the mind of the person to whom the offer was made, and that therefore a revocation sent by post does not operate from the time of posting it.

Held, therefore (reversing the decision of the Vice-Chancellor of the County Palatine), that a binding contract was made on the posting of H's acceptance, that the revocation of the offer was too late, and that H. was entitled to specific performance.

IN 1891 the Plaintiff was desirous of purchasing from the Huskisson Benefit Building Society certain houses in Flamank Street, Birkenhead. In May he, at the office of the society in Chapel Street, Liverpool, signed a memorandum drawn up by the secretary, offering £600 for the property, which offer was declined by the directors; and on the 1st of July he made in the same way an offer of £700, which was also declined. On the 7th of July he again called at the office, and the secretary verbally offered to sell to him for £750. This offer was reduced into writing, and was as follows:–

"I hereby give you the refusal of the Flamank Street property at £750 for fourteen days."

28	CHANCERY DIVISION	[1892]

The secretary, after signing this, handed it to the Plaintiff, who took it away with him for consideration.

On the morning of the 8th another person called at the office, and offered £760 for the property, which was accepted, and a contract for purchase signed, subject to a condition for avoiding it if the society found that they could not withdraw from the offer to the Plaintiff.

Between 12 and 1 o'clock on that day the secretary posted to the Plaintiff, who resided in Birkenhead, the following letter:

"Please take notice that my letter to you of the 7th instant, giving you the option of purchasing the property, Flamank Street, Birkenhead, for £750, in fourteen days, is withdrawn, and the offer cancelled."

This letter, it appeared, was delivered at the Plaintiff's address between 5 and 6 in the evening, but, as he was out, did not reach his hands till about 8 o'clock.

On the same 8th of July the Plaintiff's solicitor, by the Plaintiff's direction, wrote to the secretary as follows:-

"I am instructed by Mr. James Henthorn to write you, and accept your offer to sell the property, 1 to 17, Flamank Street, Birkenhead, at the price of £750. Kindly have contract prepared and forwarded to me."

This letter was addressed to the society's office, and was posted in Birkenhead at 3.50 p.m., was delivered at 8.30 p.m. after the closing of the office, and was received by the secretary on the following morning. The secretary replied, stating that the society's offer had been withdrawn.

> The procedural history of the case is given next, in very brief outline. The headnote of a more modern law report may well contain a more detailed procedural history, including, for example, dates of previous hearings. The procedural history is tedious and – in the vast majority of cases – of very little interest to anybody, least of all to students on academic courses.

The Plaintiff brought this action in the Court of the County Palatine for specific performance. The Vice-Chancellor dismissed the action, and the Plaintiff appealed. Farwell, QC, and TR Hughes, for the appellant:

> The names of the advocates, and summaries of their arguments, come next. Both sets of advocates refer to the same cases but they construct different legal arguments based on those authorities. (For the law reports which contain summaries of the advocates' arguments, see p. 85.) As Lord Herschell demonstrates here, judges are perfectly willing to interrupt advocates.

We say that a binding contract was made when the Plaintiff's letter of acceptance was posted: *Dunlop v Higgins* (1); *Harris's Case* (2); *Adams v Lindsell* (3). We do not dispute that, though

(1) 1 HLC 381 (i.e. House of Lords Cases, before the introduction of the series cited as App Cas, which in turn became AC).
(2) LR 7 Ch 587 (i.e. reports of cases in the Court of Chancery, which is now the Chancery Division of the High Court, and which would now appear under the abbreviation *Ch*).
(3) 1 B & Al 681 (i.e. Barnewall & Alderson, the reporters who produced this series).

the option was given for fourteen days, it could be withdrawn within that time: *Dickinson v Dodds* (1); but if a binding contract is entered into, there cannot be a withdrawal. Where an acceptance is to be signified by doing some particular thing, as soon as that particular thing is done there is a contract: *Brogden v Metropolitan Railway Company* (2). Where it must be in the contemplation of the parties that an answer will be sent by post, the posting an acceptance makes a contract. In the case of *Household Fire and Carriage Accident Insurance Company v Grant* (3) it was considered that, according to the usages of mankind, an acceptance would be sent by post; and it was held that posting an acceptance made a contract, though the acceptance was never received. Here, as the parties lived in different towns, it was to be expected that the Plaintiff would post his answer. In *Byrne v Van Tienhoven* (4) a withdrawal was held too late which was not received till after the offer had been accepted, though it was posted before the acceptance; and so in *Stevenson v McLean* (5) it was held that a withdrawal of an offer was of no effect until it reached the other party.

Neville, QC, and PO Lawrence, for the Defendant:

We submit that the Vice-Chancellor has drawn a correct inference – that there was no authority to accept by post; and if that be so, the acceptance will not date from the posting. *Dunlop v Higgins* (6) went on the ground that it was the understanding of both parties that an answer should be sent by post. In *Brogden v Metropolitan Railway Company*, Lord Blackburn puts it on the ground "that where it is expressly or impliedly stated in the offer that you may accept the offer by posting a letter, the moment you post the letter the offer is accepted." It would be very inconvenient to hold the post admissible in all cases. Here, Liverpool and Birkenhead are at such a short distance from each other, that it cannot be considered that the Plaintiff had an authority to reply by post. If the offer had been sent by post, that would, no doubt, be held to give an authority to reply

(1) 2 ChD 463 (i.e. reports of the Chancery Division of the High Court, before the introduction of the current abbreviation *Ch*).
(2) 2 App Cas 666, 691 (i.e. reports of House of Lords' decisions which would still appear in the Appeal Cases reports but the series would now be abbreviated to *AC*).
(3) 4 ExD 216 (i.e. reports of the old Exchequer Division of the High Court, which no longer exists).
(4) 5 CPD 344 (i.e. reports of the old Common Pleas Division of the High Court, which no longer exists).
(5) 5 QBD 346 (i.e. reports of the Queen's Bench Division of the High Court before the introduction of the current abbreviation *QB*).
(6) 1 HLC 381 (see above).

by post; but the offer was delivered by hand to the Plaintiff, who was in the habit of calling at the Defendants' office, and lived only at a short distance, so that authority to reply by post cannot be inferred. The post is not prohibited; the acceptance may be sent in any way; but, unless sending it by post was authorized, it is inoperative till it is received. Suppose, immediately after posting the acceptance, the Plaintiff had gone to the office and retracted it, surely he would have been free.

[LORD HERSCHELL : It is not clear that he would, after sending an acceptance in such a way that he could not prevent its reaching the other party. Possibly a case where the question is as to the date from which an acceptance which has been received is operative may not stand on precisely the same footing as one where the question is whether the person making the offer is bound, though the acceptance has never been received at all. More evidence of authority to accept by post may be required in the latter case than in the former.]

Dickinson v Dodds (1) shows that a binding contract to sell to another person may be made while an offer is pending, and that it will be a withdrawal of the offer.

[LORD HERSCHELL: In that case the person to whom the offer was made knew of the sale before he sent his acceptance.]

Farwell, in reply.

> At this point we leave the headnote and move on to the judgment itself. Lord Herschell begins by identifying the facts of the case. However, they are not all material facts. For example, the legal issue in this case does not depend on the location of the property or the precise times at which things happened (although the times would have been material if they were such that the building society had been able to communicate its withdrawal of the offer – and had in fact done so – before Henthorn posted his acceptance). (Material facts are explained more fully at p. 101.)

1892. March 26. LORD HERSCHELL:

This is an action for the specific performance of a contract to sell to the Plaintiff certain house property situate in Flamank Street, Birkenhead. The action was tried before the Vice-Chancellor of the County Palatine of Lancashire, who gave judgment for the Defendants. On the 7th of July, 1891, the secretary of the building society whom the Defendants represent handed to the Plaintiff, in the office of the society at Liverpool, a letter in these terms:- "I hereby give you the refusal of the Flamank Street property at £750 for fourteen days." It appears that the Plaintiff had been for some time in negotiation for the property,

(1) 2 ChD 463 (see above).

2 Ch	CHANCERY DIVISION	31

and had on two previous occasions made offers for the purchase of it, which were not accepted by the society. These offers were made by means of letters, written by the secretary in the office of the society, and signed by the Plaintiff there. The Plaintiff resided in Birkenhead, and he took away with him to that town the letter of the 7th of July containing the offer of the society. On the 8th of July a letter was posted in Birkenhead at 3.50 pm, written by his solicitor, accepting on his behalf the offer to sell the property at £750. This letter was not received at the Defendants' office until 8.30 pm, after office hours, the office being closed at 6 o'clock. On the same day a letter was addressed to the Plaintiff by the secretary of the building society in these terms: "Please take notice that my letter to you of the 7th inst. giving you the option of purchasing the property, Flamank Street, Birkenhead, for £750, in fourteen days, is withdrawn and the offer cancelled." This letter was posted in Liverpool between 12 and 1 pm, and was received in Birkenhead at 5.30 p.m. It will thus be seen that it was received before the Plaintiff's letter of acceptance had reached Liverpool, but after it had been posted. One other fact only need be stated. On the 8th of July the secretary of the building society sold the same premises to Mr Miller for the sum of £760, but the receipt for the deposit paid in respect of the purchase stated that it was subject to being able to withdraw the letter to Mr. Henthorn giving him fourteen days' option of purchase.

> From Lord Herschell's summary of the facts, we can identify the following as being material: (1) the seller offered to sell certain property to the buyer, for a fixed price within a specified time; (2) the buyer accepted the offer, at the set price and within the time limit, using the post to communicate his acceptance; (3) before receiving the buyer's acceptance, the seller revoked the offer, once again using the post as the means of communication.

In the next part of his judgment, Lord Herschell turns to the legal issues in the case. The first issue concerns the revocation of the offer. By identifying a series of cases which establish that postal acceptance of an offer is effective as soon as it is posted, Lord Herschell explains why he thinks the same principle does not apply to postal revocations of offers.

If the acceptance by the Plaintiff of the Defendants' offer is to be treated as complete at the time the letter containing it was posted, I can entertain no doubt that the society's attempted revocation of the offer was wholly ineffectual. I think that a person who has made an offer must be considered as continuously making it until he has brought to the knowledge of the person to whom it was made that it is withdrawn. This seems to me to be in accordance with the reasoning of the Court of King's Bench in the case of *Adams v Lindsell* (1), which was approved by the Lord Chancellor in *Dunlop v Higgins* (2), and also with the opinion of Mellish LJ in *Harris's Case* (3). The

(1) 1 B & Al 681 (see above).
(2) 1 HLC 381, 399 (see above).
(3) LR 7 Ch 587 (see above).

32   CHANCERY DIVISION   [1892]

very point was decided in the case of *Byrne v Van Tienhoven* (1) by Lindley LJ, and his decision was subsequently followed by Lush J.

The grounds upon which it has been held that the acceptance of an offer is complete when it is posted have, I think, no application to the revocation or modification of an offer. These can be no more effectual than the offer itself, unless brought to the mind of the person to whom the offer is made.

Lord Herschell then turns to the second legal issue he has to settle, namely whether acceptance of an offer is complete once it is posted. This is quickly resolved by reference to the binding precedent of Dunlop v Higgins. However, there remains a sub-issue of whether the postal rule applies to all cases or only in particular circumstances. His Lordship concludes that authorisation was implied here because the parties lived in different towns and the offer was to remain open for several days. In other words, from that point onwards, it was too late for the offer to be revoked.

But it is contended on behalf of the Defendants that the acceptance was complete only when received by them and not on the letter being posted. It cannot, of course, be denied, after the decision in *Dunlop v Higgins* (2) in the House of Lords, that, where an offer has been made through the medium of the post, the contract is complete as soon as the acceptance of the offer is posted, but that decision is said to be inapplicable here, inasmuch as the letter containing the offer was not sent by post to Birkenhead, but handed to the Plaintiff in the Defendants' office at Liverpool. The question therefore arises in what circumstances the acceptance of an offer is to be regarded as complete as soon as it is posted. In the case of the *Household Fire and Carriage Accident Insurance Company v Grant* (3), Baggallay LJ said (4): "I think that the principle established in *Dunlop v Higgins* is limited in its application to cases in which by reason of general usage, or of the relations between the parties to any particular transactions, or of the terms in which the offer is made, the acceptance of such offer by a letter through the post is expressly or impliedly authorized." And in the same case Thesiger LJ based his judgment (5) on the defendant having made an application for shares under circumstances "from which it must be implied that he authorized the company, in the event of their allotting to him the shares applied for, to send the notice of allotment by post." The facts of that case were that the defendant had, in Swansea, where he resided, handed a letter of application to an agent of the company, their place of business being situate in London. It was from these circumstances that the Lords Justices implied an authority to the company to

(1) 5 CPD 344 (see above).
(2) 1 HLC 381 (see above).
(3) 4 ExD 216 (see above).
(4) *Ibid* 227.
(5) 4 ExD 218 (see above).

2 Ch   CHANCERY DIVISION   33

accept the defendant's offer to take shares through the medium of the post. Applying the law thus laid down by the Court of Appeal, I think in the present case an authority to accept by post must be implied. Although the Plaintiff received the offer at the Defendants' office in Liverpool, he resided in another town, and it must have been in contemplation that he would take the offer, which by its terms was to remain open for some days, with him to his place of residence, and those who made the offer must have known that it would be according to the ordinary usages of mankind that if he accepted it he should communicate his acceptance by means of the post.

At this point Lord Herschell could have disposed of the case but chooses to make some additional comments about implied authorisation as the basis for acceptance of an offer by post. Since this discussion is not essential to the outcome of the case, it follows that they must be obiter dicta. (*Obiter dicta* are explained more fully at pp. 100; 104–105.)

I am not sure that I should myself have regarded the doctrine that an acceptance is complete as soon as the letter containing it is posted as resting upon an implied authority by the person making the offer to the person receiving it to accept by those means. It strikes me as somewhat artificial to speak of the person to whom the offer is made as having the implied authority of the other party to send his acceptance by post. He needs no authority to transmit the acceptance through any particular channel; he may select what means he pleases, the Post Office no less than any other. The only effect of the supposed authority is to make the acceptance complete so soon as it is posted, and authority will obviously be implied only when the tribunal considers that it is a case in which this result ought to be reached. I should prefer to state the rule thus: Where the circumstances are such that it must have been within the contemplation of the parties that, according to the ordinary usages of mankind, the post might be used as a means of communicating the acceptance of an offer, the acceptance is complete as soon as it is posted. It matters not in which way the proposition be stated, the present case is in either view within it. The learned Vice-Chancellor appears to have based his decision to some extent on the fact that before the acceptance was posted the Defendants had sold the property to another person. The case of *Dickinson v Dodds* (1) was relied upon in support of that defence. In that case, however, the plaintiff knew of the subsequent sale before he accepted the offer, which, in my judgment, distinguishes it entirely from the

(1) 2 ChD 463 (see above).

present case. For the reasons I have given, I think the judgment must be reversed and the usual decree for specific performance made. The Respondents must pay the costs of the appeal and of the action.

Specific performance is explained at p. 23.

Additional commentary on the report

Introduction
In addition to the commentary contained in the text boxes, a number of other points may usefully be made.

Material facts
We have already discussed the importance of deciding which facts are material (see p. 101). You will recall that a useful test of the materiality of a specific fact is to ask the question: 'If this fact had not been present, or had been different, would the outcome of the case still have been the same?' If the answer to this question is 'No', it follows that the fact is material.

In many cases, the materiality of one or more of the facts will often be the essential difference between the opposing advocates, as it is central to the technique of *distinguishing* other decisions (so that they are no longer binding on the court hearing the case). Applying this approach to the facts in *Henthorn v Fraser*, we can see that the fact that the property was in Flamank Street, Birkenhead, is immaterial. If the property had been in another street in Birkenhead, or for that matter in any other place in England or Wales, the outcome of the case would have been the same. Likewise, removing or varying the details of the postal transactions would not change the outcome of the case *unless* the changes of time were such that the building society had been able to communicate – and had in fact communicated – its revocation of its offer before Henthorn posted his acceptance. This would, of course, make the case significantly different *from a legal point of view* and therefore it helps us identify the materiality of the fact that the appellant had posted his acceptance of the offer before the respondent's revocation had reached him.

Ratio decidendi
The most difficult challenge when reading a law report is identifying the *ratio* of the case. The main reason for this difficulty is that when judges make statements of law in a judgment they are not expounding the law in general but are making qualified statements of law which are conditioned by the particular facts of the case. It follows that the descriptive *ratio* of a case will require both a consideration of the facts that the court determined material and any statements of law that the court articulated concerning these facts. Having completed both of these tasks in our analysis of Lord Herschell's judgment we can now turn to formulating the descriptive *ratio* of *Henthorn v Fraser* in the following paragraph.

Where a seller offers an option to purchase property at a fixed price, and agrees to keep the offer open for a specified time, the offer continues for the time specified or until any withdrawal is brought to the attention of the potential buyer. If, before it is revoked, the buyer accepts the offer using the post to communicate his acceptance, the contract is completed when the buyer places his acceptance in the post where (1) use of the post is impliedly authorised or (2) where the parties know, or ought to know, that post might ordinarily be used in such dealings.

This *ratio* is, of course, based only Lord Herschell's judgment, but since Lindley LJ explicitly concurs with Lord Herschell it represents the majority view in the case. On a cautionary note it is worth observing that identifying or formulating the *ratio* of a case is a matter of interpretation rather than a scientific task with a single correct answer. Much legal argument may turn on identifying the *ratio* of a particular case. At the same time, it cannot be denied, that the *ratios* of most leading cases are so well established that they are rarely questioned.

Obiter dicta
We have already noted (see pp. 100 and 104) that *obiter dicta* (which are often called simply *dicta*) are never, strictly speaking, binding on later courts, but may be persuasive. However, as we also noted, it is seriously misleading to leave it at that. The truth of the matter is that *dicta* have widely varying degrees of weight, ranging from lightweight, mere throwaway, remarks at one end of the spectrum, to substantial and very strongly persuasive state-ments – so strongly persuasive, indeed, as to be practically binding – at the other end. In most cases, the weight of most *dicta* lies somewhere between these two poles, with the real weight of individual *dicta* not becoming ap-parent until they have been considered in later cases.

In *Henthorn v Fraser*, Lord Herschell's remarks on implied authorisation are clearly an attempt to clarify and develop the relevant law, and are a considered response to a point raised in argument by counsel for the ap-pellants (p. 29 of the report), rather than being simply off the cuff. They can, therefore, reasonably be argued to be closer to – although by no means at – the 'practically binding' end of the spectrum of possible weights, rather than the mere 'lightweight throwaway' end.

Distinguishing
Lord Herschell concludes his judgment by *distinguishing* the case of *Dick-inson v Dodds* (p. 33 of the report). When judges *distinguish* an earlier case

they are simply saying that the case cited has no relevance to the present case because its material facts were different. Lord Herschell had already indicated (p. 30 of the report) that he thought *Dickinson v Dodds* was distinguishable when he intervened in the respondent's arguments before the court. Closer consideration of both cases shows that two material facts in *Dickinson v Dodds* and *Henthorn v Fraser* were the same, because both cases involved a prospective buyer who was granted an option to purchase land and in both cases the owner of the land entered into a contract to sell the land to someone else before receiving the buyer's acceptance. However, the material fact which distinguishes *Dickinson v Dodds* from *Henthorn v Fraser* was that in *Dickinson v Dodds* (but not in *Henthorn v Fraser*) the prospective buyer knew about the contract to sell the land to the other person before he tried to accept the offer. It was this difference in the material facts which made the two cases essentially different, with the result that the earlier case was distinguishable (and was, therefore, not binding) in the later one. In fact, as Lord Herschell acknowledges (p. 30 of the report), even the judge at first instance could – and should – have distinguished *Dickinson v Dodds* on this basis.

Marginal markings and neutral citations
Some series of law reports use marginal markings, in order to make it easier to provide pinpoint citations, while others do not. The original report of *Henthorn v Fraser* contains no such markings, while the most common system in the 20th century was to provide marginal letters, evenly spaced down each page. The system of marginal letters worked reasonably well, but it was rather cumbersome for true pinpoint citations, which had to take a form such as 'page 234, letter D, line 3'. More importantly, this citation would vary from one set of law reports to another, according to the page numbering of the report in question.

The modern judicial practice (dating from 2001 and being an important part of the system of *neutral citation*, which is explained at pp. 87–88) is for official transcripts of judgments to number each paragraph. Since these numbers are part of the text, rather than depending on the page numbering of each series of reports, they can safely be relied upon, whichever series of law reports is being used. Unless judges use very long paragraphs, marginal markings are, therefore, superfluous in reports of modern cases.

Why not just read headnotes rather than full reports?
As we have just seen, a headnote contains formal details, such as the date or dates of the hearing and the names of the advocates, as well as the

reporter's summary of the decision. One very good reason for reading the reporter's summary is that it enables you to decide whether it is worth investing further time and energy in reading the decision itself. However, it is tempting to go beyond this, and simply read the summary as a substitute for reading the decision. The first of these reasons is perfectly respectable; the second is not.

Looking at the matter in more detail, there are two reasons why you should not rely unquestioningly on the summary part of a headnote as a substitute for reading the decision itself.

First, no matter how long and detailed it may appear to be, a headnote can only be a summary; and, therefore (although the standard of modern law reporting is almost uniformly very high), there is always the possibility that accuracy may have been sacrificed to brevity. (It is for this reason that some – but only a very few – purists insist on never reading the summary section of a headnote, preferring to decide for themselves exactly what a case is about and what it decides, rather than having their perception of these matters clouded by reading the reporter's version.)

Secondly, becoming a successful law student requires you to develop the skills of legal analysis and expression. One of the best ways of developing these skills is to undertake extensive reading of how the judges themselves analyse cases and express the results of their analyses, because this helps you to develop your sensitivity to the way in which judges function. Of course, having read a law report, it is only natural that you should write your own note, as an aid to remind you of what you have just learned, and this note will also be no more than a relatively brief summary. However, you will be using this note as a reminder of the understanding which you gained at the time, and you are very unlikely to have gained full understanding of a judgment which you have not read.

Nevertheless, it must be conceded that the advice given here is a counsel of perfection, and that many students do – at least from time to time – rely on headnotes. It must also be conceded that although using headnotes in this way – even in conjunction with your lecture notes and any other teaching materials you have been given – is bad practice, it is nevertheless preferable to never opening a law report at all. In short, therefore, it is up to you to decide whether you want to take the easy way out and, with luck, become a more or less adequate law student, or whether you want to become a good law student, in which case there is no alternative to doing things properly.

Returning specifically to *Henthorn v Fraser*, a minor inaccuracy may be found in the first line of the reporter's summary (p. 27), where reference is made to a 'land society'. Further study of the case shows that the body in question was, in fact, a 'building society'. While it seems that nothing turned on the precise nature of the prospective seller of the property in question, if you referred to a 'land society' when writing an essay, you would (without realising it) be betraying the very limited extent of your reading – which is not the best thing to communicate to anyone who is marking your work.

Conclusion

Having read the general discussion of the structure of a law report, together with both the excerpt from *Henthorn v Fraser* and the analysis of Lord Herschell's judgment, you should know how to identify the key elements in a report. Developing the skills of formulating the *ratio decidendi* of a case and assessing the weight of *obiter dicta* will not come quite so easily and will require perseverance and practice. Making your own notes on cases which you have read in full does, however, pay lasting dividends when it comes to preparing coursework and mooting, and – perhaps even more importantly – embarking on examination revision, because your notes will remind you of what *you* have read and know, rather than what someone else has said or written. More generally, reading law reports will also help you to develop your sensitivity to legal language and your skills of common law reasoning. The technique of answering problem questions (see Chapter 11) differs in degree rather than kind from the technique of judgment writing. Both involve identifying the material facts that give rise to the legal issues, selecting and applying the relevant law, and reaching a conclusion.

● **Reading statutes**

Introduction

We have chosen the Dealing in Cultural Objects (Offences) Act 2003 to illustrate many of the standard features of statutes because it is very short and does not require any prior knowledge of any other statutes.

The offences created by the Act have obvious similarities with the offence of dishonestly handling stolen property, knowing or believing it to be stolen, under the Theft Act 1968, but the new offence also applies to property which cannot be proved to have been stolen, as well as to events which occur abroad. It is relatively rare for an Act to have extra-territorial effect (or, in other words, to apply to events outside the United Kingdom). On the more restrictive side, when you read the Act you will see that it applies only to a relatively small class of objects.

The Dealing in Cultural Objects (Offences) Act 2003 and the boxed commentary

The presentation of the text of the Dealing in Cultural Objects (Offences) Act 2003 follows the same pattern as the presentation of the judgment in *Henthorn v Fraser* (pp. 116–125), with the text itself being punctuated with text boxes containing our commentary.

Dealing in Cultural Objects (Offences) Act 2003
2003 Chapter 27

CONTENTS

Section

An Act to provide for an offence of acquiring, disposing of, importing or exporting tainted cultural objects, or agreeing or arranging to do so; and for connected purposes.

> This is the long title. It can be used to resolve ambiguities within the text of the Act. But if the meaning of the text of the Act is clear, that meaning must prevail over the long title: see *R v Galvin* [1987] 2 All ER 851.

[30th October 2003]

> This is the date on which the Act received the Royal Assent, which means the date on which it was passed.

BE IT ENACTED by the Queen's most Excellent Majesty, by and with the advice and consent of the Lords Spiritual and Temporal, and Commons, in this present Parliament assembled, and by the authority of the same, as follows:-

This is the standard enacting formula.

1 Offence of dealing in tainted cultural objects

(1) A person is guilty of an offence if he dishonestly deals in a cultural object that is tainted, knowing or believing that the object is tainted.

The Act does not define *dishonesty* but the meaning of this word for the purposes of other offences involving dishonesty would probably be held to be so strongly persuasive as to be practically binding. The Act does, however, go on to define certain other key words.

(2) It is immaterial whether he knows or believes that the object is a cultural object.

(3) A person guilty of the offence is liable-

(a) on conviction on indictment, to imprisonment for a term not exceeding seven years or a fine (or both),

(b) on summary conviction, to imprisonment for a term not exceeding six months or a fine not exceeding the statutory maximum (or both).

Conviction on indictment means conviction at the Crown Court. Summary conviction means conviction by a magistrates' court. The statutory maximum fine on summary conviction is £5000: see the Magistrates' Courts Act 1980.

2 Meaning of "tainted cultural object"

(1) "Cultural object" means an object of historical, architectural or archaeological interest.

Because the phrase *cultural object* and the word *tainted* have no obvious meanings, this section defines them for the purposes of this Act. As far as the words which are not defined are concerned, the court will have to fall back on the basic proposition that the meaning of an ordinary word of the English language is a question of fact: see *Brutus v Cozens* [1973] AC 854. The advocates may base their arguments on the meanings that certain words have in the context of other statutes, such as the meaning of *building* in the context of some environmental protection legislation. However, it is important never to lose sight of the proposition that the meaning of a word for the purpose of one statute will be no more than persuasive as to its meaning in the context of another statute: see *Carter v Bradbeer* [1975] 1 WLR 1204.

(2)   A cultural object is tainted if, after the commencement of this Act-

The commencement of an Act is the date on which it comes into force. This may be – but hardly ever is – the date of the Royal Assent. For the commencement of this Act, see s. 6.

      (a) a person removes the object in a case falling within subsection (4) or he excavates the object, and

      (b) the removal or excavation constitutes an offence.

(3)   It is immaterial whether-

      (a) the removal or excavation was done in the United Kingdom or elsewhere,

      (b) the offence is committed under the law of a part of the United Kingdom or under the law of any other country or territory.

(4)   An object is removed in a case falling within this subsection if-

      (a) it is removed from a building or structure of historical, architectural or archaeological interest where the object has at any time formed part of the building or structure, or

      (b) it is removed from a monument of such interest.

(5)   "Monument" means-

      (a) any work, cave or excavation,

      (b) any site comprising the remains of any building or structure or of any work, cave or excavation,

(c) any site comprising, or comprising the remains of, any vehicle, vessel, aircraft or other movable structure, or part of any such thing.

(6) "Remains" includes any trace or sign of the previous existence of the thing in question.

(7) It is immaterial whether-

(a) a building, structure or work is above or below the surface of the land,

(b) a site is above or below water.

(8) This section has effect for the purposes of section 1.

3 Meaning of "deals in"

(1) A person deals in an object if (and only if) he-

> In everyday English, the phrase *deals in* indicates commercial transactions. This section extends the meaning of the phrase beyond buying and selling, and (perhaps surprisingly) includes the giving and receiving of gifts.

(a) acquires, disposes of, imports or exports it,

(b) agrees with another to do an act mentioned in paragraph (a), or

(c) makes arrangements under which another person does such an act or under which another person agrees with a third person to do such an act.

(2) "Acquires" means buys, hires, borrows or accepts.

(3) "Disposes of" means sells, lets on hire, lends or gives.

(4) In relation to agreeing or arranging to do an act, it is immaterial whether the act is agreed or arranged to take place in the United Kingdom or elsewhere.

(5) This section has effect for the purposes of section 1.

4 Customs and Excise prosecutions

(1) Proceedings for an offence relating to the dealing in a tainted cultural object may be instituted by order of the Commissioners of Customs and Excise if it appears to them that the offence has involved the importation or exportation of such an object.

(2) An offence relates to the dealing in a tainted cultural object if it is-

(a) an offence under section 1, or

(b) an offence of inciting the commission of, or attempting or conspiring to commit, such an offence.

(3) Proceedings for an offence which are instituted under subsection (1) are to be commenced in the name of an officer, but may be continued by another officer.

(4) Where the Commissioners of Customs and Excise investigate, or propose to investigate, any matter with a view to determining-
(a) whether there are grounds for believing that a person has committed an offence which relates to the dealing in a tainted cultural object and which involves the importation or exportation of such an object, or
(b) whether a person should be prosecuted for such an offence,
the matter is to be treated as an assigned matter within the meaning of the Customs and Excise Management Act 1979 (c. 2).

(5) Nothing in this section affects any powers of any person (including any officer) apart from this section.

(6) "Officer" means a person commissioned by the Commissioners of Customs and Excise under section 6(3) of the Customs and Excise Management Act 1979.

> After this Act was passed, the Commissioners for Revenue and Customs Act 2005 merged the functions of the *Commissioners of Customs and Excise* with those of the *Commissioners of Inland Revenue* to create the *Commissioners for Her Majesty's Revenue and Customs* (or *HMRC* as they are commonly known). The 2005 Act also created the office of the Director of Customs and Excise Prosecutions. Although the original text of the 2003 Act is reproduced here, Schedule 4 to the 2005 Act enacts a number of technical amendments to this text (along with the texts of many other statutes) to reflect the scheme which it introduces.

5 Offences by bodies corporate

(1) If an offence under section 1 committed by a body corporate is proved-
(a) to have been committed with the consent or connivance of an officer, or
(b) to be attributable to any neglect on his part,
he (as well as the body corporate) is guilty of the offence and liable to be proceeded against and punished accordingly.

(2) "Officer", in relation to a body corporate, means-
(a) a director, manager, secretary or other similar officer of the body,
(b) a person purporting to act in any such capacity.

(3) If the affairs of a body corporate are managed by its members, subsection (1) applies in relation to the acts and defaults of a member in connection with his functions of management as if he were a director of the body.

> *Bodies corporate* are organisations such as companies, local authorities, professional bodies and learned societies. Subsection (3) is most likely to be relevant to some learned societies.

6 Short title, commencement and extent

(1) This Act may be cited as the Dealing in Cultural Objects (Offences) Act 2003.
(2) This Act comes into force at the end of the period of two months beginning with the day on which it is passed.
(3) This Act does not extend to Scotland.

> The short title of an Act is a useful label by which it can be known. However, it should be regarded as no more than an approximate guide to the contents of the Act, because it may be too short to be entirely accurate: *Re Boaler* [1915] KB 21. Acts of Parliament may or may not become law in Scotland. This one does not extend to Scotland because its subject matter lies within the scope of the powers which have been devolved to the Scottish Parliament.

Additional commentary

Introduction
In addition to the comments contained in the text boxes, the following comments will help you when you start to read other statutes.

Interpreting the Act generally
Since the Act creates criminal offences, whenever there are two or more possible meanings, the defendant will seek to rely on the presumption that Parliament intended the meaning which is most favourable from his or her point of view. (See p. 107.)

When identifying the purpose of the Act, regard may be had to the Explanatory Notes which accompanied the Bill (which became the Act) during its progress through Parliament. Explanatory Notes are available at http://www.legislation.gov.uk/.

Headings and marginal notes
As you have seen in the Dealing in Cultural Objects (Offences) Act 2003, sections may appear under headings (which are sometimes known as crossheadings). In longer and more complicated statutes, these headings may introduce groups of sections rather than every individual section. Additionally, until 2001, the statutory text was accompanied by *marginal notes* (also known as *side-notes* or *shoulder notes*), which, obviously enough, appeared in the margin. Although the use of marginal notes has now been discontinued, you will, of course, still encounter them in pre-2001 statutes. The question, therefore, arises as to their status in the process of interpretation.

The most recent, and most authoritative, answer to this question was given, unanimously, by the House of Lords in *R v Montila* [2005] UKHL 50, [2005] 1 All ER 113:

[34] ... Account must, of course, be taken of the fact that these components were included in the Bill not for debate but for ease of reference. This indicates that less weight can be attached to them than to the parts of the Act that are open for consideration and debate in Parliament. One cannot ignore the fact that the headings and sidenotes are included on the face of the Bill throughout its passage through the legislature. They are there for guidance. They provide the context for an examination of those parts of the Bill that are open for debate. Subject, of course, to the fact that they are unamendable, they ought to be open to consideration as part of the enactment when it reaches the statute book.

[35] ... It has become common practice for their Lordships to ask to be shown the explanatory notes when issues are raised about the meaning of words used in an enactment.

[36] The headings and sidenotes are as much part of the contextual scene as these materials, and there is no logical reason why they should be treated differently.

Schedules
Many longer and more complicated statutes conclude with schedules. Whether there are schedules (and if there are, what goes into them) is a

matter of style. However, in general terms, it can be said that schedules generally contain details that are unlikely to change very often. For example, a statute which creates a new public body may well state its function in the main part of the text, with the detailed arrangements for the appointment and removal of members being put in a schedule. This arrangement makes the statute much easier to read, since the reader can grasp the overall scheme first, without having to wade through a mass of detail which can be read as and when it is necessary to do so. It follows, therefore, that schedules are integral parts of the statutes in which they appear, and must be interpreted as such. (*Attorney-General v Lamplough* (1878) 3 ExD 214.)

In passing, it may be worth mentioning that some other kinds of detail may well appear in delegated legislation (see p. 25), rather than in the statute itself. It is impossible to lay down hard and fast rules as to what sort of details should be left to delegated legislation. However, experience shows that details which are likely to change relatively frequently (such as fees payable to public bodies by users of their services) and details which can be finalised only after extensive consultation (such as the layout and precise contents of prescribed forms) are best enacted in this way. (The alternative would be to pass an amending statute every time a fee was increased to take account of inflation, or delaying the enactment of the statute until the last practical detail had been settled, or both.)

For a much more detailed treatment of the principles of statutory interpretation, see, for example, McLeod, *Legal Method*, 8th edn 2011, Palgrave Macmillan.

● Conclusion

The skills involved in reading law reports and statutes need to be learned and practised. Both sets of skills require careful and analytical reading of the relevant texts, but both also involve a degree of creativity in developing arguments based on those texts.

When reading cases, it is always important to identify the material facts, so that you can analyse the judgments in terms of the concepts of *ratio decidendi* and *obiter dictum*. When reading statutes, the context within which the words are used is always of great importance.

9 Written English

All writing is an attempt to communicate something to
the reader. If your writing is to be effective, you must
make your meaning plain. Following the appropriate conventions of grammar, punctuation, spelling, and style, will
all help improve the clarity of your writing. One important
by-product of any improvement you achieve is that your
marks will be better than they would otherwise be.

● Introduction

Written English can be used in a wide variety of contexts, with equally widely
varying degrees of formality. An example drawn from one end of the scale
would be a simple note to remind yourself of something you need to do (in
which more or less anything goes, including, for example, abbreviations which
only you would understand, and from which grammar may be wholly absent).
At the other end of the scale there are instruments such as wills and Acts of
Parliament where a very high degree of formality is appropriate. Between the
two extremes, there are of course many intermediate stages.

This chapter is about writing English in the relatively formal context of
academic work. Many readers of this book will have highly developed skills
in written English; but experience shows that there will be many others who
lack the ability to express themselves clearly and accurately when writing
formal English. Unfortunately, experience also shows that the latter category not infrequently includes students who embark on degree-level study
with good A-level grades behind them, as well as students on postgraduate
conversion courses whose degrees did not require much, if anything, in the
way of essay writing in either coursework or examinations.

This chapter, therefore, provides a basic survival guide to the standard conventions of grammar, punctuation and spelling which will usually be expected

when you are writing law essays and examination answers, together with some guidance as to the kind of style which will be appropriate. However, before turning to the substance of these topics, it must be conceded that those readers who have the greatest need to improve their written English are likely to find that a good deal of hard work is required. Nevertheless, these readers can be confidently assured of three things. First, the craft of good, formal writing can be learned by anyone who is prepared to work sufficiently hard at it. In the words of Alexander Pope, in his *Essay on Criticism*:

> True ease in writing comes from Art not Chance,
> As those move easiest who have learn'd to dance.

Secondly, once the craft has been learned, its practice becomes very largely automatic. Thirdly, the effort of learning how to write formal English well will not be wasted. As Dr Johnson put it, 'what is written without effort is in general read without pleasure'. From the student's perspective, of course, there is the additional – and not unimportant – point that material which is written in a way that pleases the examiner is likely to be rewarded with a higher mark than the less appropriately written offerings of other students.

Two problems face anyone who tries to teach people how to write formal English well. First, they lay themselves open to the charge of linguistic (and even cultural) fascism. After all, conventions of grammar, punctuation, spelling and style all change with the passing of time. Moreover, it is in the nature of things that most of those who teach and examine are likely to be older than most of those whom they are teaching and examining. Therefore, while it is reasonable to ask why the conventions which examiners absorbed – perhaps twenty, thirty or even forty years ago – should be regarded as being more appropriate than those absorbed much more recently by their students, the psychological fact of the matter is simply that many examiners do tend to see things this way. And wise students will accept this fact as being one which they cannot change. More particularly, as we have already said, pleasing the examiner is likely to pay dividends in terms of marks. Furthermore, as you move out of the world of education and into the world of employment, many of the people under whom you will be working will share the expectations which your examiners had.

Secondly, those who provide guidance as to what constitutes good, formal writing always put themselves at risk of being criticised for failing to follow their own prescriptions. In this case it is the teachers who are called upon to display wisdom by accepting that they are unlikely to maintain the highest standards all the time. However, few teachers should object to having their shortcomings drawn to their attention, since it is only capable students who will be able to do this; and there are few things more gratifying than teaching capable students.

Before we proceed to the substance of grammar, punctuation, spelling and style, it will be well worthwhile to introduce the *mongoose principle*, which will provide you with the solution to many of the problems you will encounter when writing formal English.

● The mongoose principle

The mongoose principle takes its name from an old story about a customer who wrote to a pet shop:

Dear Sirs,

Please send me two mongooses.

Yours etc.,
A. Customer.

However, on reading the letter over, the writer felt that perhaps the plural of *mongoose* was not *mongooses*, and accordingly tore the letter up and wrote the following:

Dear Sirs,

Please send me two mongeese.

Yours etc.,
A. Customer.

After a few more moments of thought, the writer felt that perhaps this was not right either, and accordingly tore this letter up as well, before writing the following:

Dear Sirs,

Please send me one mongoose.

Yours etc.,
A. Customer.

PS: On second thoughts, make it two.

The *mongoose principle*, therefore, states: *if in difficulty or doubt, rewrite it.* The principle provides a simple solution to many problems and you ignore it at your peril.

● Sentence structure

Simple sentences

Reduced to an absolute minimum, a sentence must have a *subject* and a *finite verb*. The subject is the person or thing who (or which) does something and the verb is what is being done. The basic form of a verb is the *infinitive*, which (as the word suggests) is *unfinished* or *open-ended*. In English, infinitives begin with *to* – for example, *to eat, to live, to sleep, to walk*. We will return to infinitives at p. 164, where the question will be whether they should or should not be split, but we are introducing them here in order to explain that, by way of contrast, the *finite* forms of a verb are no longer open-ended but have been *finished* in the sense that they show when something is (or was or will be) done. In other words the verb will have a *tense*, which will place the action in the present, the past or the future. Take the following example:

The boy rode.

Here the subject (the boy) did something (rode) in the past. If we had used the infinitive (to ride) we would have produced something which is unfinished to the point where it is nonsense:

The boy to ride.

On the other hand, we could have used the finite verb in other tenses and said, for example

The boy rides,

or

The boy will ride.

The first, third and fourth examples are very simple sentences, but we could make them more complicated by saying, for example

The boy rode a bicycle.

In this example, we have added an *object*. In grammatical terms, the word *object* simply signifies the person or thing to which the activity of the verb is done.

Another common form of sentence has no object but does have a *complement*. For example, in the following sentence *round the block* is the complement:

The boy rode round the block.

In English, unlike many other languages, the order of the words is crucial. The following two sentences use exactly the same words but mean fundamentally different things.

The boy killed the girl.
The girl killed the boy.

The basic principles to remember about simple sentences are:

- they begin with a capital letters (even when the first word is not the name of a person or a place);
- they have a finite verb,
- the order of the words determines the meaning of the sentence; and
- the subject and the verb must *agree as to number*.

Your response to these four points may be that you have no problem with the first three, but that you do not understand the fourth one. In fact, the fourth one has a very clear meaning: it is simply expressed in technical language. All it means is that if the subject is singular, the verb must also be singular; and if the subject is plural, the verb must also be in the plural. Most people find that, most of the time, they instinctively use language in such a way as to satisfy this need for agreement. So (leaving aside some dialect usages) most people would not have to think about any matters of grammar before saying

the boy was riding

rather than

the boy were riding;

or

the boys were riding

rather than

the boys was riding.

However, some words present a very common source of error in relation to agreement between subject and verb. Test yourself on the following two sentences:

There are a number of reasons why you should read this book.
There is a number of reasons why you should read this book.

Many people feel, intuitively, that the first version is correct on the basis that the plural *reasons* requires the plural verb *are*. As a matter of strict grammar, however, the second version is correct because it is the singular *number* which governs the verb, which is, therefore, also required to be in the singular. In fact, so many people would instinctively use the first version that you may wish to say that it constitutes an exception to the rule that a singular subject requires a singular verb. However, if you make this assertion implicitly by simply following this usage in your written work, you will be adopting a high-risk strategy. Some of your readers may have a stricter view of grammar that will lead them to conclude that you are writing ungrammatically as a result of ignorance. If you feel that the grammatically correct version sounds awkward, but you wish to avoid the grammatically incorrect version, the solution lies in the mongoose principle: rewrite your sentence. Nobody could object to

there are many reasons why you should read this book.

Therefore, rewriting it in this way will offend nobody, while avoiding a form of words which sounds awkward, and without having had to complicate your expression or compromise your meaning in any way.

A second trap for the unwary when making subjects agree with their verbs as to number is the apparently innocuous word *none*. Once again, test yourself on the following two sentences.

None of them were right.
None of them was right.

Many people would happily use the first version; and, if they heard it, would feel intuitively that it is grammatically correct. However, as with the previous example, this is an illusion. As a matter of strict grammar, the second example is preferable. The explanation is that, once again, people are misled by a grammatically irrelevant plural (in this case *them*), and have overlooked the fact that the grammatically relevant *none* originated as a shortened version of *not one* and is, therefore, singular. Of course, if you feel the grammatically correct version sounds awkward or pedantic, the answer is simple: remember the mongoose principle and write:

They were all wrong.

The final commonly encountered difficulty with singulars and plurals arises from *collective nouns*. These are singular in form but nevertheless refer to a number of people or things. Examples of collective nouns include *army*, *jury*, and *team* (each of which consists of a number of members), as well as companies and local authorities such as *Marks and Spencer* and *Camden London Borough Council* (which consist, respectively, of all the shareholders and all the councillors).

The basic principle is that either a singular or a plural verb may be used, provided internal consistency is maintained. So, for example, the following are both equally acceptable:

When the army comes home, it will be welcomed by the local community.

When the army come home, they will be welcomed by the local community.

However, it would be wrong (because it would be internally inconsistent) to say either of the following:

When the army comes home, they will be welcomed by the local community.

When the army come home, it will be welcomed by the local community.

This freedom of choice is limited in some cases, where the crucial issue is whether the collective noun is being used to identify a single entity, or as shorthand for all the members of the group. So, for example, the following are both wrong:

The family are an important social unit. (The *are* must be replaced by *is*.)

My family is the kindest people I know. (The *is* must be replaced by *are*.)

Finally, collective nouns which refer to inanimate objects (such as *cutlery*, *crockery* and *luggage*) are always singular. For example, it is correct to say:

the cutlery is in the drawer

and wrong to say

the cutlery are in the drawer.

Compound sentences

Simple sentences are all very well. They can convey meaning perfectly adequately. But they quickly become tedious to read. A succession of simple sentences will not please your examiners. Therefore you must be able to write compound sentences, consisting of two (or more) clauses, both (or all) of which could stand as simple sentences; or, in other words, both (or all) of which are main clauses. For example:

John rode his bicycle but Janet drove her car.

When writing compound sentences, you need to be careful with your use of the *joining* words (or *conjunctions*) which you use to link the two clauses. The most common are

- and;
- or;

and

- but.

The use of *however* presents a difficulty. Technically, it is an adverb and not a conjunction, although in *informal* communication this distinction is often lost and it tends to be used as a conjunction. For example, *I missed my train, however I still got home on time*. Clearly, in contexts such as this, *however* is being used interchangeably with *nevertheless*, and it is unlikely that anyone with any knowledge or intuition of grammatical convention would write *I missed my train, nevertheless I still got home on time*, without breaking it into two sentences. Bearing in mind, therefore, that this chapter is concerned with *formal* usage, our advice must be to avoid using *however* as a conjunction. This leaves you with a straightforward choice. The first possibility is to use a genuine conjunction:

I missed my train but I still got home on time.

Alternatively, you could retain *however* but use two simple sentences

I missed my train. However, I still got home on time.

(The use of the comma after *however* in the second example is explained at p. 154.)

There is an old-fashioned 'rule' that *and* and *but* cannot properly be used to begin sentences, because (being conjunctions) their function is to join clauses together. Like many other 'rules', this one is based on a sound principle. However, also like many other 'rules', this one can be applied too strictly. The occasional use of *and* and *but* as opening words can be very striking. For example:

He was handsome. And I do mean handsome.

Similarly:

She had only one talent. But what a talent it was.

You will relatively seldom need such rhetorical devices in academic writing, but the possibility is worth noticing. In any event, of course, such usage may occasionally be justified on the ground of variation of sentence structure.

Just as *compound* sentences are one stage on from *simple* sentences, so *complex* sentences are one stage on from *compound* sentences. It is, therefore, to complex sentences that we now turn.

Complex sentences

Like *compound* sentences, *complex* sentences consist of at least two clauses. However, the distinction between the two categories lies in the fact that compound sentences contain two (or more) main clauses, while complex sentences contain a main clause and at least one *subordinate* clause. For example:

John rode the bicycle *that his parents had given him for his birthday*.

In this example, the words *his parents had given him for his birthday* could not stand as a sentence on their own and therefore they cannot be a main clause. To put it another way, they are dependent upon, or *subordinate to*, the main clause. At a functional level, they provide the reader with more information about the topic that is the subject of the main clause.

Subordinate clauses are introduced by a sub-group of words known – for obvious reasons – as *subordinating conjunctions*. The most common examples include:

after	once	until
although	since	when
as	than	where
because	that (*or* which)	whereas
if	unless	while

As a footnote to this list, it must be said that if you read more detailed discussions of grammar than we have space for here, you may well find extensive discussion of the uses of *that* and *which*. For our purposes, however, we need say no more than that, in practice, they are both widely used interchangeably as subordinating conjunctions. (Try seeing how the grammar-check on your word-processing programme treats these two words. You may well find that it wants you to use *that* much more often than *which*. There is nothing intrinsically wrong with this, but if writing is to be more than a mere mechanical exercise, and provided the basic conventions are respected, some scope for individuality is a good thing.)

● Spelling

Introduction
It is widely believed that English spelling is an arbitrary mish-mash, devoid of principles. However, according to David Crystal, a leading academic authority on the English language, it has been estimated that

- only about 3% of commonly used English words have spellings which are so divorced from principle that they must simply be learned;
- the spellings of over 80% of words are regular (in the sense of conforming to established patterns); and
- whether the spelling of the remaining 15% or so of words can be said to be regular is open to discussion. (See *The Cambridge Encyclopaedia of the English Language*, Cambridge University Press, 2nd edn, 2003, p. 272.)

However, everyday users of language (as distinct from those skilled in the science of linguistics) may understandably remain unconvinced. Take, for example, what is probably the best known 'rule' of English spelling: *I before e except after c*. While this 'rule' undoubtedly helps you with the correct spelling of words like *believe, relieve, conceive, deceive*, and *receive*, it equally clearly has no application to words such as *ancient, conscience, efficient, science* and *society*, not to mention *eight, either, foreign* and *heir*. Of course, linguistics (like law) is a complex subject, and specialists in spelling will formulate and qualify their rules in such a way that they can identify regularity of spelling in many cases where it is not apparent to the untrained eye. All of which means that readers who find English spelling confusing are in a difficult position.

Two practical suggestions

Since this is not the place to launch forth upon a detailed discussion of the complex rules of spelling to which, according to Crystal, at least 80% of words conform, only two practical suggestions can be made.

First, the best way of learning how to spell is simply to read good writers carefully and learn from their example. Secondly, if this seems too haphazard, or your tastes are such that you seldom, if ever, read good writers, you may simply have to learn the correct spellings of a number of words which are commonly spelt incorrectly.

In terms of law, few things annoy examiners more than students who are unable to spell words which they should have read dozens, if not hundreds, of times. The following is a non-exhaustive list of common errors:

arguement (for *argument*),
contractural (for *contractual*),
defendent (for *defendant*),
enviroment (for *environment*),
goverment (for *government*),

interpretate (for *interpret*),
Parliment or *Parlament* (for *Parliament*),
perogative (for *prerogative*),
president (for *precedent*),
priveledge (or something similar) for *privilege*,
sovreign (for *sovereign*),
Westminister (for *Westminster*).

In more general terms, the following words are commonly misspelt in various ways:

accommodate;
committee;
definitely;
discipline;
embarrass;
exaggerate;
excellent;
except;
gauge;
guarantee;
guard;
harass;
necessary;
occasion;
opportunity;
recommend;
separate;
succeed.

In ordinary usage, *judgment* and *judgement* are normally regarded as being straightforward alternative spellings, with the only requirement being that you should be consistent as to which one you use within a single piece of work. However, in legal usage, *judgment* is always used when referring to a decision of a court. Therefore, there is much to be said for adopting this version as your standard usage in all cases, because this will give you one fewer thing to think about when you are trying to write well.

Two pairs of words which are commonly confused are *principle/principal* and *practice/practise*.

Principle can only be a noun, as for example, in *the mongoose principle*. Principal can be either a noun or an adjective. For example, *The principal of the college*, and *the principal reason for buying this book is to improve your study skills in law* are both correct.

Practice is a noun; *practise* is a verb. For example, you would talk about *a solicitor's practice*, but you would say *I used to practise criminal law*.

This distinction between the noun form and the verb form also appears in a number of other words, including *advice/advise* and *licence/license*. For example, you give someone *advice* when you *advise* them; and when you have a *licence* to do something, you are *licensed* to do it.

Initial capitals

Few people have any difficulty with using initial capitals for the names of people (such as *John Smith*), places (such as *London*), and the days of the week and the months of the year (such as *Monday* and *August*). However, many people do find difficulty when the words in question are institutions or offices.

Traditionally, the basic rule has been perfectly clear and straightforward. The key distinction lies in writing about institutions or offices generally and writing about specific examples of institutions or offices. In the former context, no initial capitals are used, while in the latter context they are. Applying this in practice, you would write 'all governments tend to ...' but 'the Government lost a vote of confidence yesterday'. Or, 'most twentieth century prime ministers said ...' but 'the Prime Minister said ... '

Clear though this distinction is, there is no doubt that it is much less commonly observed now than it used to be, with the result that many people (including journalists writing for what have traditionally been called 'quality newspapers') will happily write, for example, *act of parliament*. However, lawyers are not bound by the style guides of newspapers and you should always write *Act of Parliament*.

● Punctuation

Introduction

Once we have made the elementary observation that a full stop must be used at the end of a sentence, it is difficult to know how much detail needs to be mastered before you can be considered competent at punctuation. For the present purposes, we will be satisfied with a few comments on commas, semi-colons and colons, together with an explanation of the correct use of quotation marks, parentheses (or round brackets) and brackets (or square brackets) and, finally, apostrophes. However, no matter how brief the discussion may be, the importance of punctuation cannot be emphasised too strongly. Punctuation can change the meaning of a sentence, and can even enable the reader to make sense of the apparently meaningless.

One frequently quoted example of the extent to which punctuation can create different meanings from the same words is:

Woman without her man is nothing.

Punctuation can make this mean two quite distinct things:

Woman: without her, man is nothing.
Woman, without her man, is nothing.

For further classic illustrations of punctuation as the linguistic equivalent of the philosopher's stone, consider the following two sentences.

The condemned man walked round the yard three minutes after he was hanged.

What this means is, of course:

The condemned man walked round the yard: three minutes after, he was hanged.

Yet another example of punctuation giving meaning to a statement which is apparently absurd, may be found in an old piece of doggerel, which is often quoted (in slightly varying forms) by writers on punctuation, and which was cited by Sir Robert Megarry V-C in *Marshall v Cottingham* [1982] Ch 82. With no more than a final full stop by way of punctuation, the piece reads:

Every lady in this land
Hath twenty nails upon each hand
Five and twenty on hands and feet
And this is true without deceit.

When punctuated – and minor differences are possible but the following suggestion is perhaps the clearest – it reads:

Every lady in this land
Hath twenty nails: upon each hand
Five, and twenty on hands and feet;
And this is true without deceit.

Punctuation may even bring meaning to a text which not only appears to be plainly wrong (as in the previous example), but also to one which is apparently meaningless. The classic example here is the truly mind boggling:

Janet where John had had had had had had had had had had had the examiners approval.

Once this is understood to be a comment on how an exercise in written English had been marked, it becomes relatively easy to punctuate the comment itself as follows:

Janet, where John had had 'had had', had had 'had': 'had had' had had the examiner's approval.

Three variations are possible. Taking them in the order in which they appear in the sentence, there is, first, the point that double quotation marks could have been used instead of single ones. Secondly, either a semi-colon or a full stop could have been used instead of a colon, although if a full stop had been used, a capital letter would be needed immediately after it, to start a new sentence. Thirdly, *examiners'* would be correct if there were two or more examiners. We will come to each of these points, albeit in a different order, shortly.

Commas, semi-colons and colons
Commas divide sentences into different types of component parts. Commas are generally used to separate grammatical units (words, phrases or clauses) from each other, as the following examples show:

By the great, grey, green, greasy Limpopo river.
On the other hand, when Sherlock Holmes considered the case ....
I came, I saw, I conquered.

If you read any or all of these examples aloud, you will immediately notice that, in addition to separating the grammatical elements from each other, the commas also indicate slight pauses. If a slightly stronger pause is needed, a semi-colon would be appropriate. Thus there is a more declamatory, perhaps even dramatic, tone to:

I came; I saw; I conquered.

There is significant variation of usage of commas where some single words are used to start sentences. For example, in

Originally, punctuation formed no part of written English ....

many highly literate writers would omit the comma after *originally*, and many commentators would regard both usages as being acceptable. Of course, the point is not limited to *originally*, but applies equally to all adverbs – such as *fortunately*, *eventually*, *slowly*, and so on – which are often used on their own to begin sentences. (Most English adverbs end in *ly*, although, as the next example will show, *however* is a very common exception.) On the other hand, there are *apparently* similar sentences where the use of a comma would be quite simply wrong by anyone's standards. For example,

However hard I try to lose weight ....

simply cannot take a comma after *however*. But the people who would regard it as optional in the previous example would also regard it as being optional in, for example

However, I found that taking more exercise helped me to lose weight.

Since the comma after *however* will sometimes be essential, sometimes optional and sometimes wrong (depending on the sentence in question), it follows that the interests of both consistency of style and immediate clarity of meaning, will be served by using it where it is optional. If you follow this practice consistently, the reader will know that when you have omitted it, you know what you are doing; and this will help to make your meaning clear in all cases without requiring too much re-reading.

The colon is the strongest pause short of a full stop, with which, in some situations at least, it is practically interchangeable. So, reverting to a previous example, it would be perfectly acceptable to write:

He was handsome: and I do mean handsome.

Indeed, by way of an aside, and as an indication of the incremental nature of these things, once you have seen this sentence written with a colon, you may realise that it could also be written with a semi-colon instead (we have already noted this possibility in the case of the *had had* example):

He was handsome; and I do mean handsome.

You could even use a comma, although this would lose a significant part of the emphasis which the other versions convey.

He was handsome, and I do mean handsome.

If you try reading all three versions aloud, varying the weight of the pause on an increasing scale of comma, semi-colon, colon, you will see clearly that, in examples such as these, the usage you choose is a question of the effect you wish to achieve, rather than of being right or wrong.

Returning to the potential interchangeability (at least in some situations), of colons and full stops, it is important to sound a note of caution. More particularly, you should not take this potential interchangeability as a licence to join long lists of clauses into very long sentences. As we shall say again in the context of style (see p. 160), there is a useful rule of thumb to the effect that any sentence of more than about 20 words should be scrutinised carefully, to see whether it could not, with benefit, be broken down into two or more sentences.

There are two final points to make about commas. First, they can be used in pairs to divide off a word, phrase or clause which could be removed without affecting the essential meaning of the sentence. Where this usage is employed, the commas function in much the same way as parentheses – see p. 158 – but without making the printed page look so cluttered. The following examples of a word, a phrase and a clause show this use.

The best writers, however, use punctuation very carefully.

The best writers, but not necessarily run-of-the-mill hacks, use punctuation very carefully.

The best writers, which is a category that unfortunately does not include all students, use punctuation very carefully.

In each case, the main point of the sentence is simply that the best writers use punctuation very carefully.

The third point to be made about commas is, in some ways, a variation on the second; but isolating it into a category of its own is a useful way of emphasising its importance. Consider the following sentence:

Essays which must be sent to the external examiner must be in a form suitable for photocopying.

This could bear either of two meanings. First, inserting two commas gives:

Essays, which must be sent to the external examiner, must be in a form suitable for photocopying.

In other words, all essays have to be sent to the external examiner *and* they all have to be in a form which is suitable for photocopying. If this is what is meant, it should be rewritten as:

Essays must be sent to the external examiner and must be in a form which is suitable for photocopying.

The second possibility is:

Essays which must be sent to the external examiner, must be in a form which is suitable for photocopying.

In this case, inserting a single comma has changed the meaning so that it is only those essays which have to be sent to the external examiner which have to be in a form which is suitable for photocopying.
If this is what is meant, it should be rewritten as:

If an essay must be sent to the external examiner, it must be in a form which is suitable for photocopying.

Quotation marks

Quotation marks (also known as *inverted commas*, *speech marks*, or simply *quotes*) are principally used to indicate *direct speech*. In other words, they are used round the actual words that someone has said or written, as in the following example:

In passing sentence the judge said to the defendant: 'You are a thoroughly evil man'.

On the other hand, they are never used to indicate *indirect* (or *reported*) speech. Assuming that the previous example is a true account of what the judge said, it would be incorrect to write:

In passing sentence, the judge said that 'the defendant was a thoroughly evil man'.

If this form of expression is preferred, no quotation marks are used, and you would simply write:

In passing sentence, the judge said that the defendant was a thoroughly evil man.

As well as being used in relation to direct speech, quotation marks are sometimes used round well-known phrases, almost as if the writer is apologising for the cliché. For example:

He was a 'Sunday afternoon' motorist.

It was an 'eleventh hour' plea for clemency.

In all the examples given here, the quotation marks are single, but they could just as well have been double. It is simply a matter of taste. However, it is important that you are consistent in your use of whichever form you choose, and that where you have a quote within a quote, you use the other form. Pursuing the second point, both the following are, therefore, correct:

She said, "Whenever I hear 'to be or not to be' I think of my school days".

She said, 'Whenever I hear "to be or not to be" I think of my school days'.

If you wish to use a quote within a quote within a quote (and so on), you should simply keep alternating between the two types of quotation marks. However, there is a danger that readers may soon lose track of your meaning. Therefore, once you are tempted to go beyond a quote within a quote, it will usually be a good idea to recall the mongoose principle and rewrite what you are trying to say.

Finally, as we will see in Chapter 10, it cannot be emphasised too strongly that scrupulous use of quotation marks, in conjunction with proper referencing, is the key to avoiding allegations of that form of cheating which is called plagiarism.

Round brackets (or *parentheses*)

Words which are enclosed in round brackets (which are technically known as *parentheses*) are an aside or explanation which can be omitted without affecting the gist what is being said. For example:

The temperature today is 68 °F (20 °C), but tomorrow will be cooler.

This is, of course, the general principle underlying the proposition (which we encountered at p. 89) that where the citation of a journal or a law report contains a date in round brackets, the date is an optional part of the citation.

Square brackets

Words in square brackets are essential to the meaning of what is being written (which, again, explains the point about square brackets in the citation of journals and law reports). One common use of square brackets is to make a quotation meaningful. For example, a judge who has heard a large number of witnesses, including the claimant's husband and son, may say, 'I did not believe either of the claimant's first two witnesses'. Unless you know who these witnesses were and their place in the succession of witnesses, this conveys practically nothing. Therefore, in writing, you would say:

The judge said, 'I did not believe [the claimant's husband or son]'.

Apostrophes

Apostrophes have two uses. They can indicate that a word is a contraction of two other words; and they can indicate a relationship of belonging. The second use is known as *the possessive*.

The first use may be illustrated by what are essentially contractions of two words into one, such as *don't* (for *do not*); *I'm* (for *I am*); and *isn't* for *is not*). Such usages need no further discussion here, because they are generally considered to be inappropriate in formal writing. (It must, however, be conceded, that this consensus is weakening rapidly. Nevertheless, we suggest that you adhere to it, on the simple ground that this will annoy no-one, whereas breaching it will certainly annoy some people.) If you want to test your eye for detail, you might like to try to find the one point in this book – apart from examples of the use and misuse of apostrophes – where we have used such a contraction.

Turning to the possessive use of apostrophes, the basic rules are:

- adding *'s* to a singular noun creates the possessive form (so *the girl's bicycle* means *the bicycle belonging to the girl*); and
- where a plural ends in *s* (as most English plurals do), adding the apostrophe on its own creates the possessive form, without the need for a further *s* (so *the girls' bicycles* means *the bicycles belonging to the girls*).

Where a singular noun ends in *s* (which is most likely to be the case where names (such as *Jones*) are concerned, either *'s* or an apostrophe on its own is acceptable: *Tom Jones' bicycle* or *Tom Jones's bicycle*). However, where a word ends with *ss*, the possessive form does require *'s*, as in *the boss's bicycle*.

The only possessive forms which do not use apostrophes are possessive pronouns, such as *his*, *hers*, *theirs* and *its*. These forms require no apostrophe because the possessive is built into the word itself. So, to take a single example, you would write *the bicycle was hers*, rather than *the bicycle was her's*.

Unfortunately, one aspect of the use and non-use of apostrophes in the context of possessives causes persistent and serious difficulty for many people. These people are tempted to apply the basic rule of adding *'s* to *it* when they wish to create the possessive form. However, this overlooks the point that, as we have just seen, with possessive pronouns the possessive form is built into the word itself (so that no apostrophe is needed). Using an apostrophe in an attempt to mean *of it* is doubly unfortunate because *it's* is a perfectly legitimate word in the context of informal English, where it is an example of the other type of use of apostrophes (namely contractions) and where it means *it is*. So if you write *the dog was playing with it's bone*, what you are really saying is *the dog was playing with it is bone*. This cannot be what you really meant.

Fortunately, the correct use of *it's* presents no difficulty provided you follow the advice to avoid all such informal expressions in academic work. If you do try to follow this advice, but carelessness nevertheless leads you to write *it's* in a first draft, you will know that it must be corrected (either by removing the apostrophe or by writing *it is*, depending on what you meant).

Style

Introduction
As a student doing a piece of academic writing, you will be hoping to make a favourable impression on your examiners. This section of this chapter

will, therefore, provide some advice on how to increase your chances of doing so.

The need for formal style

Academic writing requires a formal style of expression. One crucial aspect of this is that you should not use anything which might reasonably be considered to be slang. Thus, for example, you might say

> The defendant was clearly somewhat inexperienced in the ways of the world.

But, even though it may mean much the same thing, you would never say:

> The defendant was clearly a bit of a wally.

Similarly, as we saw at p. 158, it is best to avoid contractions such as *don't*, *I'm* and *isn't*. Avoiding these forms will not only add to the formality of your style, but will also avoid the errors which flow from the common inability to distinguish between *its* and *it's*. (If you never use the latter form, the distinction will never trouble you.)

On the other hand, you should never use any form of words merely because you think it 'sounds good'. A very common error of this sort is to say *prior to* when you mean *before*.

Finally, you would be unwise if you allow the requirement of formality to act as a straitjacket. Even in formal writing, good style requires variation in sentence structure, so that, for example, you use a mixture of simple, compound and complex sentences (see pp. 142–148).

The importance of clarity

As with any other form of communication, if you are to be effective you must make your meaning plain. You could do a great deal worse that follow H. L. A. Hart (the leading English legal theorist of the 20th century), who almost said (and the following version is slightly edited in order to emphasise the point) 'Where I am clearly wrong, I hope that I may at least be wrong clearly'.

One important contribution to achieving clarity is to keep your sentences fairly short. As we have already said at p. 155, there is a useful rule of thumb to the effect that the clarity of a sentence which contains more than 20 words can often be improved by breaking the sentence down into two (or more) separate sentences.

The pursuit of clarity is hard work and requires a talent for self-criticism. It is alarmingly easy to say something which you did not quite mean, as evidenced by the old story of a judge who had to pass sentence on a man who had trussed up a teenage boy like a chicken before sexually molesting him. Clearly outraged by the defendant's conduct, the judge began passing sentence by saying 'I should very much like to give you a taste of your own medicine'. Of course, in oral communication what has been said cannot be unsaid, although instant feedback can result in equally prompt clarification or correction. In the case of written communication, you will, equally obviously, lack the benefit of instant feedback, but provided you develop the ability to be self-critical, this may be counterbalanced by the opportunity to read over what you have written and thus avoid putting the faulty version into circulation in the first place.

Some forms of words repeatedly cause difficulty and are, therefore, best avoided altogether unless you are absolutely confident that you have mastered them. Three examples will suffice.

First, suppose you are given a *Subject Handbook* at the beginning of your course, which tells you that the course is being delivered through a programme of lectures and tutorials. Basically, there is to be one lecture and one tutorial each week but, because of the difficulty of having a tutorial before (or very soon after) the first lecture, there is to be no tutorial in the first week. This is a common situation and one which can be easily explained with perfect clarity. Unfortunately, it can also be presented very ambiguously as the following form of words shows:

There will be a lecture every week. There will be no tutorial in the first week, but there will be one in the second week and every other week after that.

Bearing in mind that you know there is to be a weekly tutorial, you will understand this to mean that there will be a tutorial *in the second week and in every week thereafter*. However, unless you already knew what it meant, you could reasonably interpret it as meaning that there will be a tutorial *in the second week and in alternate weeks thereafter*.

A second example is illustrated by the following sentence.

Smith is the second greatest goalkeeper in the world after Brown.

Does this mean that Brown is number one and Smith is number two; or that Brown is number one, followed by someone else who is the greatest goalkeeper after him, with Smith tagging along in third place? Most people would probably assume the first meaning is the intended one; but if this really is the intended meaning, the word *second* is superfluous. In order to avoid the doubt, it would be useful to invoke the mongoose principle and rewrite the sentence. There are two obvious possibilities, one of which requires only additional punctuation rather than true rewriting. The punctuation possibility merely requires the use of parentheses, to produce

Smith is the second greatest goalkeeper in the world (after Brown).

The rewriting possibility requires an almost equally light touch, namely the omission of the word *second*, to produce

Smith is the greatest goalkeeper in the world after Brown.

The third and final example involves the use of the word *only*, which causes repeated difficulties, as the following sentences show.

Only she imagined the threat was real. (This suggests that nobody else took the threat seriously.)

She only imagined the threat was real. (This suggests that there was no evidence to support her view that the threat was real.)

She imagined only the threat was real. (This suggests that she had been on the receiving end of something else as well as the threat – such as a promise – but that it was only the threat which she had taken seriously.)

Using the active and passive forms of verbs

The active form of a verb deals with *doing something*, while the passive deals with *something being done*. For example, the first of the following two sentences contains an active verb, while the second contains a passive one.

Janet drove the car.
The car was driven by Janet.

The classic advice is to use the active and avoid the passive wherever possible, because the active is both shorter and more direct. Unfortunately, there is a very long tradition among lawyers of using the passive as their standard style, which means you will have to make a special effort not to find yourself slipping into the same bad practice. However, the effort is well worthwhile for two reasons. First, the active genuinely is a more direct – and, therefore, better – means of communication in most cases. Secondly, habitual use of the active means that, on those occasions when you feel the passive would make your point more clearly, it will stand out much more effectively. The following two sentences show how the emphasis of a sentence can depend on whether the verb is used actively or passively.

Janet drove the car, while John rode the bicycle.
The car was driven by Janet, while the bicycle was ridden by John.

The first sentence emphasises the identities of the people, while the second emphasises the means of transport.

Gender-neutral language
It is now well established that formal writing should be composed in gender-neutral terms.

One way of doing this is to use *he or she* (or *she or he*), coupled with *his or her* (or *her or his*) as appropriate. However, many people feel this is unduly cumbersome.

Another frequently encountered solution is to write *s/he* (coupled again with *her or his*), but this has at least three disadvantages compared with *he or she* and *she or he*:

- it has no obvious pronunciation except for *ess stroke he*, which not only betrays its origins as a non-word but also has the additional weakness of leaving the masculine form as the only one which is recognisable, which in turn means that this formula is not quite gender-neutral;
- it leaves no choice as to whether the masculine or the feminine is placed first;
- it has no associated forms corresponding to *his or her* (or *her or his*).

Some people might add a fourth objection, namely that it is grossly inelegant, but this would be nothing more than a matter of taste.

Fortunately, applying the mongoose principle provides a very simple formula that will almost always avoid the problem: *write in the plural*. Thus

a student will receive his or her marks within three weeks of the end of the examination period becomes

> students will receive their marks within three weeks of the end of the
> examination period.

The rewritten version is not only simpler and more elegant than the original, but it also has the advantage of containing nothing which could offend anyone.

Some people take a halfway house approach to the plural solution, which produces:

> a student will receive their marks within three weeks of the end of
> the examination period.

While this usage has a pedigree stretching far beyond the origins of political correctness (with examples being found even in the works of Shakespeare), its mixture of singular and plural forms (*a student* and *their*) nevertheless grates on many an educated ear and has nothing to recommend it over the straightforward plural solution.

Splitting infinitives

The infinitive form of a verb begins with *to*. For example, *to stop*, *to go*, *to love* and *to hate* are all infinitives. This raises a question of where you should place an adverb. For example, should you say *suddenly to stop*, *to suddenly stop*, or *to stop suddenly*? The traditional view is that both the first and the third can be correct, but the second one is always wrong. Whether or not you subscribe to the traditional view, it is probably wise to pretend that you do and develop the habit of avoiding split infinitives. The reason is simple: split infinitives do (rightly or wrongly) annoy many people, and it is never a good idea to annoy people (such as examiners) when you want to make a favourable impression upon them.

Unfortunately, however, considerable care is needed when avoiding split infinitives, because the alternatives can give rise ambiguity. Does *he decided to stop suddenly* mean that it was the *decision* or the *stopping* which was sudden? Of course, the mongoose principle can, as always, provide a solution. You could say either *he made a sudden decision to stop*, or *he made a decision to stop suddenly*, depending on your meaning. If you still detect a hint of ambiguity in the latter version, you could be even more explicit and say *he decided that stopping suddenly was a good idea*.

● Conclusion

It is important to write English which is sufficiently formal to be appropriate to academic work, without falling into the trap of being pretentious. Essentially, this requires you to follow the conventions of grammar, punctuation, spelling and style, while ensuring that your vocabulary avoids anything that might reasonably be considered to be slang.

If you ever encounter difficulty or doubt when writing anything, remember the mongoose principle: *if in difficulty or doubt, rewrite it.*

10 Answering Essay Questions

Essay writing is a distinctive form of communication which requires you to interpret the instructions you are given, undertake the relevant research and structure your answer according to the demands of the particular question. The presentation should follow accepted conventions of footnoting, referencing and legal citation to assist the reader and avoid allegations of plagiarism or cheating.

● Introduction

Writing, like speech, is a form of communication, an attempt to convey meaning. To be an effective communicator you have to speak or write in a way that the people who hear or read your words will understand; and therefore you have to ask yourself, 'who is my audience?'.

Most of the time, when you speak or write you will naturally use language which is appropriate for your audience. If you are chatting informally with friends you do not speak in the same way as you would if you were presenting a seminar paper in class or presenting an argument to the court. If you are writing a letter of complaint to a business organisation, you approach it quite differently from the task of writing a brief note to a boyfriend or girlfriend.

Much of the written work you produce as a student will be assessed and the audience will be your lecturers and tutors. Your language and style must both be appropriate to this academic context. This means that your arguments must not only be logical, coherent and supported by authority, but also that you must present them in an *impersonal* way.

Expanding for a moment on the need for impersonal presentation, a lawyer addressing a court would never say, 'I believe my client should win this appeal', but would adopt the more impersonal style of 'I submit that the law in this appeal is all in favour of my client', before going on to cite the authorities which would enable the court to agree. And you should present your essays in the same style. So, for example, if you consider an outcome to be unfair, you must construct an argument to show why it is unfair, drawing on examples from sources such as dissenting judgments and academic criticism of the relevant law. What you should never do is simply say 'I think this outcome is unfair'.

Clarity and accuracy should be your aims in all your writing, but these are not always easy goals to reach. As we saw (in Chapter 7), much legal wrangling concerns the interpretation of words, but as we then went on to see (in Chapter 9), you can improve the clarity of your work by developing good habits of linguistic style and following the standard conventions of grammar, spelling and punctuation.

If you have not written in this way before, you may find it an uphill struggle in the early stages of your studies. However, it is a skill you need to master, since you will find that until you can write in a coherent, academic style, the real merit of your arguments will often go unappreciated. Crucially, this will be reflected in your marks, because examiners cannot know whether a muddled piece of work represents clear understanding that has been poorly presented, or poor understanding that has been clearly presented. From the point of view of assessment, however, this distinction is unimportant, because neither will be given a good mark.

As well as being clear, your writing should follow a consistent system of footnoting and referencing. Your lecturers and tutors will probably have a preferred system and you may be obliged to use that. You must be rigorous in citing your sources and providing references to all the materials you have used when preparing your work. This is not only good academic practice in its own right, but is also essential if you are to avoid allegations of *plagiarism*, or to put it another way, *academic dishonesty*, or – to put it even more bluntly – *cheating*.

● Cheating

Plagiarism, which is the most common form of academic dishonesty or cheating, is essentially the act of taking the work of another and passing it off as your own. The work of others can include their thoughts and inventions, but by far the most common form of plagiarism is using the words and ideas of others without proper acknowledgement. Increasingly, with the advent of the World Wide Web and word processing, students claim that written work is their own when, in fact, the work includes the words and ideas of others which are not acknowledged. Clearly, therefore, plagiarism is a form of theft, because plagiarists are dishonestly taking the work of others and using is as if it were their own. This is a serious matter for any student because, quite apart from any penalty which may be imposed by your college or university, the fact that you have been found guilty of dishonest conduct is likely to be mentioned in any reference which your college or university provides in connection with any applications you may make for jobs or for postgraduate study. It is particularly serious for students who intend to enter the legal profession, because findings of dishonesty will also be reported to the legal professions' governing bodies.

While every college's or university's regulations will reflect what has been said so far, we now move on to matters where there may be differences of terminology. However, the important thing to grasp is that whatever terminology your college or university adopts, they will still be talking about *cheating*. Some institutions simply give an extended meaning to the word *plagiarism*, to include what others would call something like *academic dishonesty*. Whatever it is called, we are now dealing with matters such as:

- falsifying or inventing material (for example, inventing case names);
- providing false information about a source you have quoted (for example, claiming to have used a later edition of a book than that which you actually used);
- copying other people's work or allowing them to copy yours (both of which are forms of what is sometimes known as *collusion*);
- failing to put direct quotations in *quotation marks* (also known as *inverted commas* or *speech marks*); and
- making only minor changes to the writings of others and then failing to acknowledge the source.

Three matters are worth particular emphasis.

First, the fact that using quotation marks and citing your sources will protect you from allegations of plagiarism must not be taken as an invitation to produce work which is simply a string of quotations, such as: *Smith says [quotation]. But on the other hand, Brown says [quotation], while Jones says [quotation]*; and so on. Dictionaries of quotations are one thing; essays are another.

Secondly, you may feel that you cannot improve on the way the leading judges and commentators have expressed complex ideas, and that you would be foolish to try to do so. The answer to this is twofold.

- It is implicit in what we have already said that there will undoubtedly be situations in which it is acceptable – and indeed, desirable – that you should use someone else's actual words. (Of course, when you do so – and we make no apology for repeating the most basic point of all – you must use quotation marks and cite your source. But, provided you do this, you may be demonstrating that you have the ability to identify the very core of the point which is being made, and that you possess the discernment to be able to identify a telling turn of phrase.)

- In situations where direct quotation is not appropriate, you may experience difficulty in putting things into your own words. More particularly, you may find it difficult to get far enough away from the original form of words to avoid plagiarism, while still saying substantially the same thing. While conceding that this can be difficult, we must also point out that it is at least part of the essence of the exercise, because expressing things accurately in your own words is one way in which you demonstrate that you really understand them. Moving to a more practical response, one very useful technique for dealing with this problem is to take notes from (but do *not* simply copy out) the original text. Then, a few days later, return to your notes and rewrite them into proper, polished prose. This two-stage removal between the original text and your own version will usually be enough to ensure that you are producing your own work in your own words.

Thirdly, you need to take particular care if you set your written work out in such a way that lengthy quotations are indented as blocks of text (as they are in this book, as well as in many others). You might assume that the fact of indentation is sufficient to indicate that you are quoting someone else; and, for everyday purposes, this assumption may well be sound. Nevertheless, if you rely solely on the fact of indentation, without the addition of quotation marks (which, once again, is the style adopted in this book as well as in many others), you run the risk that a particularly strict marker may decide that you are guilty of plagiarism. While you may succeed on appeal (assuming – which will not always be the case – that the members of the appeal committee are less strict than your original marker), you will find the mere fact of being subjected to the allegation is stressful. Additionally, the time-scales for processing appeals can extend to many months in some colleges and universities. Apart from prolonging the exposure to stress, such delays can have serious consequences in terms of progression to the next stage of your studies and even, at final year level, in terms of graduation. Fortunately, the solution is simple. Whatever the prevailing fashion in the typographical design of books may be, all you have to do, in order to put your academic integrity beyond doubt, is to add quotation marks at the beginning and end of your indented quotations.

Fourthly, a particular difficulty arises in the context of discussing assessed coursework with other people. More particularly, there is always the danger that, once you enter such discussions, you will cross the line which divides the offence of collusion from the kind of legitimate discussion which is a healthy part of belonging to any academic community. Where coursework requires you to collaborate with others (for example, in group presentations or any other form of teamwork) there will, of course, be no problem, provided you limit your discussions to other members of your own group or team. However, in the much more common case where coursework is required to be an individual effort (or, in the case of group or team work where you are tempted to discuss the work with people from outside your own group or team), you need to be very much more careful.

Ultimately, in many cases the distinction between collusion and discussion is a matter of degree, but in practical terms a disciplinary panel must draw a line and decide on which side of that line your conduct falls. A useful test is to ask yourself whether the discussion provides you (or others) with ideas that you (or they) would not otherwise have had. Giving yourself a scrupulously honest answer to this question should enable you to avoid straying into the forbidden territory of collusion.

The most important piece of advice is simply this: make sure you

- know,
- understand, and
- follow

your college's or university's regulations in relation to all forms of cheating, whatever terminology they may use.

Having emphasised the importance of acknowledging your sources, we must now turn to the nuts and bolts of how you do this, and discuss the techniques of *referencing* and *footnoting*.

● Referencing and footnoting

Referencing and footnoting your work should, as we noted in the introduction to this chapter, follow whatever guidelines your college or university provides. If you are given a choice of systems to follow, it is important that you follow your chosen system consistently.

We dealt at length with the citation of cases and statutes in Chapter 6. Here we will look at referencing books, articles and Internet resources using both the Oxford Standard Citation of Legal Authorities (OSCOLA, available at http://www.law.ox.ac.uk/publications/oscola.php) and Harvard system (which, as we shall see in a moment, has no definitive form). OSCOLA, as the name suggests, is a comprehensive guide to legal citation, providing extensive guidance on matters well beyond footnoting and referencing. Many institutions use variants on OSCOLA or the Harvard system. For example, some colleges and universities use a variant on Harvard citation, recommending the use of double rather than single quotation marks for the title of a journal article, whereas other institutions advise using single quotation marks. The examples below follow the OSCOLA system precisely (which is possible, since a definitive version is available), and (since no definitive version exists) the British Standards Institution interpretation of the Harvard system (BS 5605:1990 *Recommendations for citing and referencing published material*). The OSCOLA system uses numbered footnotes and the OSCOLA illustrations in the citations below would appear consecutively numbered throughout the essay at the bottom of the relevant page. The Harvard system uses brief citations within the body text and provides the full citation in a reference list at the end of the work. An example of a short paragraph, which includes a direct quotation from a book, illustrates the different approaches. Taking OSCOLA first:

> When speaking of the *ratio decidendi* of a case it is tempting to think in terms of a fixed and single entity with an objective and continuing existence, which merely needs to be located and identified, just as a treasure hunter may seek to locate and identify a sunken wreck within a given area of the seabed. As we shall see in the remainder of this chapter, however, this model is seriously misleading.[1]

The Harvard system, on the other hand would produce:

> When speaking of the *ratio decidendi* of a case it is tempting to think in terms of a fixed and single entity with an objective and continuing existence, which merely needs to be located and identified, just as a treasure hunter may seek to locate and identify a sunken wreck within a given area of the seabed. As we shall see in the remainder of this chapter, however, this model is seriously misleading. (McLeod 2011 p. 132).

Whichever system of citation you use, the same basic information must be included. When citing books you need to include the author's name (or authors' names), the title of the book (in *italics*), the edition, publisher, place and date of publication and, if quoting directly from the work or referring to a specific point, the relevant page number. The OSCOLA system discourages the use of full stops and commas in citations and includes the full reference in a numbered footnote at the bottom of the page. This would be footnote 1 from the example given above:

¹Ian McLeod, *Legal Method* (8th edn, Palgrave Basingstoke 2011) 132.

The same citation using the Harvard system would not include the page number, since this is cited in the short reference in the main body of the text. The full reference would be included in a reference list at the end of the work and could be cited thus:

McLeod, I., 2011. *Legal Method*. 8th ed. Basingstoke: Palgrave.

The basic information for journal articles is the author's name (or authors' names), the title of the article (in single quotation marks) and the year, volume and page reference of the article. Most law journals have preferred abbreviations of the journal title. The OSCOLA system encourages the use of the standard abbreviations where possible. An example of an OSCOLA journal article citation, from the *New Law Journal*, is:

JR Spencer, 'Retrial for reckless infection' (2004) 154 NLJ 762

The Harvard citation for this article could use either the accepted abbreviation, as in the OSCOLA form, or the full title of the journal, with the latter appearing thus:

Spencer J. R., 2004. 'Retrial for reckless infection'. *New Law Journal* vol. 154, p. 762.

Internet resources often provide very little citable information and frequently disappear into cyberspace as quickly as they appeared online. Include the author (if identified), the title of the article or the title of the page, the URL and the date the resource was accessed. In OSCOLA this would be:

Richard Garner, 'Electronic tags used to beat the A-level cheats' *The Independent* (London, 11 May 2007) <http://education.independent. co.uk/news/article2530771.ece> accessed 14 May 2007

A Harvard style citation could be:

Garner, R. (2007, 11 May) 'Electronic tags used to beat the A-level cheats' (*The Independent*), Available: http://education.independent. co.uk/news/article2530771.ece (Accessed: 2007, 14 May).

Footnoting and referencing, like grammar that follows standard conventions, makes your work easier to read. Inconsistent footnoting and referencing in your work will undermine your attempts to create a well-presented composition and give the impression that your work is the product of an erratic and disorganised mind. Finally, it is worth repeating that full referencing and citation is also fundamental to avoiding allegations of plagiarism.

● Writing good law essays

Introduction
The focus of this chapter is on how to write coursework essays, but most of the discussion is also relevant to examination essays. The only real dif ferences (apart from length) between a coursework essay and one written under examination conditions are that you have time to research the coursework questions, while in the case of examinations your revision will be the equivalent of research and you can cite much less detailed authority.

The hallmarks of a good law essay
While most students will have written many essays before coming to the study of law, it is equally true that many law students experience difficulty in understanding exactly what they are being asked to do when they are required to write an essay. Perhaps the key difference between writing essays in law (and for the moment we include not only essays as such, but also case notes, dissertations and answers to problem questions) and writing in most other subjects within the general area of arts, humanities and social sciences, is the extent to which every proposition you make must be expressed with precision and supported by authority. We are well aware that, in saying this, we will annoy both teachers and students of other subjects, who will almost certainly feel that we are claiming law to be the only truly

academically rigorous subject. Of course, we are not asserting that at all. We are merely recording the fact that many students, when coming to law for the first time, experience difficulty with the degree of precision and the extent of authority which is required. Furthermore, the fact that this applies even to those doing postgraduate conversion courses would seem to suggest that success in degree-level study of other subjects does not necessarily ensure success in law. No doubt those who embark on the study of other subjects will have to learn the kind of academic rigour that those subjects require; but our concern is only with the law.

Law essays must not only be logically structured presentations of coherent arguments, but must also answer the question and be supported by authority. An essay should not simply be a series of paraphrases of the material you have been referred to, but a critical review of that material. Although your understanding of the relevant material is a prerequisite to success in essay writing, it will not, on its own, be enough. What you must do is *demonstrate* your understanding; and you will do this by

- interpreting the question,
- doing the relevant research, and
- writing a well-argued answer which demonstrates that you have interpreted the question perceptively and rigorously and done the relevant research thoroughly.

Before elaborating each of these points, it may be worth commenting briefly on two classically bad types of essay.

The more common type is known as the *£10 Note Answer*, where the student summarises the whole of the law on the topic, rather than selecting and applying only the relevant parts. In other words, the student is effectively saying to the examiner 'take it out of that and keep the change'.

The other type, which while less common is still too common, is known as the 'Kings of Israel Answer', and takes the form of an answer to the question which the student wishes had been set, rather than the one which has actually been set. The name of this type of answer comes from the story of the divinity student who had calculated that an essay on the Kings of Israel was bound to come up in the examination. Unfortunately for the student, this turned out to be a miscalculation, but there was a question which required candidates to distinguish between the major and the minor prophets. Accordingly, our student began his (or was it her?) essay thus: 'Who am I to distinguish between the major and the minor prophets? However, the Kings of Israel are very interesting … ' and then proceeded to reproduce the essay which he (or she) had meticulously prepared.

With these cautionary tales in mind, we can now return to the topic of how to write *good* essays.

Interpreting the question

Generally
Interpreting an essay question is the first step towards writing a good essay. In practice, what it means is that you must ask yourself these questions and sub-questions:

1. What is the question about?
   Sub-questions: Are there any presumptions, approaches or sub-issues implicit in the question?
2. What does the question ask me to do?
   Sub-questions: Are there any expansions or limitations in the question?

Until you can identify the main ideas or key concepts in the question, *and* clearly understand what you are being asked to do, you risk falling into the trap of reciting all you know on a given subject and producing a £10 Note Answer. And you will never be asked to do this in a law essay.

Identifying the key concepts tells you what the question is *about*, while the instructional words in the question tell you *what you are being asked to do*. Often the instructions will ask you to *evaluate* or *critically analyse* a particular topic. Alternatively, they may ask you to *discuss* or *explain* a specific issue. All these terms require you to do a great deal more than simply *describe* the relevant law and you must be clear from the outset about their meanings. (The most commonly used instructions are explained at the end of this section.) When thinking about the key concepts in the question, it is important to take into account whether you are being asked to look at the issues from a particular angle, and whether any statements in the question make presumptions or have implications that you need to address. When reflecting on what the question is asking you to do, you will find that identifying the scope of the question will also tell you what you are *not* being asked to do.

Consider the following essay question which we will use as a working example throughout this chapter:

'The Human Rights Act 1998 effectively gives the people of England and Wales a bill of rights... the Act is of enormous significance in

that it has bestowed "higher law" status on most Convention rights.'
Critically discuss.

One way to begin interpreting the question is to highlight the text of the question, identifying the component parts as we have done below. We have done this for the present question as follows:

- the key concepts are in **bold** text,
- the approach which the question invites is in ***bold italics***,
- the three sub-issues are in **bold** and each is asterisked*, while
- the instructional words are <u>underlined</u>, and
- a limitation on the scope of the essay is *italicised*.

'The **Human Rights Act 1998** *effectively gives* the people of *England and Wales* a **bill of rights***... the Act is of enormous significance in that it has bestowed "**higher law**"* **status** on most **Convention rights***.' <u>Critically discuss</u>.

Another way to interpret the question is to rewrite it in your own words. This is a little harder than highlighting the key terms in the title, but has the advantage of improving your analysis and understanding of the question. You might rewrite the question to read:

The way in which the Convention rights in the Human Rights Act 1998 are protected and elevated as 'higher law' means that to all intents and purposes the English and Welsh peoples have, in the Human Rights Act, a bill of rights.

By rewriting the question you have made explicit a link which is only implicit in the original question, namely that it is only because the Human Rights Act 1998 (HRA 1998) is a higher form of law that England and Wales now has something akin to a bill of rights.

An alternative to rewriting the question in your own words is to expand on the component parts of the question as a series of bullet points:

- What the statement says:
    - The Convention rights protected by the HRA 1998 have been given special status in English law, thus the HRA 1998 is to all intents and purposes a bill of rights.

- Approach:
  - The words 'effectively gives' make it clear that the HRA 1998 is not a bill of rights but indicate the angle the essay should take, i.e. an examination of whether:
    - The HRA 1998 protects the human rights of citizens in the same way as a bill of rights might.
    - The HRA 1998 is protected in the same way as a bill of rights would be protected or entrenched.
- What the question asks me to do:
  - Explain the scheme of the HRA 1998 and 'Convention rights'.
  - Explain what is meant by a bill of rights and whether the HRA fits that mould.
  - Interpret the concept of 'higher law' and consider whether the HRA 1998 is such a 'higher law'.
- Limitations:
  - Question is limited to England and Wales, i.e. English law.

This interpretation and analysis of the question produces something that has the beginnings of a plan, but in reality this is merely a sketch map for your research, rather than the plan you will use when you write your essay.

The instructional words ask for *critical discussion* of the statement, which calls for a consideration of a range of viewpoints, both for and against the statement, together with an assessment of the strengths and weaknesses of each of these perspectives. A lecturer or tutor setting this question would expect you to explain (among other things) what a bill of rights is. He or she would not be looking for a detailed description of a bill of rights, but would want to see whether you can identify the fundamental features of such basic constitutional documents, and then evaluate the HRA 1998 in order to detect whether it shared or lacked those necessary features. To reach such a judgment you will first need to have examined the views of authors and the courts. Having thus considered the strengths and weaknesses of each perspective, you will be able to make your own assessment. More particularly, it is not enough to present the arguments of authors who support the statement and those of authors who oppose the statement. *Critical discussion* requires the essay writer to express a judgment as to the merits of the arguments, together with a convincing argument in support of that judgment.

Before moving on to consider the topic of *researching the question*, it may be useful to consider, briefly, what is meant by a variety of other commonly used instructional words.

Some commonly used instructional words

Unfortunately, many students never achieve their full potential in course-work and examination essays because they fail to understand what the question is asking them to do. This selection of commonly used instructional words should help you to interpret most of the essay questions you encounter. Learning to interpret instructional words when you have a term-time essay to complete will help you produce an answer appropriate to the question, but it will also prepare you for when the same instructions appear in examination questions.

Analyse: Analysis involves separating or breaking down something into its component parts *and* discussing the relationships between each of the parts.

Criticise: Criticising something involves coming to a judgement about a particular argument, point of view or theory, through a process of discussion in which you examine both the strengths and weaknesses of the particular argument *and* provide justification for your own assessment.

Discuss: The instruction to discuss something is often used interchangeably with the instruction to *critically discuss* something. Either instruction involves both description *and* interpretation. It requires you to explain the relevant ideas and arguments and examine them through reasoned argument, supported by authority, in order to reach a conclusion. A discussion should not be one-sided but a consideration of the arguments on *all* sides of the debate.

Distinguish: A question that asks you to distinguish one thing from another will usually focus on concepts that are commonly muddled. Distinguishing requires you to explain the *similarities and differences* between two or more things and provide illustrations wherever possible.

Evaluate: Evaluation involves reaching a *reasoned judgment* about the value or legitimacy of a particular argument, concept or theory. In doing this, you must scrutinise, with reference to appropriate evidence, the advantages, failings and limitations of the argument, concept, or theory.

Illustrate: Illustrating something involves giving concrete examples (such as decided cases) that support and help to explain your line of reasoning.

Justify: Justifying something involves providing and explaining relevant reasons to support your conclusions.

Researching the question

Once you know what the question is about, and what you are being asked to do, you can then begin to research the question. Just as the question is not an invitation to tell the reader all you know about the topic, so the research is not a quest to read everything in print, or on the Internet, about the topic. Researching the question is a search for *relevant* materials so, if you were answering the question on the HRA 1998, you would look for articles about the HRA 1998 and in particular at authors who suggest that the HRA 1998 has 'higher law' status, or shares the characteristics of a bill of rights or similar constitutional document, and authors who reject such views.

Essentially, the task at the research stage is to

- locate,
- read, and
- make notes on,

the materials that are relevant to your answer. Much of the material you need will be readily available, but there may well be many other students looking for the same information and working to the same deadline. You could, therefore, usefully photocopy journal articles as early as possible after receiving the question, and reserve books from the library as necessary.

Reading and making notes on the materials can be very time-consuming and to make the best use of the time available you will need to employ effective reading strategies while remaining focused on the question. To get a general impression of the issues you will first need to read broadly, though the extent of the overview reading you need to do will very much depend on the level of your existing knowledge of the essay topic. This general reading should help you discover the important themes around the key concepts of the essay and the range of possible answers to the question. When your understanding is such that you can take a stance on the answer you should then narrow the focus of your reading and concentrate in detail on the arguments that support your view. The detailed reading should, however, be a critical evaluation of the materials and you need to note the flaws as well as the strengths of the arguments you intend to rely on in your essay.

At this stage we can usefully return to the SQ3R technique which we first encountered at pp. 15–17. When using this technique to research an essay question, *surveying* and *questioning* the material are done at the same time by skim reading or quickly scanning the materials you think might be suitable for your essay, while always keeping the key concepts of the essay question at the forefront of your mind. To survey a book in this way, you would flick through the table of contents, and (if they are not included in the table of contents) the main headings and subheadings within each of the relevant chapters. You may also scan the most promising pages, looking for words and phrases which are relevant to your essay topic. When reading, you should ask yourself the following questions:

- is the material relevant to the key concepts of the essay?
- does the material support or contradict what I already know?
- is there anything new or interesting here that is worth pursuing further? (Remember that everything *must* be *relevant* to the question.)

You will then be in a position to progress to the *reading*, *recalling* and *reviewing* stages of the SQ3R process in the usual way.

Planning and writing the answer

Planning the answer

Planning your answer helps you create the direction and structure of your essay. Your efforts at this stage should focus on using the research materials to build a logical, coherent, well-structured essay. Remember, the essay is *your* work and *only you* can provide readers with the directions they need to find their way through your composition. A plan will help you to help them.

The form of your plan might be graphical, or it might simply use headings and subheadings. In practice it is helpful to use a piece of paper large enough to contain your complete plan so that you can both see the overall picture and ensure the component parts fit together. Here is part of a plan we will use at the writing stage. It includes the points we will discuss when creating a main body paragraph.

A. HRA 1998
    1. 'Convention rights'
        (a) From European Convention of Human Rights (ECHR)
            (i) Not all ECHR rights – arts 1 and 13 are excluded.
            (ii) Less far-reaching and more qualified than other bills of rights – e.g., German basic law – art 3 EHCR only absolute right.

(b) ECHR not incorporated into English law but 'Convention rights' given special status by HRA 1998:
    (i) Courts cannot quash primary legislation – statutes declared incompatible with ECHR by courts still remain law – scheme retains legislative supremacy of Parliament. But
    (ii) Courts required – where possible – to interpret legislation (post and pre HRA 1998) compatibly with ECHR.
(c) Not entrenched/protected in same way as constitutional documents:
    (i) Bill of Rights in United States Constitution – Congress and 75% of states must agree to amendments.
    (ii) German Basic Law – cannot be changed.
(d) Does not bind Legislature
    Other constitutional documents bind legislature executive and judiciary.

The level of detail you need in your plan will vary. At some points, shorthand terms that remind you of arguments you are familiar with will suffice; but where you are less sure, longer explanations will be necessary. What is important is that your plan must illustrate both the line and order of your argument(s) in a way that you understand and be sufficiently detailed to be genuinely useful when you write your essay. The plan is a tool to help you build an effective essay, just as an architect's plan directs the builder of a house. At first you might find it hard to construct and use the plan, but with increasing use you will learn how to customise the tool and make it work for you.

Writing the answer
Writing the answer is the place where many students start when tackling an essay question, and this is probably the most common reason for underperformance (and even failure) in assessment. Writing your essay will not always be easy, but it will be a great deal easier to write if you have properly *interpreted* and *researched* the question, and equally carefully *planned* your answer.

The introduction should be short and simple. It needs to tell the readers what the essay is about and prepare them for the journey through your essay. What you are doing here is interpreting the question for your readers, and providing markers (or signposts) to give them an idea of the ground you are going to cover. This will enable them to build their own mental map of the territory they will be covering before they start on the journey itself.

Here is an example of how the essay question we have considered through-out this chapter might be introduced:

> The United Kingdom was, when it ratified the European Convention for the Protection of Human Rights and Fundamental Freedoms (ECHR), one of the first member states of the Council of Europe to do so. Those rights guaranteed in the ECHR which are now protected in English law by the Human Rights Act 1998 (HRA 1998) have been labelled by that Act as 'Convention rights'. This essay will discuss whether the HRA's approach to Convention rights can properly be described as giving those rights the status of 'higher law'; and whether, to all intents and purposes, this provides the citizens of England and Wales with a constitutional document comparable to a bill of rights.
>
> A consideration of the scheme of the HRA 1998 will show that the legislative supremacy of Parliament is left intact. An examination of the Bill of Rights in the Constitution of the United States of America and the fundamental law of Germany will reveal that the Act lacks the conventional protection of legal entrenchment usually seen in bills of rights. On the face of it, this would suggest that the HRA 1998 does not have the 'enormous significance' the statement claims but an analysis of the impact and effect that the Act has had on English law reveals a new culture of human rights among citizens, an increased willingness on the part of the judiciary to protect human rights[1] and a sensitivity to human rights on the part of the government.[2]
>
> [1]See the comments of Lord Hoffmann on the principle of 'legality' in *R v Secretary of State for the Home Department ex parte Simms* [1999] UKHL 33, [2000] 2 AC 115, 131-32.
>
> [2]For example, the government's response to the decision in *R v Secretary of State for the Home Department (Respondent) ex parte Al-Hasan* [2005] UKHL 13, [2005] 1 WLR 688.

Having set the scene for the readers, you then need to write the main body of the essay, taking up each of your themes in linked paragraphs or sections. Treat each paragraph as a separate unit of thought or mini-essay, while ensuring that it is clearly related to the themes of your essay. Follow the order of your plan to move smoothly from one point to the next.

A tried and tested method for creating an effective paragraph is to begin with a *topic* sentence, followed by *supporting* sentences and then a *concluding* sentence. However, all good writing contains varying structures, so you should not treat this model as one to be followed on all occasions, although it will serve to sharpen your perception of what needs to be achieved in a paragraph. The topic sentence introduces the key idea you will discuss in the paragraph and helps connect the paragraph to the overall plan. Sometimes it may be preceded by a transitional clause or sentence, but the topic sentence should always appear early on in the paragraph. If you look back to the first sentence of this paragraph, you will see that we use a few transitional words (linking this paragraph to the preceding one), followed by a topic sentence which tells you that in this paragraph we are going to discuss writing the main body paragraphs of an essay.

The supporting sentences of a paragraph are where the critical discussion takes place. The topic is analysed and the evidence is critically examined to develop and advance the arguments of your essay. The concluding sentence of a paragraph does not require you to come to a conclusion, but it does require you to evaluate or indicate how the argument has moved on. This will keep your arguments alive and keep readers on track. If readers fail to follow your arguments, you will lose their attention; and in an assessed essay or an examination you will also lose marks. Where a point is developed over a series of paragraphs, the concluding sentence of each one will act as a bridge to the next, until your final paragraph contains a concluding evaluation. Here are two paragraphs based on our essay plan above:

The 'Convention rights' identified in the HRA 1998 are contained in Arts 2–12, and 14 ECHR, Arts 1–3 of the First Protocol and Arts 1 and 2 of Protocol 6. The HRA does not add to these Convention rights, which, after 50 years and the increasing remoteness of the specifically post-World War II perspective, might be criticised for having the limited aim of protecting the citizen from state interference. Many constitutional documents, such as the basic law of Germany, are more far reaching. German basic law includes a general right to equality[3] and a number of social rights such as the right of mothers to the 'protection and care of the community'[4]. Convention rights do not embrace social rights such as the right to a free education[5]; or minority rights like the right to be educated in one's own language[6]; nor does the HRA protect minority cultures[7]. Only one Convention right is absolute, namely Art. 3, the right not to be 'subjected to torture or to inhuman or degrading treatment or punishment', whereas a large part of Germany's basic law is 'inviolable'[8]. In enacting the HRA 1998, it seems Parliament did not intend to create a bill of rights along the typical lines of a constitutional document like Germany's basic law or Sweden's Instrument of Government. This is particularly apparent from the approach which is adopted towards Convention rights.

The scheme of the HRA which is often, albeit wrongly, described as 'incorporating' the ECHR into English law[9] preserves the legislative supremacy of Parliament and was designed, in the words of the Lord Chancellor of the day, 'to give the courts as much space as possible to protect human rights, short of the power to set aside or ignore Acts of Parliament'.[10] Ultimately, like every other statute, the Act could be repealed by the present or any future Parliament. However, unlike any other statute, it places an interpretative obligation upon the courts in relation to their interpretation of all other statutes, by requiring them to read all legislation, whenever passed, in such a way as to be compatible with Convention rights, wherever it is possible to do so. It may be objected that the HRA is not truly unique in this respect, since the Interpretation Act 1978 imposes a whole range of interpretative obligations in respect of all other statutes – except, in each case, 'where the context otherwise requires'. The answer to this objection is that the Interpretation Act is limited to matters of technical convenience – such as the meaning of 'day' and 'month' and the presumption that the singular includes the plural and so on – whereas the HRA deals with a matter of constitutional principle. Thus this interpretative obligation, imposed by Parliament on the courts, is what gives the HRA its 'special status' in English law.

[3]Art. 3.

[4]Art. 6(4).

[5]Sweden: Instrument of Government, Chapter 2 Art. 21.

[6]Canadian Charter of Rights and Freedoms s. 23.

[7]Sweden: Instrument of Government Chapter 2 Art. 20.

[8]Arts 1, 4, 10, 13.

[9]Lord Clyde, *R v Lambert* [135].

[10]HL Debs, 3 November 1997, col. 1228.

In each of these paragraphs the topic is identified in the first sentence. Looking at the first paragraph, we see that it deals with Convention rights; the supporting sentences then analyse these rights and criticise them by a comparison to the rights protected in other constitutional documents. The evaluation in the concluding sentence is that Convention rights are not comprehensive and that Parliament did not intend to create a bill of basic rights in the HRA. The end of the last sentence in the first paragraph also acts as a transition clause, or bridge, between it and the next paragraph. This transition is maintained in the first sentence of the second paragraph, which then unfolds following a similar pattern to the first.

By the end of your essay your conclusions should be fairly easy to write. The key thing is that they must fit the preceding discussion. This has two main elements. First, do not introduce new material into the conclusion. Secondly, do not express opinions that are not substantiated by the evidence; and, in particular, do not come to a firm view unless it is very clearly supported by the evidence. Other ways of rounding an essay off include linking the conclusion to the introduction by picking up a phrase, quotation or anecdote again, or using a quotation from a primary source to amplify your point. Above all, remember that a conclusion does not need to tie together every strand of the essay into a neat bow. If the evidence is equivocal, or the arguments finely balanced, then you should present that to the readers and allow them to reach their own conclusions. For example:

> The HRA is not so wide ranging in the kind of human rights it protects as many constitutional documents, and the Act lacks the legal entrenchment usually found in such fundamental or basic laws. In a strict legal sense, the HRA is not analogous to a bill of rights and Convention rights have not been given any 'higher status' than the provisions of any other Act of Parliament. Nevertheless, the HRA has placed the protection of basic human rights firmly on the public agenda and while Parliament may still 'as a matter of constitutional legality ... be sovereign ... as a matter of constitutional practice [the HRA] has transferred significant power to the judiciary'[11], a move which Flinders[12] claims 'represents an unprecedented transfer of political power from the executive and legislature to the judiciary'. The enormity of the significance of the HRA is yet to unfold fully, and it remains to be seen whether it turns out be such a major constitutional change. In the nature of the British constitution, the HRA may evolve as a peculiarly British bill of rights, but only time will show whether the HRA will be listed with the likes of 'Magna Carta... as a "revolutionary" legal and historical document in the sense that it changed man's and woman's thinking [turning] the UK's

political and legal culture upside down [and perhaps] the right way around'[13].

[11]KD Ewing, 'The Human Rights Act and Parliamentary Democracy' (1999) 62 MLR 79, 79.

[12]M Flinders, 'Mechanisms of judicial accountability in British central government' [2001] *Parl. Aff.* 54, 63.

[13]D McGoldrick, 'The United Kingdom's Human Rights Act 1998 in Theory and Practice' (2001) 50 *ICLQ* 901, 953.

This conclusion returns to the themes identified in the introduction and, in so far as is possible, it provides an answer to the question set. It also reminds those readers who have to mark your work for assessment purposes that you understand that the question is multi-layered and that the constitutional implications of the HRA are still being worked out. The essay ends with a forward-looking quotation, leaving the reader to continue thinking about the question as the journey ends.

Editing the answer

The final stage in the journey of writing (rather than reading) is *editing* and *reviewing* your answer. This is not an easy task. It is often far easier to spot mistakes in the work of others than those in your own work. Ideally you should put the essay aside for a day or two after writing it, before turning your hand to the task of editing. There is a tendency when reading your own work to read what you think you wrote rather than reading the words printed on the page; and even if you do limit yourself to the words on the printed page, it is easy to assume that they mean what you intended them to mean, rather than meaning what they do actually say.

If you write your essay using word processing software, most obvious spelling errors will be identified by proprietary spell checks, although it is always a good idea to ensure that the spell check is set to British English. However, most standard word processing packages do not contain many legal terms or proper names, so you will still need to keep an eye out for spelling mistakes when reviewing your work.

When editing your work, look in particular at the

- structure,
- content,
- grammar, and
- style,

bearing in mind especially the need to ensure *coherence* while eliminating *inaccuracies* and *irrelevant material*. Additionally, you must always ensure that you have complied with any specific presentation instructions you have been given and that all your sources are properly referenced and acknowledged.

● Conclusion

A good essay will be well written, well presented and contain only relevant material. And, above all, it will *answer the question*. Preparing your work thoroughly will help you to interpret the question, undertake appropriate research and formulate a plan. At the end of the planning stage, the content should have been adequately sifted so as to be *relevant* to the question and *directed* to an appropriate answer.

Writing your essay following the recognised conventions of grammar, spelling, punctuation and referencing will improve the style and presentation of your work. A careful final editing of the essay will pick up most of the errors that remain. This method of essay writing will not produce perfection and one or two errors will evade even the most meticulous editor. Nevertheless, if you plan and write essays following this approach you should begin to produce good law essays; and for your labours you should receive good marks.

11 Answering Problem Questions

Legal problem solving involves a number of distinct steps. First, you must identify both the legal and factual issues in a given situation. Secondly, you must select the relevant law from a wide range of cases and statutes. Thirdly, you must apply this law to the specific facts of the problem. Fourthly, you must conclude by either advising the parties of the probable outcome of the case, or summarising your discussion of the issue raised by the problem, depending on the instructions you have been given. As well as being an essential skill for students, problem solving is a skill used by professional lawyers on a daily basis. Ultimately, it is a skill best gained by practice.

● Introduction

Although many people accept the truth of the saying that *knowledge is power*, the reality of the matter is a great deal less clear-cut. In fact, there is much to be said for the view that knowledge, like money, is intrinsically worthless. After all, taking the example of money, why should anyone want to accumulate mass-produced little metal discs carrying embossed images, words and figures, and mass-produced pieces of printed paper bearing one of a range of identical designs? The answer is obvious: *if the discs of metal and pieces of paper are coins and banknotes, you can spend them*; but if you were shipwrecked on a desert island, even the most immense fortune would be worthless *because you would not be able to use it*. Similarly, no matter how extensive your knowledge of law may be, it will be worthless *unless you can use it*. In this chapter we show you how to *use* your knowledge of the law to answer problem questions.

Law students are often given problem questions in the form of a factual scenario. They are then required to advise one or more of the parties, or to discuss the legal issues which arise. We will look at two problem questions shortly, but before doing so it is worth saying something about how you should approach them.

● Planning and writing an answer

Introduction

The building blocks for answering a problem question are your *knowledge* and *understanding* of the relevant law. However, examiners do not want to see a pile of raw materials: they want to see the finished product. In this context, the finished product is the answer you have created using the building blocks of knowledge and understanding. The construction of a good answer, like the construction of a good building, requires careful planning and skilful execution. In the hands of the unskilled the best materials are not fully exploited. If you give an unskilled builder good bricks and mortar you will still end up with a badly constructed building, albeit one made of good materials. The four-stage process we outline below is a technique for developing the skills to construct a good answer to problem questions using your building blocks of knowledge and understanding. It is used first at the planning stage; it is then used again at the writing stage.

Identifying the issues

The first step in producing a good answer to a problem question is to *identify the issues*. This is a matter of identifying *what the question is about from a legal point of view*. At the *planning* stage, you will be reading through the question with a view to spotting and noting the issues. Identifying the issues is essentially a process of *analysis*, which in this context means separating the question into its distinct parts, recognising each fact and issue, and then ranking those facts and issues in terms of relevance and importance. At the *writing* stage you will write a short opening paragraph, setting out the issues you have identified and will then address in your answer.

The testing of skills begins with the reading of the problem question. First, you need to break down the problem and identify the *material facts*. Always read the question *questioningly*. If, in the facts of the problem question, you are told a child is seven years old ask, 'why have I been told this? What is the legal significance of this fact in the context of the question?' The only true exception to the proposition that all the facts are included for a reason (namely to be commented upon in answering the question) is that some facts are included simply to make the story more readable. The name of the café in the first example discussed below falls into this category. There is, however, also a quasi-exception, where facts are introduced by way of red herrings. Some students regard this as a form of cheating by the examiner, on the basis that such facts do not relate to the answer; but this is to misunderstand the point. Red herrings will only distract those who do not really understand the relevant law, and therefore their introduction is a perfectly legitimate way of testing the true extent of the students' understanding. In other words, and being perfectly consistent with the general principle that all facts are mentioned for a reason, red herrings are introduced so that you may comment on them, even though your only comment will be to identify their irrelevance.

Secondly, you need to identify the *legal issues* raised by the *facts*. It may be that you consider the facts to be too far-fetched to be taken seriously. Two points arise. First, the facts of some of the most important legal cases are themselves quite improbable, as the discussion of *Donoghue v Stevenson* (below) illustrates. Secondly, and perhaps more importantly, you must understand that the questions are constructed in order to bring out certain points which the examiner expects you to be able to identify and discuss. This may well result in an intrinsically improbable storyline; but problem questions never pretend to be essays in social realism anyway.

Finally, you need to identify any *legal claims* and *defences* that the parties may have. A party who has no recognisable legal claim, or a party who does have such a claim but who will be met with a cast-iron legal defence, will have no legal redress. Evaluating possible claims and defences at the planning stage will not only help you to identify the contentious legal issues raised by the problem, but will also enable you to dispose of any straightforward and uncontentious issues in a sentence or two.

Selecting the relevant law

At the planning stage, step two requires you to *select the law* which is relevant to the issues identified at stage one. At the writing stage, this is made explicit when you *state* the law you have selected to support the legal claims and defences you have identified. Selecting the relevant law is a filtering process where you sift out any irrelevant law and retain only the law which is pertinent to your answer.

The principal authorities in English law (and other common law jurisdictions) are statutes, delegated legislation, and case law, although in many subjects it will also be necessary to ask whether there are any relevant provisions of EU law or of the European Convention on Human Rights as made relevant to the English legal system by the Human Rights Act 1998. (The EU dimension and the impact of the European Convention on Human Rights, together with the Human Rights Act, are discussed in Chapters 2 and 5, respectively.) It is important to bear in mind the weight of the various authorities (in terms of the level of court) when selecting the law to support your arguments. Remember that no court can quash primary legislation, and *persuasive authorities* (for example, cases decided by the Privy Council or the High Court of Australia) might influence a court to follow a particular line of reasoning but do not bind it to do so.

Applying the law

The third step in the problem-solving process requires you to *apply* the *relevant* law to the *material* facts. It is your ability to do this convincingly that demonstrates the true extent of your *understanding*. One type of classically bad answer simply reproduces, more or less accurately depending on the extent of your knowledge and understanding, *all* the law on the topic, with no attempt at selection or application. (In other words, it is a *£10 note answer*, of the kind we identified in the context of essay writing at p. 174.) In terms of professional practice, the equivalent would be simply to read aloud to the client the whole of the relevant chapter from a textbook and then claim that this amounts to giving the client legal advice.

Applying the law at the *planning* stage means considering how the law you have selected fits the material facts. Later, at the *writing* stage, you will apply the law to support your discussion, and thus demonstrate that you can construct a logical argument.

Concluding with advice

In most problem questions (as in the examples we shall be considering shortly) you will be asked either to advise one or more of the parties, or to discuss the legal issues which arise from the facts. If you are required to give advice, you may feel that once you have identified the issues, selected and applied the relevant law and produced a logical answer following the steps outlined above, it will be obvious to the examiner what your advice will be. Nevertheless, you should conclude your answer with a short paragraph containing your advice. Similarly, if the question requires you to *discuss the legal issues arising from the facts*, you should conclude with a short summary of the issues you have been discussing.

This four-fold approach to answering problems is not a quick fix solution. It does not help you avoid attending lectures and tutorials or seminars, nor does it exempt you from extending your knowledge of the law through appropriate library work. However, it does help you put your knowledge to good use.

● Worked examples

Introduction

Having discussed the skills you will require when planning and writing answers to problem questions we will now look at some worked examples to illustrate the planning and writing process. We will do this by looking at two questions based on the type of work you will be doing in tutorials or seminars, for coursework and in examinations. In the first question we will establish the importance of planning if you are to construct a good answer to a problem question; in the second question we provide a step-by-step illustration of the planning and writing of an answer following our suggested four-fold approach. Of course, by the time you are answering actual questions, you will have studied a substantial body of law, and therefore those questions may be more complex than our examples. Nevertheless, our examples will provide a useful introduction to the skills you will need to master if you are to impress the examiners with the extent of your understanding of the law. Furthermore, since problem solving is a transferable skill, your study of our examples will also provide you with the basis for a structured approach to problem solving in other contexts, which will be invaluable to you in your future career, whether or not this lies within the legal profession.

Problem 1

Our first problem provides a relatively simple illustration of the points raised so far, but in order to understand it we must first consider the case of *Donoghue v Stevenson* [1932] AC 562.

The facts were that May Donoghue went with a friend to the Wellmeadow café in Paisley, Scotland, where her friend bought her an 'ice cream float'. This treat consisted of ice cream in a tumbler, into which ginger beer was poured. After Mrs Donoghue had consumed some of the drink, her friend topped up the tumbler with more ginger beer. This action revealed that the bottle, which was opaque, contained not only ginger beer but also the decomposed remains of a snail. (It is, of course, relevant that the bottle was opaque, because, if it had been clear, the remains of the snail would have been plainly visible.) Mrs Donoghue suffered prolonged and acute stomach pain, together with repeated vomiting and depression.

Since Mrs Donoghue had not bought the drink herself she could not sue in contract so she brought a claim in tort against the manufacturer. The basic elements of the tort of negligence were well known to the common law before *Donoghue v Stevenson*, and can be summarised thus:

- the defendant must owe the claimant a *duty of care*;
- this duty must have been *breached*;
- the breach must be the *cause* of the claimant's damage (or loss);
- the damage must *not* be too *remote*.

(Since *Donoghue v Stevenson* did not involve the question of *remoteness of damage*, we will not be exploring that idea here.)

The problem Mrs Donoghue faced was that the case law did not establish a general rule defining the relationships between parties that gave rise to a *duty of care*, but simply identified certain factual situations as creating duty relationships. For example, the cases established that dock-owners owed a duty of care to some (but not all) people using the gangways between docked ships. The cases also established that people who put into circulation 'articles dangerous in themselves' (like loaded firearms) owed a duty of care to people who might come within the vicinity of the dangerous articles. The decision of the House of Lords in *Donoghue v Stevenson* (which, incidentally was in Mrs Donoghue's favour) led to the development of the modern tort of negligence, based on the *neighbour principle*. According to this principle, which is contained in the speech of Lord Atkin, you owe a duty of care to your neighbour. Crucially, this general formula goes on to define *neighbours* as *those people who are so closely and directly affected by your actions (or omissions) that, when you are considering your actions (or omissions), you would reasonably have these people in mind*.

Influential though Lord Atkin's *neighbour principle* has been in the subsequent development of the law, the actual *ratio* of *Donoghue v Stevenson* is somewhat narrower, and is neatly summed up in the headnote of the report.

The manufacturer of an article of food, medicine or the like, sold by him to a distributor in circumstances which prevent the distributor or ultimate purchaser or consumer from discovering by inspection any defect, is under a legal duty to the ultimate purchaser or consumer to take reasonable care that the article is free from defect likely to cause injury to health.

For present purposes, this necessarily brief consideration of *Donoghue v Stevenson* will suffice and the first problem question can now be considered. In other words, having gained some useful legal *knowledge*, we are now in a position to *apply* it. Consider the following facts.

Adam buys a bottle of soda water from Cobra's café. Eve drinks some of the soda water. Later that day Adam discovers the decomposing remains of a slug in the bottle. Advise Eve of any claim(s) she may have in the tort of negligence.

A cursory reading of the problem might lead to an answer based simply on knowledge of *Donoghue v Stevenson*. Such an answer might read:

> *Donoghue v Stevenson* [1932] AC 562 establishes that the manufacturer of a product owes a duty of care to the ultimate consumer. Where, through the carelessness of the manufacturer, a consumer is caused damage by a defect in a product (and the consumer had no opportunity to identify the defect) the manufacturer will be liable in the tort of negligence.

This is not a good answer. It makes no reference to the facts or the issues raised in the problem and simply repeats the material as originally presented. It demonstrates the ability to recall and reproduce information, but nothing more. A student who produced such an answer could be said to *know* about the law, but this is not enough: we need to get beyond this and show the examiner that we have *identified* the legal issues and *selected* the relevant law, and can *apply* it in the context of this particular factual situation. Consider this answer:

> Eve can sue Cobra's Café in the tort of negligence. The facts of this case are very similar to those in *Donoghue v Stevenson* [1932] AC 562; the slug in the soda water is as much a defect in the product as the snail was in the ginger beer. In *Donoghue* the court held that even though the claimant did not buy the product the manufacturer owed her a duty of care; thus even though Eve did not buy the soda water, the manufacturer will not escape liability.

A student who produced an answer like this is demonstrating some *understanding* of the law. One way of showing that you understand something is to rewrite it in your own words; this answer shows a familiarity with the case law and the capacity to reword and explain this comprehension to others. The issue (negligence) has been *identified*, the relevant case has been *selected* and there is some attempt to *apply* the law to a different set of circumstances. However, several criticisms may be made. First, in terms of *issue identification*, the answer does not set out the elements of the tort or identify the contentious issues in the problem. Secondly, in terms of style, it is much better to state the principle of law first and then apply this to the facts. Thirdly, and most importantly, the answer reveals that the student has not read the question with sufficient care.

You will recall that we said that, at the *planning* stage, *analysis* of the question requires a *careful* and *questioning* reading. Consider the problem and ask: do any facts that could have a bearing on your answer appear to have been omitted? Are there are any uncertainties in the facts we are given in the problem? An essential part of the planning stage is to break the problem apart so that we can identify the relationships between the parties and distinguish between relevant and irrelevant facts.

Careful analysis of the problem reveals three key issues:

- we are not told whether anyone has suffered any damage or sustained any losses;
- we do not know whether the bottle is clear or opaque or how Adam discovered the slug; and
- we do not know who the manufacturer is.

Since the facts of a problem question are to be taken as stated and cannot be investigated, it is a matter of judgment as to whether alternative analyses should be considered or whether to make a reasonable assumption on the facts. Consider this answer to the problem:

The issue here is whether Eve (E) has a claim in the tort of negligence against the manufacturer of the soda water. To establish a claim, E will need to show that the defendant owed her a duty of care; that this duty was breached; that the breach caused her damage; and that this damage is not too remote. The main points here are whether E is owed a duty of care and if, as a matter of fact and of law, she suffered any damage.

A manufacturer of a product owes a duty of care to the ultimate consumer of a product where through the manufacturer's negligence the consumer, who had no opportunity to inspect the product, suffers loss or damage (*Donoghue v Stevenson* [1932] AC 562).

In *Donoghue v Stevenson*, the claimant could not see the decomposing snail in the opaque bottle; thus she was denied the opportunity to inspect the contents of the bottle before drinking the ginger beer. This was an important factor in the court's reasoning which led to the imposition of liability on the manufacturer. Although we know that Adam discovered the slug in the bottle of soda water, we do not know how he did this. If the soda water (a clear liquid) was in a transparent bottle the manufacturer may escape liability, since one of the central facts of this case would present an essential difference from the situation in *Donoghue v Stevenson*.

We do not know from the facts whether E has suffered any damage. This is important because it is only if she has sustained losses as a result of drinking the soda water that her claim in negligence will succeed.

E is, therefore, advised that unless (1) it is established that she could not inspect the contents of the soda water bottle and (2) that she suffered damage, she should not pursue a claim in the tort of negligence.

In this answer, the legal issues are clearly *identified* in the first paragraph and the elements of the tort are summarised. The most pertinent issues are highlighted and in three short sentences the scene is set. This can only be achieved by careful analysis at the *planning* stage. In the second paragraph the law which we *selected* (and which, of course, is somewhat limited in this example) is *stated* in so far as it is relevant to the facts. Note that there is no reference to the facts of *Donoghue v Stevenson*: only the applicable principle of law is stated. In the third paragraph the emphasis is on *application* of the law and building up an argument. At the *planning* stage, this involves asking how the facts of this problem differ from (or are similar to) the selected law. Here, at the writing stage, the material facts are evaluated against the law stated. The response concludes with advice to Eve. This is brief and not contrived: it simply answers the question posed.

The importance of understanding what you should be doing when answering a problem question is that, whenever you answer such a question, you can ask yourself: *have I demonstrated to the examiner that I know and understand the law and that I can employ the skills of analysis and evaluation in applying the relevant law to the problem*? Unless you can truthfully answer *yes* to this question, you should try again.

Problem 2

In Problem 1 we looked at some typical answers to a question on the basic elements of the tort of negligence and *Donoghue v Stevenson*. In Problem

2 we will look at a more complex factual scenario and work step-by-step through the four-fold approach to planning and writing in order to construct an answer to the problem. First, we will add to our knowledge of the tort of negligence by looking in more detail at the breach of duty point, and in particular at the standard of care owed by the drivers of motor vehicles.

We have already seen that in an action for negligence the first thing a successful claimant must establish is that the defendant owed him or her a duty of care. In many situations there will be no problem. For example, it is now well established that manufacturers owe a duty of care to the ultimate consumer of their products and that doctors owe a duty of care to their patients. Coming closer to the problem which we are about to consider, it is also well established that road users owe a duty of care to other road users. As Kennedy J stated, in *Dulieu v White* [1901] 2 KB 669, 671–672, a driver on a road owes a duty to use 'reasonable and proper care and skill so as not to injure either persons lawfully using the highway or property adjoining the highway, or persons ... occupying that property'.

Once the existence of a duty of care is established, the question of whether the defendant is in breach of that duty must be addressed. This is decided by judging the defendant's conduct against that of a hypothetical 'reasonable person'. This is primarily an *objective* test, because essentially the court asks, 'what would a reasonable person have done in these circumstances?' rather than seeking to enter the mind of the defendant in an attempt to identify what he or she was actually thinking. (There are many areas of law where the court will, indeed, seek to enter into the mind of a particular person: this is called applying a *subjective* test.) If the answer is that, on the particular facts of the case, the defendant's conduct fell below the standard of the 'reasonable person' then the defendant will be held to be in breach of the duty which he or she owed; and, if that breach of duty caused damage to the claimant, the defendant will usually be liable. With these points in mind, we will now look at two cases, in both of which the 'reasonable person' is the 'reasonable driver'.

In *Roberts v Ramsbottom* [1980] 1 WLR 823, the defendant suffered a stroke shortly before leaving his house to drive to work. Although the stroke had no obvious physical consequences, it did impair the functioning of his brain. The result was that Mr Ramsbottom drove off, without being conscious of the fact that he was ill. His journey lasted less than twenty minutes. In that time, he crashed into the back of a stationary van, narrowly missed running over two men working in the road, knocked a cyclist off his bicycle, and collided head-on with a parked car. The question for the High Court was whether the defendant could escape liability for the damage he had caused on the basis that his actions were completely beyond his control, or if he should be judged by the objective standard of care of an ordinary reasonable driver. Neill J, relying on a number of criminal cases, found that the courts had been reluctant to absolve drivers of liability where the disabling event was not sudden, and concluded, therefore (at p. 832), that 'nothing less than total loss of consciousness' would enable the defendant to avoid liability. Since Mr Ramsbottom's consciousness had only been impaired, rather than completely lost, he was held liable for the damage which he caused. Significantly, Mr Ramsbottom had got out of his car after crashing into the stationary van and had engaged in a brief discussion with the van's occupants before continuing his journey. The judge considered this would allow the claimants to succeed on a second ground, namely that the defendant had continued to drive not only when he was unfit to do so, but when he should have been aware of his unfitness.

The later case of *Mansfield v Weetabix* [1998] 1 WLR 1263, concerns a lorry driver who, unknowingly, suffered from a condition known as malignant insulinoma. As a consequence of this condition the driver's brain was starved of glucose, resulting in improper brain functions. The lorry's 40 mile journey ended when the driver approached a bend too quickly and crashed into the claimant's shop. The driver had been seen driving erratically at two earlier points in his journey, and had been stopped by the police after he collided with the rear of a trailer which he was following. The question for the Court of Appeal was whether the judge at first instance had correctly interpreted the law in applying *Roberts v Ramsbottom* to the case. Leggatt LJ, delivering the unanimous judgment of the court, said *Roberts* was wrongly decided on the first ground, preferring to say (at p. 1267) that, in civil cases, a driver could escape liability where 'the disabling event [was] gradual, provided that the driver [was] unaware of it'. The court went on to hold (at p. 1268) that although the driver suffered from only 'an impaired degree of consciousness' as a result of his malignant insulinoma, the fact that he was unaware that he suffered from the condition meant that he was not to be held liable for the damage that he had caused. The standard of care in the case was that of 'the reasonable competent driver [who is] unaware that he is or may be suffering from a condition that impairs his ability to drive'. (*Ibid.*)

Before reading the problem question that follows you might find it useful to check your knowledge of the law we have examined thus far. In particular, you will find it helpful to note the differences between *Roberts v Ramsbottom* and *Mansfield v Weetabix*.

Now, consider the following question.

Amber was diagnosed some years ago as being diabetic. She received a great deal of advice at that time, which placed particular emphasis on the importance of taking her medication conscientiously and eating regular meals, and how to identify the symptoms of hypoglycaemia (low blood sugar level), such as dizziness and blurred vision. One morning she oversleeps and in the rush to leave her house and get to work she gets into her car and drives off without eating any breakfast. On the way to work, Amber suffers from increasingly severe bouts of blurred vision and fails to stop at a red traffic signal. Amber narrowly avoids knocking Jade off her bicycle, but collides with Emerald's car.

Meanwhile, Beryl, having crashed her car into a lamppost, is stationary some 200 metres ahead of the traffic signal. Jade stops when she sees the accident and finds Beryl collapsed and unconscious in her seat. While Jade is calling the emergency services, Beryl regains consciousness and attempts to drive off, running over Jade's bicycle before bringing the car to a halt. Medical tests reveal that Beryl has suffered an epileptic seizure. Beryl has never had an epileptic seizure before and had no reason to believe she was susceptible to epilepsy.

Advise Amber and Beryl as to their liabilities in the tort of negligence.

To answer this question we first need to plan. *Identifying* the issues means re-reading the question, noting as we do so the *material facts* and the *legal issues* raised by those facts. Remember to read *questioningly*. For example, you might ask 'Is it significant that Amber did not eat breakfast?' The answer is 'Yes'. It is significant that Amber did not eat anything, because diabetics who skip meals increase their chances of hypoglycaemia. If you cannot answer all the questions you raise during re-reading the question, do what research you can in the circumstances. If you are in an examination, your general knowledge, your dictionary (if you are allowed to use one) and your wits may be your only resources. If you are answering the problem question as a piece of coursework, a quick search on the Internet will often provide the answer.

Returning to the question, and dealing first with Amber, we note:

- she knows that she suffers from diabetes and knows (or should know) that skipping meals might lead to hypoglycaemia;
- she knows (or should know) that blurred vision is a symptom of hypoglycaemia;

- she owes a duty of care to other road users;
- she might be in breach of that duty by failing to stop at the red traffic signal (with the key issue here being whether she should be judged by the objective standard of care of the reasonable driver and, if so, whether she fell below that standard of care);
- she caused damage to Emerald's car; and
- she might raise the defence that she had an impaired degree of consciousness.

Turning to Beryl, we note:

- she had a sudden epileptic seizure while driving her car and as a result of this has crashed into a lamppost;
- she had no knowledge of her condition;
- she owes a duty of care to other road users;
- she may be in breach of that duty by (i) crashing into a lamppost and (ii) driving over Jade's bicycle (with the main issue here being whether she fell below the standard of care of a reasonable driver suffering a sudden disability);
- she caused damage to the lamppost;
- she caused damage to Jade's bicycle;
- in respect of the damage to the lamppost (presumably owned by the Highway Authority), she could raise the defence that she suffered a sudden and total loss of consciousness and was not aware of the condition that caused her disability; and
- in respect of the damage to Jade's bicycle, she could raise the defence that through impaired consciousness she did not know she was unfit to drive.

Now that we have *identified* both the *material facts* and the *legal issues* arising from those facts, we need to *select* the relevant *law*. In our example this is straightforward, since we have only looked at relevant cases. In the problem questions you will answer during your studies there are three reasons why this process will not be so simple. First, you will have to select the relevant law from a much larger body of law drawn from both cases and statutes. Secondly, having selected the applicable cases and statutes, you will need to examine these materials in detail, and perhaps carry out further research to discover whether there are other cases or statutes which are relevant to the legal issues raised by the problem. (Clearly this point does not apply to examinations.) Thirdly, the level of the court that made the decision might be relevant to the arguments you intend to develop and therefore you should note this. For example, in the cases we have selected here, we note that *Roberts* is a first instance decision of the High Court and that *Mansfield* is a decision of the Court of Appeal.

The third step in the planning process to consider how to *apply the law to the facts* of the problem question. What we are doing here is seeing how the selected law fits (or does not fit) the facts. We have done this by constructing a simple table (below) that we can readily refer to when we come to the writing stage. In the left-hand column we note the law and in the right hand column we consider how it applies to the facts of the problem.

Dulieu v White (High Court) A driver owes a duty of care to other road users.	Amber Beryl	– Owes a duty of care to other road users. – Owes a duty of care to other road users.
Roberts v Ramsbottom (High Court) (1) The standard of care is the ordinary 'reasonable driver' unless the driver suffers a sudden and total loss of consciousness. (2) A driver who continues to drive when unfit to do so or when he should be aware of his unfitness to drive will not escape liability.	Amber Beryl Amber Beryl	– Suffers a gradual impairment of consciousness. – Liable under Roberts. – Suffers a sudden and total loss of consciousness causing her to crash into a lamppost. – Not liable under Roberts. – Continues to drive when she experiences blurred vision. – Liable under Roberts. – Drives over Jade's bicycle when she might have known she was unfit to drive. – Liable under Roberts?
Mansfield v Weetabix (Court of Appeal) The standard of care is the 'reasonable driver' who is unaware that he is suffering from a condition (that transpires gradually or suddenly) which impairs his ability to drive.	Amber Beryl	– Her condition gradually worsened but she knew she suffered from diabetes and knew/should have known that blurred vision is a symptom of hypoglycaemia. – Liable under Mansfield. – Did not know that she had epilepsy; thus she could not anticipate an epileptic seizure. – Not liable to Highway Authority under Mansfield. – Not aware of the disabling condition which impaired her consciousness and her ability to drive. – Not liable to Jade under Mansfield.

In this question we have been asked to advise Amber and Beryl as to their liabilities in the tort of negligence. Our answer will *conclude* with advice drawing on our application of the law to the facts. Some points are uncontroversial and we effectively drew our conclusions on these points as we applied the law to the facts in the table. Other issues are less clear-cut and it is these points that we need to discuss in our answer if we are to gain high marks.

The planning stage is now complete and we are now ready to write our answer. You might be wondering how you will ever manage to plan in this way under examination conditions. The simple answer is to prac- tise throughout your course by using this method to prepare for seminars and tutorials and when doing coursework. You will also find that using this structure when planning answers to old examination questions will be a great help to you when revising for your examinations, because this will ensure that you revise actively, engaging with the kind of material you will encounter in the examination itself. You will also find that, if you plan ef- fectively, you will spend less time writing; and, more importantly, you will answer the question in a structured fashion which will ensure that you keep the focus on the relevant issues. Here is our answer to the problem:

The issue for Amber (A) in this scenario is whether she is liable to Emerald (E) for the damage she caused to E's car. Ultimately this will turn on whether A can successfully raise a defence, based on her impaired consciousness, in order to avoid liability in any negligence claim E might bring. Beryl (B) is likely to be sued by Jade (J) for the damage B caused to her bicycle; and by the owner of the lamppost, presumed to be the Highway Authority (HA). B will want to know whether she can resist these claims on the basis of her sudden and complete loss of consciousness and the fact that she was unaware of her unfitness to drive. To succeed in a claim in the tort of negligence, the claimants will need to show that the defendants owed them a duty of care; that this duty was breached; that the breach caused their damages; and that the damage was not too remote.

In *Dulieu v White* [1901] 2 KB 669 it was held that road users owe a duty of care to other road users and to persons and property close to the highway. On this authority it is clear that A owes a duty of care to E and B owes a duty of care to HA and J. Having established that defendants owe the claimants a duty of care, the next issue to address is whether the defendants breached the duty of care owed. This is a key issue for both A and B and the court would determine the matter by measuring the defendants against the requisite standard of care. Two possible routes are open to the court. First it could judge the defendants against the objective standard of the ordinary 'reasonable driver'; secondly, it could use the more subjective test of the 'reasonable driver' who is unaware that she is suffering from a condition which impairs her ability to drive.

Looking first at A, she has suffered a gradual impairment of consciousness due to a hypoglycaemic attack which is a classic symptom of diabetes. A knew that she was a diabetic and skipped eating breakfast, which is the probable cause of her hypoglycaemic attack.

In *Roberts v Ramsbottom* [1980] 1 WLR 823 Neill J held that a defendant should be evaluated by the standard of care of the ordinary 'reasonable driver' unless the driver suffered a sudden and total loss of consciousness. Since A has suffered only a gradual and partial loss of consciousness, she would be judged by the standard of the 'reasonable driver' under *Roberts*. The requirement for a sudden and total loss of consciousness was, however, overruled by the Court of Appeal in *Mansfield v Weetabix* [1998] 1 WLR 1263. The court applied the 'reasonable driver' test subjectively holding that the lorry driver in the case was to be judged by the standard of the 'reasonable driver' who is unaware that he is suffering from a condition, which transpires gradually or suddenly, that impairs his ability to drive. The difficulty A faces is that, although the law no longer requires the sudden and total loss of consciousness, the court in *Mansfield* limited the subjective test to drivers who are unaware of their condition. A is not unaware that she suffers from diabetes and should know that not eating her breakfast might lead to a hypoglycaemic episode. Further, applying the second element of the decision in *Roberts* (which was not overruled by the Court of Appeal in *Mansfield*), A could also incur liability for driving when she was unfit to do so, or when she should have been aware of her unfitness to drive. Applying this test, A ought to have stopped driving as soon as she realised that her vision was blurred.

Turning to B and considering first her potential liability to HA, B crashed into HA's property after a sudden epileptic seizure, causing complete loss of consciousness. This would satisfy the requirement for a sudden and total loss of consciousness under *Roberts* and the modified standard of care in *Mansfield*, making it highly probable that B would escape liability for the damage she caused to HA. This was

B's first epileptic seizure and she did not know she was susceptible to epileptic seizures. She would be judged as the 'reasonable driver' who is unaware of a condition that impaired her ability to drive.

B was not, however, unconscious when she damaged J's bicycle, and the Court of Appeal did not criticise the second element of *Roberts* in *Mansfield* so it remains good law. If B were judged on this second part of *Roberts*, namely that she drove when unfit to do so or when she should have been aware that she was unfit to do so, the decision would turn on whether B was actually *aware* that she was unfit to drive. B is clearly unfit to drive, but given the seriousness of her condition it may well be that B was unaware of her unfitness to drive. The facts of the problem differ from those in *Roberts*, where the defendant never lost consciousness at any point and actually got out of his car and held a short conversation with the workmen whose van he crashed into before continuing his journey. Here, there is no evidence that B was ever roused to that level of consciousness and it may be that B was still very dazed and confused when she drove her car over J's bicycle. While the claimant might argue that B's ability to put the car into gear suggests some degree of consciousness, there is no indication that B's level of awareness is any higher (and some suggestion that it may well be lower) than that of the defendant in *Mansfield*. In that case, the defendant drove his lorry some 40 miles before crashing into the claimant's shop: here B has moved her car only a very short distance.

A is advised that she is likely to be held liable for the damage she caused to E's car, since she suffered no sudden and total loss of consciousness and either was aware or should have been aware that she was unfit to drive. B is advised that the sudden and total loss of consciousness will absolve her of fault and liability in respect of the damage to HA. B's liability to J is more problematic. However, it is submitted that she should not be held liable on the basis that she was not aware of her disabling condition and that her level of consciousness was seriously impaired to a degree at least equal to, and probably greater than, that of the defendant in *Mansfield*.

● **Conclusion**

Having read this chapter you should have a satisfactory understanding of how to approach answering problem questions. If you want to move on from simply understanding *how* to answer problem questions and progress to actually *answering them well*, you will need to practise. Tutorials and seminars will provide ample opportunity for such practice. Practising the technique of answering questions will not only improve the structure and content of your work but will also help you to develop your written English skills (as discussed in Chapter 9) into an appropriate style of academic writing. A logical structure that draws on only relevant material is the key to a good answer, but to score high marks the structure and content need to be revealed through a written style which demonstrates your ability to use correct grammar, spelling and punctuation, as well as appropriate vocabulary.

12 Oral Skills

An effective oral presentation requires thorough preparation and real familiarity with the subject matter. A successful presentation will have explicit goals, be appropriately structured for the needs of the audience and make creative and sensitive use of visual, verbal and non-verbal communication. When approached in a careful way, delivering oral presentations need not be as stressful an activity as many students find it to be.

● Introduction

Your career as a student is likely to give you many opportunities for participating in oral presentations, some of which may well count for assessment. The nature of these presentations, whether assessed or not, will vary quite widely: some will involve working with other students and making joint or group presentations, while others will be undertaken and presented alone. Certain presentations will be quite informal and take place in small group sessions, whereas others may require a more formal setting, such as a moot court. Some contexts, such as mooting, require you to follow a particular code of etiquette, but the basic skills and sensitivities required for fluent and effective oral communication, which we discuss in this chapter, remain the same whatever the situation.

As with every skill, you will find that the best way to improve your mastery of oral presentation skills is through practice. Every oral presentation you make is an opportunity to develop your skills, refine your technique and build up your self-confidence. Improving your oral skills will help you in your academic studies and beyond. At the most obvious level, effective oral communication skills are essential to the advocacy work of many barristers and solicitors. Additionally, however, these skills are increasingly tested and valued by employers, which means you may well find that you are asked to make oral presentations in a variety of job interviews, and not only in the selection processes for aspiring trainee solicitors and pupil barristers.

● Preparing the presentation

Identifying the purpose

The first thing you need to do is to identify the purpose of your presentation. This involves consideration of two questions:

- who is my audience? and
- what do I want to achieve?

In order to determine what you want to achieve, you will first need to clarify your goals and understand your role in the presentation. If, for example, you are asked to make an oral presentation, in a small group session, to other students, the purpose (in terms of what you want to achieve) might be to share your perspective on the topic. Your role in this case will be that of a teacher and will involve imparting information, explaining concepts or ideas and stimulating the group's understanding. If, however, your presentation requires you to participate in a debate, your role will be that of an advocate and you will concentrate on developing a compelling argument and persuading the audience to share your point of view. In each case you will want the audience:

- to understand what you are saying; and
- be interested in what you say.

Additionally, in some situations at least, you will want to

- convince your audience by the quality of your arguments.

You will, however, only achieve these goals if you take into account the expectations and needs of your audience.

People will listen to what you have to say when the subject matter is intrinsically interesting to them, or where you make it interesting to them by arousing their curiosity. Audiences will also listen to material that is likely to be useful to them. If you have a free choice of topic you might choose one that you think will interest the audience. If the topic is specified, you can still take a particular stance on the topic to engage the audience's attention. If your presentation requires expert knowledge of a subject, and the majority of your audience lack that expertise, pitch your presentation at a level that most people will understand. Keeping an eye on the audience's body language will often help you to keep track of whether they are following you, or whether you need to explain the technical aspects of the topic more clearly. Always bear in mind the simple fact that if you forget the needs of your audience, they will also forget you.

Sometimes your audience will be a mixed group in terms of ability and topic interest. When this happens, it is important to decide which groups in the audience are most valuable to you. Imagine, for example, that you are a student approaching graduation, who is appearing in the final of a prestigious mooting competition, and that the case concerns an issue of shipping law (which is an area of law in which you ultimately wish to specialise). The first, and most important, person to consider is the moot judge, even if you know that the audience also contains some first year students (who know nothing about shipping law), as well as a number of shipping law practitioners, who are your potential employers. Not surprisingly, most people, faced with such an audience, would focus on the judge, in the hope that this will deliver the double reward of winning the competition while also impressing the practitioners. (The topic of mooting is discussed in more detail at pp. 214–220.)

At a more mundane level, where a course is assessed by oral presentation, it is worth emphasising that a vital part of the purpose of your presentation will be to comply with the marking criteria and presentation rubric produced by your college or university. It is important to discover how your presentation will be evaluated, particularly in terms of the weighting between subject knowledge, analysis of the topic, and oral presentation skills.

Researching and planning

Once you have determined the purpose of your presentation, you can begin the research. You may find it helpful to formulate the purpose of your presentation as a question, or to draft a presentation title, to ensure that you know the boundaries of your research before you begin the process. The research method for an oral presentation is in some ways like that for an essay, in that it calls for active and selective reading (see the discussions of the SQ3R technique at pp. 15 and 179), where the emphasis is on identifying *only* that material which is relevant to your presentation. However, the processes also differ, since an oral presentation gives you the opportunity to use materials such as pictures, graphics, statistics and anecdotes. In particular, illustrations, whether graphic or anecdotal, are useful ways of varying the content of your presentation, since they provide your audience with breaks from the heavier material and thus increase your chances of keeping their attention.

Tailor your research to the length of the presentation: if your presentation is only seven or eight minutes long you will not be able to cover very much material and should not try to do so. Do not exceed the time limit for your presentation simply because you have too much material, nor for any other reason within your control. Audiences react badly to speakers who overrun their allotted time, and if the presentation is assessed you will lose marks.

Plan the presentation using the results of your research to build a logically ordered and coherent presentation. One commonly cited method for ordering material in an oral presentation is the 'three times rule' which says that when addressing your audience you should 'tell them what you are going to tell them; tell them; tell them what you have told them'. The introduction is the place to tell the listeners 'what you are going to tell them', the main body of the presentation is where you 'tell them' and the conclusion is where to 'tell them what you have told them'. In the conclusion you should take particular care to demonstrate that you have achieved all you promised in your introduction.

In one sense, there is nothing remarkable about the 'three times rule'. It simply reminds the speaker that a presentation must have a beginning, a middle and an end. However, it serves the additional, and very important, function of emphasising the need for *planned repetition* in public speaking. For this reason many people plan the main body of their presentation first. This reduces the risk of making claims in the introduction that cannot be achieved in the time available and also helps to ensure that only the aims that have been fulfilled in the presentation are featured in the conclusion.

Plan the main body of the presentation by listing the issues and sub-issues you need to cover, and then arrange them into some kind of order. Use headings and subheadings to represent each point and sub-point, and sketch out your plan on a single side of paper if at all possible. Ideally, you should provide yourself with an overview of what you are aiming to achieve. This will help you to identify not only any gaps in your material and flaws in your argument, but also any aspects of your material or argument that you can jettison because they do not contribute anything useful to the overall enterprise. Some topics work best if they are presented in a chronological order, while others lend themselves to a thematic, topic-based, structure.

Where you need to develop an argument, your presentation should follow a logical order revealing each step of your line of reasoning. Above all, the content and structure of your presentation needs to be planned for delivery as speech, in a way that makes sense of the topic and in a manner which makes it as easy as possible for your listeners to follow what you are saying. Once the main body of the presentation is in order, create an outline of your introduction and conclusions, before starting to make notes for your presentation.

Using notes

One of the biggest temptations when preparing for oral presentations, especially for the inexperienced public speaker, is to produce a written text. This is not an appropriate or helpful way to prepare for oral presentations and should be avoided. The appeal of having a written text in front of you is easy to understand and is frequently justified by a comment like 'I just want it as a back-up in case I get lost or nervous'. Two problems usually emerge. First, when people get nervous during presentations and have the text to hand they cannot always quickly locate the information they want (since they have not actually been following the text word for word) which results in greater anxiety and, at times, complete panic. Secondly, once people turn to the text they never leave it; and, moreover, they begin to speak too quickly, their eyes remained glued to the script and all engagement with the audience is lost. Consequently, the oral presentation starts to sound like an essay being read aloud and the listeners are lost.

This does not mean that you should avoid using notes, but simply that they should be appropriate for the task. Most experienced public speakers use some kind of notes when speaking, if only to stay on track and maintain the balance of their presentation. One way of doing this is to use index cards of a size small enough to hold discreetly in your hand. Many Parliamentarians favour this system of notes; and, provided you do not cram the cards with text, you will readily be able to see, at a glance, the points you want to discuss, and the order in which you want to discuss them. An alternative method is simply to have a copy of your plan or extended outline of your presentation on a single piece of paper that you can glance at from time to time. Visual aids, such as overhead projector transparencies or slides produced in a presentation graphics program such as PowerPoint, can also be used as prompts. If you do use visual aids, however, you would do well also to print paper copies for yourself and keep them in front of you during the presentation. In most rooms and lecture theatres the projection screen is behind the speaker and you do not want to get into the habit of turning your back on your listeners and talking to the projection screen. It is poor style and does little to endear you to the audience.

Before you deliver your presentation, you should try to spend some time familiarising yourself with your notes. Ideally, your preparation schedule should allow enough time for you to put your notes aside for a few days, so that you can return to them with a relatively fresh mind. This will give you a more realistic idea of whether your notes are detailed enough to remind you of all you need to say, as well as giving you time to make any necessary changes. If you are making a presentation for the first time, you may find it helps if you practise by having a trial run in front of a friend. This should give you a fair idea of what the task entails, as well as, hopefully, providing you with some constructive feedback on the content and style of the presentation.

● Delivering the presentation

First impressions
Whenever people meet other people for the first time, they make judgments about them very quickly. First impressions really do count, as people evaluate you by your dress, appearance and body language in a matter of minutes. As the saying known by all sales people goes: *you only get one chance to make a first impression.* If your oral presentation is made in a small group session your audience will, for better or worse, already have an impression of you and will not usually expect you to dress up for the occasion. If you are taking part in a moot, the audience may expect you to dress in formal attire, such as a dark suit; and even if they do not expect this, the judge will. The three key things are to:

- be sensitive to the occasion;
- dress appropriately; and, above all,
- remember that the audience begins evaluating you as soon as they see you.

An oral presentation involves direct face-to-face communication; your words are delivered in person, rather than through the medium of the written word. It is therefore an essential part of the exercise that you will be assessed (formally or informally) not only on *what* you say, but also on *how* you say it. Your audience will judge your delivery by the way you use your voice, maintain eye contact, and use body language such as posture and gestures. Behaviour such as standing with your hands in your pockets, or fiddling with jewellery, will project the wrong image.

Verbal communication

The first words you say will either confirm the audience's initial impression or give you at least some opportunity to alter it. Introduce yourself clearly and confidently, smile and make eye contact with the audience; and then tell them, quite briefly, the purpose of your presentation, before providing an outline of how you will proceed. Your voice is the principal tool through which you will communicate with your listeners and a number of factors need to be taken into account here, namely:

- volume;
- clarity;
- pace; and
- tone.

Your voice should be loud enough for people to hear without them having to struggle to listen. Straining to hear is very tiring and people will stop listening very quickly if they cannot easily hear what you are saying. If you are using a microphone to amplify your voice, or are speaking in unfamiliar surroundings, it is perfectly acceptable to ask the audience if they can hear you. Asking this question straight after you have introduced yourself is also a good way of engaging with the audience at an early stage of the presentation.

Your words will need to be more clearly enunciated when you speak in public than in your ordinary speech. Pronounce the syllables in words clearly and avoid dropping letters at the end of words and allowing words to merge together. A common difficulty is the letter 'g' at the end of words, thus 'going around' ends up sounding like 'goin-round'. Numbers can also be very difficult to hear unless they are clearly pronounced: for example, 'fifteen' and 'fifty' are readily confused.

As well as enunciation, the pace at which people speak affects the clarity of what they say. When addressing other people, even in a small group, you need to speak more slowly than you would in everyday conversation. This does not mean that you need to have long pauses and breaks in your delivery but it does mean that your delivery should be slow enough for your listeners to hear every word and at the same time should flow smoothly. Pauses should, of course, be inserted; both to give people time to consider points you have made, and for dramatic effect.

Finally, you need to vary the tone of your voice to emphasise important points and to keep the audience engaged. Speaking in a monotonous voice will send your audience to sleep and communicate a complete lack of interest in the subject on your part. Voice tone, pitch and pace can be used to deliver a number of signals to your listeners. For example, if you slow down or make a slight pause before increasing the volume of your voice slightly, the audience will realise that you are about to make an important point. Such implicit clues are much better than pausing and saying 'Now this point is very important, please listen carefully'. An audience will soon tire of such interventions.

Non-verbal communication

We have already noted that your dress and body language contribute to the first impression. Body language is, however, culturally specific and what is acceptable behaviour in one country or society may be rude or offensive in another. It is important to recognise, therefore, that first impressions can also be the result of cultural misunderstandings, and that you may need to be sensitive to a variety of cultural norms if you have to address a multicultural audience.

Whatever the cultural setting, your gestures need to match your words; a wide grin will not usually help communicate the gravity of a serious point. You should use your hands, body posture and eye contact only to facilitate communication and you should avoid any gestures that positively distract or annoy your audience. Fiddling with pens, buttons or jewellery, and swaying to and fro at a lectern will undermine the effectiveness of your presentation, whereas a timely and appropriate hand gesture will reinforce your point. Avoid body language which communicates nervousness, such as covering part of your face with a hand or constantly clearing your throat, as well as anything that might suggest that you are untrustworthy, such as looking away from the audience when speaking. Above all, maintaining eye contact with the audience is vital for creating trust and sustaining engagement when addressing a Western European or North American audience.

Using visual aids and handouts

Visual aids can be very powerful presentation tools. They can help to reinforce ideas, compare information and to illustrate points that you make in your presentation. Any visual aids you use should match and enhance your words: an oral presentation should never be overshadowed by cutting edge graphics. PowerPoint slides should not be used as a shield to hide behind, and you should never simply read from the slides. Make sure the audience can read your slides by keeping colour combinations simple (light colours on dark backgrounds or dark colours on light backgrounds work best), and avoid red–green colour combinations since some 10% of the male population are red–green colour blind. The text should be large enough and the fonts clear enough for all the audience to see, and you should avoid cramming text onto slides, since white space on the screen makes the text easier to read. Always check in advance if you will be permitted to use visual aids for an assessed presentation; and, if so, what facilities are provided. There is no mileage in creating PowerPoint slides unless the room you will be speaking in has appropriate computer projection facilities. Finally, never be totally reliant on technology – it sometimes fails.

Handouts are a more difficult issue. A copy of your slides can save people writing notes and help them focus on what you are saying, but if you give the audience too much information in advance you run the risk that they will simply read the handout and not listen to what you have to say. Perhaps the best strategy is to distribute only outlines in advance and, where needed, provide fuller handouts at the end of the presentation.

● Mooting

Introduction

A moot is a role-play exercise, in which two pairs of advocates (or sometimes two single advocates) conduct legal argument, based on an imaginary factual scenario, in front of a judge (or sometimes a bench of two or more judges). For the sake of simplicity, the rest of this section is written on the basis that there are two pairs of advocates and one judge, since this is by far the most common situation. At the end of a moot the judge will decide not only which side has won on the law, but also – and for the participants much more importantly – which side has won in terms of being the better mooters.

Most law schools offer at least some opportunity to moot, while many go further and incorporate mooting into your programme of assessment. In addition to any internal provision, there are also several inter-institutional mooting competitions. Either your law school or the promoters of inter-institutional mooting competitions will lay down the specific rules for the moots which they cover (for example, there will always be a time limit – typically 30 or 40 minutes for each side); but the advice contained in the rest of this section is offered by way of more general guidance to mooting.

Preparing for a moot

In academic terms, preparing for a moot is similar to preparing to write an answer to a problem question (see Chapter 11). This may sound odd, because in a problem question you have to discuss both the basis of any liability and the possibility of any defences which the facts may disclose, while in a moot you are required to argue only on one. In practice, however, this distinction between problem questions and mooting is more apparent than real, since each side in a moot must foresee – and be able to counter as best they can – the arguments which the other side will put forward

Mooting problems are almost always couched in terms of appeals. This enables the person who sets the problem to identify the grounds of appeal. You will be told which side of the case you have to argue and you will be given the name of your co-advocate. (You may or may not be told which of you is to be the leader and which the junior. If you are not told this, you will have to agree between yourselves.) The grounds of appeal you are given will, typically, contain two points of law, so that each advocate can argue one of them.

The person who is organising the moot (whose traditional title is Master – or Mistress – of Moots, but who will here, for the sake of simplicity, be called the organiser) may be a fellow student, a member of staff, or a fellow student with the support of a member of staff. After you have decided how you are going to argue your point of law, but before the moot itself, you must give both the organiser and your opponents a list of the authorities on which you will be relying. Naturally, your opponents must reciprocate.

Someone (it may be you, the organiser or someone who has been specifically allocated this task) must collect the authorities. Ideally, this will involve the law reports and the statutory material itself, but in some colleges and universities it will not be possible to take this material out of the library, so you will have to make do with photocopies or printed downloads. Even if you have the original source, you will still need a photocopy or a duplicate download as well, so that the judge can have one copy while you have another.

Advocacy for mooters

Introduction

Just as preparing for a moot has much in common with preparing to write an answer to a problem question, so performing as an advocate draws heavily on the advice given previously in this chapter in the context of oral skills generally. However, four points which are specifically relevant to mooting must be mentioned here, namely, addressing the judge, citing authority, using authority, and dealing with questions from the judge.

Addressing the judge

Moots are almost always located in either the Court of Appeal or the Supreme Court. While there is no reason in principle why a moot should not be heard by a bench of three or five judges (depending on which court is involved), constraints of sheer practicality often mean that only a single judge will sit.

When addressing the judge, inexperienced advocates often have difficulty in handling the distinction between *My Lord* (or *My Lady*) and *Your Lordship* (or *Your Ladyship*). The easy way to work out the correct form is that, with one exception, *My Lord* (or *My Lady*) is appropriate only where you would use the name of the person you are addressing in a less formal relationship. So, for example, if a friend asks you how soon you will be ready to go out, you might say 'About another ten minutes, Mary'. Imagining this in the formal context of the High Court, the Court of Appeal or the Supreme Court, with the judge asking you how much longer you need to complete the presentation of your case, you would say 'About another ten minutes, My Lord'. The exception is where you are addressing a bench consisting of two or more judges and you need to refer to one judge while speaking to another. Responding to the same question in this context, you would say, for example, 'I hope to be no more than another ten minutes, My Lord, but it may take me a little longer to provide a full response to the point which My Lord, Lord Justice Blank, raised a few moments ago'.

Turning to the correct use of 'Your Lordship' or 'Your Ladyship', the principle is, once again, clear. This usage is appropriate only where, in a less formal context, you would say 'you'. So, for example, if your housemate says 'shall we have pizza tonight?' you might reply 'if you like'. In the context of the courtroom, if the judge says 'I do not need to hear any further argument on this point', you would reply 'as Your Lordship (or Your Ladyship) pleases'.

When speaking about another judge at the level of the High Court or above who is not involved in the instant hearing, the correct usage is *His Lordship* (or *Her Ladyship*). So, for example, when citing an earlier case as an authority, you would say

> I refer Your Lordship to the speech of Baroness Hale of Richmond in the case of *R (Williamson) v Secretary of State for Education and Employment* in the second volume of the Appeal Cases reports for 2005, at paragraph [58], where Her Ladyship said '...'

Where the case dates from before the introduction of numbered paragraphs, the pinpoint citation would be to the page number and – where the series of law reports offers the opportunity – a marginal letter. In any case, an adjustment to *Lord* (or *Lady*) *Justice Blank* or *Mr* (or *Mrs*) *Justice Blank*, as appropriate, will be obvious.

When speaking of a circuit judge, you would say *His* (or *Her*) *Honour Judge Blank*, or, when speaking of the judge from whose court the instant appeal has come, you could simply say *the learned judge* or (if the judge was sitting at first instance) an alternative would be *the learned judge at first instance*, or even *the learned trial judge*.

Citing authority
Many students fall into the trap of thinking that textbooks and journal articles contain the law, even though it is clear (see pp. 81–82) that they do not do so. All that any textbook or journal article can ever contain is what its author thinks the law is, with the law itself being contained in the relevant cases, statutes, treaties and so on. It follows, therefore, that when citing authority, you should cite an original source wherever possible, reserving the citation of textbooks and journal articles for those situations where the law is unclear, in which case the opinion of authors may well be useful as 'fertilisers of thought' (a phrase which comes from the judgment of Sir Robert Megarry in *Cordell v Second Clanfield Properties Ltd* [1969] 2 Ch 9). However, even when it is appropriate to cite textbooks and journal articles, it is important that you let the judge know that you understand the limited status of the material you are using.

Where a case is reported in the 'official' Law Reports you should cite that reference (see pp. 83–84). When giving the reference orally, you should use the relevant words in full rather than articulating the established abbreviations. (The citation of *R (Williamson) v Secretary of State for Education and Employment* (above) shows how this is done.) When citing statutes, the short title is sufficient (see p. 92).

Using authority
Many students who study legal method (or whatever it may be called in their college or university) seem to regard it as an introductory chore which has been imposed upon them by the designers of their curriculum gratuitously, rather than as the foundation of their subsequent studies. If mooting achieves nothing else, it will at least dispel this misunderstanding, since a sound grasp of the principles of both binding precedent and legislative interpretation will prove indispensable when you are constructing and

arguing your case – and perhaps even more so when you are trying to per-suade the judge that your opponents' case is flawed. (Chapter 7 contains a useful overview of legal method, although by the time you are mooting you will be likely to have read a more substantial treatment of the subject, such as McLeod, *Legal Method*, 8th edn, 2011, Palgrave Macmillan.)

Dealing with questions from the judge
Every mooter must expect to be interrupted at least once by the judge. It is important to realise that this is not done out of spite or frustration, but because it is an essential part of the mooting exercise to find out how the advocates deal with questions. (As many an experienced mooter has dis-covered, preparing an address on the law is one thing: responding to ques-tions may be quite another.) If you do not understand the question which is being asked, you should say so, although it is always good psychology to adopt a form of words which suggests that the lack of effective communica-tion is your fault rather than the judge's. ('I am afraid I do not quite follow your Lordship's point' is likely to produce a much better response than 'If your Lordship could manage to express the question more clearly, I might be able to answer it'.)

The two-fold nature of the decision
The facts of life in relation to mooting are that, however hard the ques-tion setter has tried to be even-handed, one side will almost always have a stronger case than the other. It follows, that the odds of winning *on the law* are likely to be stacked in favour of one side rather than the other. However, while it is always pleasing to win on the law, what really matters in mooting is *who wins the moot*. In this connection – although it may seem perverse to say so – the side with the weaker case may even be in the stronger position in terms of mooting. After all, presenting a strong case well is likely to be less challenging (and, therefore, less impressive) than making the best of a bad job by putting up a creditable – even if ultimately unsuccessful – per-formance when presenting a weak one.

Once the judge has given his or her decision as to who wins the case, therefore, you will receive a distinct decision as to who has won the moot. This will normally follow on immediately from the decision on the case itself. Therefore, unless the rules under which you are operating make specific provision to the contrary, you can assume that you will not have to take part in the sort of wrangles which usually arise in real-ity, concerning matters such as applications for leave to appeal and for orders as to costs.

The difference between moots and mock trials

Although moots are sometimes referred to as *mock trials*, the two exercises are, in fact, quite distinct from each other.

More particularly, a mock trial is really a form of amateur dramatics which relies heavily on improvisation. Although mock trials will usually be staged in the context of the Crown Court, there is no reason why a scenario taken from civil law should not be used, with the trial being placed in a county court However, the model of a criminal case in the Crown Court is so common that the remaining comments here will assume, for the sake of simplicity, that this is the kind of mock trial which is being staged. On this basis, therefore, the idea is that someone will be charged with an offence, for which he or she will then be tried.

Turning to the nuts-and-bolts of staging a mock trial, the offence itself may have been enacted, with potential witnesses being placed strategically so that they can give witness statements and – ultimately – evidence; or someone may simply write a set of witness statements, which are then treated as a script. As with mooting, there may be a pair of advocates for each of the prosecution and the defence, or there may be only one on each side. There will, of course, be a jury. Whoever conceives the mock trial (if the offence is enacted) or whoever writes the witness statements (where it is not) will take care to include at least one point of law which is capable of being argued either way. Whether the offence has been staged or merely scripted, much of the fun of a mock trial comes from the way in which the witnesses improvise answers to the questions put to them by the advocates in respect of matters which arise on an unforeseen basis as the trial unfolds.

The advantages of mock trials over moots is that they give far more students the opportunity to become involved, since witnesses, jurors and at least one defendant will be required, as well as the advocates. However, the disadvantages are substantial. First, a mock trial is much more complicated to set up (especially if the offence is enacted) and the actual performance takes much longer (it being difficult to get through any mock trial in less than two hours, with three being more realistic, in which time four or five moots could have been heard. Secondly, the advocates must have at least some knowledge of the law of evidence (and since this is typically taught at Level Three, the pool of students from which the advocates may be drawn is inevitably restricted). Thirdly, even where the offence has been enacted, it has clearly not been actually committed. (Even in the interests of artistic integrity, it would not be practicable to stage an actual murder or rape, for example; and if the offence is one of dishonesty there will equally clearly have been no actual dishonesty because the defendant would simply have been playing a part.) Finally, and leaving aside whether it is an advantage or a disadvantage, the practical difficulties in staging mock trials makes it impracticable to incorporate them into programmes of assessment.

● Conclusion

Having read this chapter, you should realise that the key to successful oral presentations, is twofold:

- ● research and plan thoroughly; and
- ● remember that an oral presentation is not simply a written presentation read out loud.

Identifying the purpose of your presentation and considering the needs and expectations of your audience are paramount if you are to deliver effective presentations. Research and planning must focus on the fact that you are working towards an exercise in communication using the medium of speech, and the content must be simply and logically structured, using planned repetition where appropriate to reinforce your message. Delivering the presentation requires attention to style, acknowledging that appearance, body language and voice control will all contribute to the degree of success or failure of the presentation.

Appendix 1
Extracts From the European Convention on Human Rights and Fundamental Freedoms

Articles 2–12 and 14 of, and Articles 1–3 of the First Protocol, and Articles 1 & 2 of the Sixth Protocol to, the European Convention for the Protection of Human Rights and Fundamental Freedoms 1950

Section 1
Article 2
1. Everyone's right to life shall be protected by law. No one shall be deprived of his life intentionally save in the execution of a sentence of a court following his conviction of a crime for which this penalty is provided by law.
2. Deprivation of life shall not be regarded as inflicted in contravention of this Article when it results from the use of force which is no more than absolutely necessary:
   (a) in defence of any person from unlawful violence;
   (b) in order to effect a lawful arrest or to prevent the escape of a person lawfully detained;
   (c) in action lawfully taken for the purpose of quelling a riot or insurrection

Article 3
No one shall be subjected to torture or to inhuman or degrading treatment or punishment.

Article 4
1. No one shall be held in slavery or servitude.
2. No one shall be required to perform forced or compulsory labour.
3. For the purpose of this Article the term 'forced or compulsory labour' shall not include:

(a) any work required to be done in the ordinary course of detention imposed according to the provisions of Article 5 of this Convention or during conditional release from such detention;

(b) any service of a military character or, in case of conscientious objectors in countries where they are recognized, service exacted instead of compulsory military service;

(c) any service exacted in case of an emergency or calamity threatening the life or well-being of the community;

(d) any work or service which forms part of normal civic obligations.

Article 5

1. Everyone has the right to liberty and security of person. No one shall be deprived of his liberty save in the following cases and in accordance with a procedure prescribed by law:

(a) the lawful detention of a person after conviction by a competent court;

(b) the lawful arrest or detention of a person for non-compliance with the lawful order of a court or in order to secure the fulfilment of any obligation prescribed by law;

(c) the lawful arrest or detention of a person effected for the purpose of bringing him before the competent legal authority on reasonable suspicion of having committed an offence or when it is reasonably considered necessary to prevent his committing an offence or fleeing after having done so;

(d) the detention of a minor by lawful order for the purpose of educational supervision or his lawful detention for the purpose of bringing him before the competent legal authority;

(e) the lawful detention of persons for the prevention of the spreading of infectious diseases, of persons of unsound mind, alcoholics or drug addicts, or vagrants;

(f) the lawful arrest or detention of a person to prevent his effecting an unauthorized entry into the country or of a person against whom action is being taken with a view to deportation or extradition.

2. Everyone who is arrested shall be informed promptly, in a language which he understands, of the reasons for his arrest and of any charge against him.

3. Everyone arrested or detained in accordance with the provisions of paragraph 1(c) of this Article shall be brought promptly before a judge or other officer authorized by law to exercise judicial power and shall be entitled to trial within a reasonable time or to release pending trial. Re-

lease may be conditioned by guarantees to appear for trial.
4. Everyone who is deprived of his liberty by arrest or detention shall be entitled to take proceedings by which the lawfulness of his detention shall be decided speedily by a court and his release ordered if the detention is not lawful.
5. Everyone who has been the victim of arrest or detention in contravention of the provisions of this Article shall have an enforceable right to compensation.

Article 6

1. In the determination of his civil rights and obligations or of any criminal charge against him, everyone is entitled to a fair and public hearing within a reasonable time by an independent and impartial tribunal established by law. Judgment shall be pronounced publicly but the press and public may be excluded from all or part of the trial in the interest of morals, public order or national security in a democratic society, where the interest of juveniles or the protection of the private life of the parties so require, or to the extent strictly necessary in the opinion of the court in special circumstances where publicity would prejudice the interests of justice.
2. Everyone charged with a criminal offence shall be presumed innocent until proved guilty according to law.
3. Everyone charged with a criminal offence has the following minimum rights:
   (a) to be informed promptly, in a language which he understands and in detail, of the nature and cause of the accusation against him;
   (b) to have adequate time and facilities for the preparation of his defence;
   (c) to defend himself in person or through legal assistance of his own choosing or, if he has not sufficient means to pay for legal assistance, to be given it free when the interests of justice so require;
   (d) to examine or have examined witnesses against him and to obtain the attendance and examination of witnesses on his behalf under the same conditions as witnesses against him;
   (e) to have the free assistance of an interpreter if he cannot understand or speak the language used in court.

Article 7

1. No one shall be held guilty of any criminal offence on account of any act or omission which did not constitute a criminal offence under national

or international law at the time when it was committed. Nor shall a heavier penalty be imposed than the one that was applicable at the time the criminal offence was committed.

2. This Article shall not prejudice the trial and punishment of any person for any act or omission which, at the time when it was committed, was criminal according to the general principles of law recognized by civilized nations.

Article 8

1. Everyone has the right to respect for his private and family life, his home and his correspondence.
2. There shall be no interference by a public authority with the exercise of this right except such as is in accordance with the law and is necessary in a democratic society in the interests of national security, public safety or the economic well-being of the country, for the prevention of disorder or crime, for the protection of health or morals, or for the protection of the rights and freedoms of others.

Article 9

1. Everyone has the right to freedom of thought, conscience and religion; this right includes freedom to change his religion or belief, and freedom, either alone or in community with others and in public or private, to manifest his religion or belief, in worship, teaching, practice and observance.
2. Freedom to manifest one's religion or beliefs shall be subject only to such limitations as are prescribed by law and are necessary in a democratic society in the interests of public safety, for the protection of public order, health or morals, or for the protection of the rights and freedoms of others.

Article 10

1. Everyone has the right to freedom of expression. This right shall include freedom to hold opinions and to receive and impart information and ideas without interference by public authority and regardless of frontiers. This Article shall not prevent States from requiring the licensing of broadcasting, television or cinema enterprises.
2. The exercise of these freedoms, since it carries with it duties and responsibilities, may be subject to such formalities, conditions, restrictions or penalties as are prescribed by law and are necessary in a democratic society in the interests of national security, territorial integrity or public

safety, for the prevention of disorder or crime, for the protection of health or morals, for the protection of the reputation or rights of others, for preventing the disclosure of information received in confidence, or for maintaining the authority and impartiality of the judiciary.

Article 11

1. Everyone has the right to freedom of peaceful assembly and to freedom of association with others, including the right to form and to join trade unions for the protection of his interests.
2. No restrictions shall be placed on the exercise of these rights other than such as are prescribed by law and are necessary in a democratic society in the interests of national security or public safety, for the prevention of disorder or crime, for the protection of health or morals or for the protection of the rights and freedoms of others. This Article shall not prevent the imposition of lawful restrictions on the exercise of these rights by members of the armed forces, of the police or of the administration of the State.

Article 12

Men and women of marriageable age have the right to marry and to found a family, according to the national laws governing the exercise of this right.

Article 14

The enjoyment of the rights and freedoms set forth in this Convention shall be secured without discrimination on any ground such as sex, race, colour, language, religion, political or other opinion, national or social origin, association with a national minority, property, birth or other status.

Articles 1–3 of Protocol 1 – Enforcement of Certain Rights and Freedoms not Included in Section 1 of the Convention

Article 1

Every natural or legal person is entitled to the peaceful enjoyment of his possessions. No one shall be deprived of his possessions except in the public interest and subject to the conditions provided for by law and by the general principles of international law.

The preceding provisions shall not, however, in any way impair the right of a State to enforce such laws as it deems necessary to control the use of property in accordance with the general interest or to secure the payment of taxes or other contributions or penalties.

Article 2
No person shall be denied the right to education. In the exercise of any functions which it assumes in relation to education and to teaching, the State shall respect the right of parents to ensure such education and teaching in conformity with their own religious and philosophical convictions.

Article 3
The High Contracting Parties undertake to hold free elections at reasonable intervals by secret ballot, under conditions which will ensure the free expression of the opinion of the people in the choice of the legislature.

Articles 1 and 2 of Protocol 6 – Concerning the Abolition of the Death Penalty

Article 1
The death penalty shall be abolished. No one shall be condemned to such penalty or executed.

Article 2
A state may make provision in its law for the death penalty in respect of acts committed in time of war or of imminent threat of war; such penalty shall be applied only in the instance laid down in the law and in accordance with its provisions. The State shall communicate to the Secretary General of the Council of Europe the relevant provisions of that law.

Note: Articles 16, 17 and 18 respectively provide that arts.10, 11 and 14 do not prohibit restrictions on the political activities of aliens; nothing in the Convention gives any right to do anything which would harm the rights which it protects; and the restrictions contained in the Convention may be applied only for the purposes for which they are prescribed.

Appendix 2
Law Reports and Journals
(Some Useful References)

AC (formerly App Cas)	Appeal Cases (Law Reports)
Admin LR	Administrative Law Reports
All ER	All England Law Reports
All ER (EC)	All England Law Reports (European Cases)
Anglo-Am	Anglo-American Law Review
BLR	Building Law Reports
CJQ	Civil Justice Quarterly
CLY	Current Law Yearbook
CMLR	Common Market Law Reports
CMLRev	Common Market Law Review
COD	Crown Office Digest
Ch. (formerly ChD)	Chancery (Law Reports)
Co Law	Company Lawyer
Con LR	Construction Law Reports
Conv.(n.s.) (or Conv. or Conveyancer	Conveyancer and Property Lawyer (New Series)
Cox CC	Cox's Criminal Cases
Cr App R (or CAR)	Criminal Appeal Reports
Cr App R (S) (or CAR(S))	Criminal Appeal Reports (Sentencing)
Crim LR	Criminal Law Review
DLR	Dominion Law Reports (a Canadian series)
EBLRev	European Business Law Review
ECR	European Court Reports
EG	Estates Gazette
EGLR	Estates Gazette Law Reports
EHRR	European Human Rights Reports
ELRev	European Law Review
ER	English Reports
FCR	Family Court Reporter
FLR	Family Law Reports

FSR	Fleet Street Reports
FTLR	Financial Times Law Reports
Fam	Family Division (Law Reports)
Fam Law	Family Law
Harv LR	Harvard Law Review
HLR	Housing Law Reports
ICLQ	International and Comparative Law Quarterly
ICR	Industrial Cases Reports
ILJ	Industrial Law Journal
Imm AR	Immigration Appeals Reports
IRLR	Industrial Relations Law Reports
ITR	Industrial Tribunal Reports
JBL	Journal of Business Law
JP	Justice of the Peace Reports
JPL	Journal of Planning and Environment Law (formerly Journal of Planning Law)
JPN	Justice of the Peace Journal (Abbreviating 'Journal' to 'N' may seem rather odd. The explanation is that this periodical was originally known as 'Justice of the Peace Newspaper', and the 'JPN' abbreviation has survived even though it is now commonly referred to as 'Justice of the Peace Journal' by way of contradistinction to 'Justice of the Peace Reports' – see 'JP') JPN was re-titled as *Criminal Law and Justice Weekly* at the beginning of 2009 but is still cited under its former abbreviation.
JR	Juridical Review
JSPTL	Journal of the Society of Public Teachers of Law
JSWL	Journal of Social Welfare Law
KB	King's Bench (Law Reports)
KIR	Knight's Industrial Reports
LGR	Local Government Reports
LG Rev	Local Government Review (renamed as *Local Government Review Reports* in November 1993, and absorbed into the *Justice of the Peace* in 1996)
LJ	Law Journal
Ll L Rep	Lloyd's List Reports (1919-1950)
Lloyd's Rep	Lloyd's Reports (1951 onwards)

LQR	Law Quarterly Review
LS	Legal Studies
LSGaz	Law Society's Gazette
LT	Law Times
MLR	Modern Law Review
Med LR	Medical Law Reports
NILQ	Northern Ireland Legal Quarterly
NZLR	New Zealand Law Reports
NewLJ	New Law Journal
OJ	Official Journal of the European Communities
OJLS	Oxford Journal of Legal Studies
P (formerly PD)	Probate (Law Reports)
P & CR	Property and Compensation Reports (formerly Planning and Compensation Reports)
PL	Public Law
QB (formerly QBD)	Queen's Bench (Law Reports)
RPC	Reports of Patent, Design and Trade Mark Cases
RTR	Road Traffic Reports
SJ (sometimes given as Sol Jo)	Solicitors' Journal
SLT	Scots Law Times
STC	Simon's Tax Cases
Stat LR	Statute Law Review
TLR	Times Law Reports
US	United States Reports
WLR	Weekly Law Reports
Yale LJ	Yale Law Journal

Index